HOME FOLKS' OLD-FASHIONED

1001 BEST
SHORT EASY
RECIPES

SWEETWATER
PRESS

1001 Best Short Easy Recipes

Copyright © 2007 Cliff Road Books, Inc.

Produced by arrangement with Sweetwater Press

ISBN-13: 978-1-58173-650-2
ISBN-10: 1-58173-650-9

Recipes collected by Jennifer Grissom

Design by Miles G. Parsons

Printed in China

Home Folks' Old-Fashioned

1001 BEST SHORT EASY RECIPES

SWEETWATER
PRESS

CONTENTS

APPETIZERS AND BEVERAGES

ITALIAN WHITE BEAN DIP

2 (14-ounce) cans Great Northern beans, drained
1 tablespoon olive oil
3 teaspoons garlic, minced
2 teaspoons rosemary
Juice and zest of 1 lemon

Combine all ingredients in a food processor or blender; blend until smooth. Makes about 2 cups.

SUN-DRIED TOMATO DIP

1 (16-ounce) carton cottage cheese
¼ cup sun-dried tomatoes
1 green onion, chopped
2 teaspoons Italian seasoning
Juice and zest of 1 lemon

Combine all ingredients in a food processor or blender; blend until smooth. Makes about 2 cups.

PEANUT-CHUTNEY SPREAD

1 (3-ounce) package cream cheese, softened
1 cup chunky peanut butter
½ cup chutney, large pieces chopped
Salt and pepper to taste
2 tablespoons milk

Combine cream cheese, peanut butter, chutney, and salt and pepper to taste, beating until smooth. Add enough milk to thin to spreading consistency. Makes about 2 cups.

GINGER DIP

1 cup mayonnaise
1 cup sour cream
1 tablespoon soy sauce
1 teaspoon rice vinegar
1 teaspoon ground ginger
2 chopped green onions

Combine all ingredients. Makes about 1½ cups.

TANGY ASIAN DIP

1 cup mayonnaise
1 cup sour cream
1 (8-ounce) can water chestnuts, drained and chopped
3 chopped green onions
1 teaspoon minced garlic
1 teaspoon soy sauce
½ teaspoon ground ginger

Combine all ingredients. Makes about 2½ cups.

OLD-FASHIONED FRENCH ONION DIP

1 cup sour cream
1 cup mayonnaise
1 (1½-ounce) package dry onion soup mix
2 green onions, chopped

Combine all ingredients. Chill before serving. Makes about 2 cups.

LEMON-DILL DIP

1 cup mayonnaise
1 cup sour cream
2 teaspoons dried dill
1 teaspoon minced garlic
½ teaspoon onion salt
Juice and zest of 1 lemon

Combine all ingredients. Makes about 2 cups.

ONION-SPINACH DIP

1 cup mayonnaise
1 cup sour cream
1 (10-ounce) package frozen chopped spinach, thawed and drained
1 (1½-ounce) package dry onion soup mix

Combine all ingredients, stirring until well combined. Makes about 3 cups.

SAVORY SPINACH DIP

1 cup mayonnaise
1 cup sour cream
1 (10-ounce) package frozen chopped spinach, thawed and drained
1 (1-ounce) envelope vegetable soup mix
½ cup grated Parmesan cheese

Combine all ingredients, mixing well. Chill before serving. Makes about 3 cups.

SPINACH AND ARTICHOKE DIP

1 cup mayonnaise
1 cup sour cream
**1 (10-ounce) package frozen chopped spinach, thawed and
  drained**
**1 (14-ounce) can marinated artichoke hearts, drained and
  chopped**
1 (1-ounce) envelope vegetable soup mix
½ cup Parmesan cheese, grated

Combine all ingredients, mixing well. Chill before serving. Makes
about 4 cups.

CREAMY CUCUMBER DIP FOR VEGETABLES

½ cup butter, softened
½ cup grated Parmesan cheese
1 teaspoon garlic salt
2 cups plain yogurt
1 cucumber, peeled, seeded, and chopped
4 chopped green onions

Beat butter and cheese until smooth. Blend in remaining ingredients.
Makes 3 cups.

COTTAGE CHEESE CUCUMBER SPREAD

1 cup cucumber, finely chopped
1 cup small curd fat-free cottage cheese
Dash pepper
1 tablespoon minced chives

Mix cucumber, cottage cheese, and pepper. Spread on low-fat whole-wheat crackers, and garnish with minced green onion. Makes about 2 cups.

CREAMY HERBED CHEESE SPREAD

2 (8-ounce) packages cream cheese, softened
½ cup butter, softened
1 teaspoon minced garlic
1 teaspoon dried oregano
1 teaspoon dried basil
½ teaspoon black pepper
½ teaspoon seasoning salt
¼ teaspoon dried thyme
¼ teaspoon dried dill

Combine all ingredients, beating well. Chill at least one hour for flavors to blend. Serve with crackers. Makes about 2½ cups.

PINEAPPLE CHEESE BALL

2 (8-ounce) packages cream cheese, softened
1 (8-ounce) can crushed pineapple, drained
Salt and pepper to taste
1 cup roasted pecans, chopped

Combine cream cheese, pineapple, and salt and pepper, mixing well. Form into a ball and roll in chopped pecans. Chill before serving. Makes about 3 cups.

SAVORY STRAWBERRY CHEESECAKE

4 cups shredded sharp Cheddar cheese
1 cup pecans, chopped
1 cup mayonnaise
1 small onion, chopped
Cayenne pepper to taste
1 cup strawberry preserves

Combine cheese, pecans, mayonnaise, onion, and cayenne pepper, mixing well. Pat into a circle, about ¾-inch thick. Spread strawberry preserves over top. Serve with crackers. Makes about 8 cups.

CHEESE BALL

1 (8-ounce) package cream cheese
1 small jar pimento cheese
1 small jar Old English cheese
Paprika

Put all cheese in a large bowl and sit at room temperature for 2 hours. Mix together with hands. Form into ball and garnish with paprika. Refrigerate. Makes about 3 cups.

CURRIED CHUTNEY CHEESE BALL

2 (8-ounce) packages cream cheese, softened
½ cup mango chutney, large pieces chopped
2 teaspoons curry powder
Dash cayenne pepper
2 cups roasted pecans, chopped and divided

Combine cream cheese, chutney, curry powder, and cayenne pepper, mixing well. Stir in 1 cup pecans. Form into a ball and roll in remaining pecans. Chill before serving. Makes about 3 cups.

GARLIC-CHEESE BALL

1 (8-ounce) package cream cheese
1 (16-ounce) package processed cheese spread, such as Velveeta
2 cups chopped pecans, divided
2 to 3 teaspoons garlic salt, to taste
¼ teaspoon cayenne pepper

Combine cheeses and mix thoroughly. Stir in 1 cup pecans, garlic salt, and cayenne pepper. Shape mixture into a ball. Roll in remaining pecans. Chill until firm. Serve with crackers. Makes 4 cups.

TANGY SHRIMP DIP

1 (5-ounce) can shrimp, drained
1 (8-ounce) carton cottage cheese
3 tablespoons chili sauce
½ teaspoon minced garlic
½ teaspoon onion powder
Dash hot sauce

Combine all ingredients in food processor or blender; blend until smooth. Makes about 2 cups.

CREAMY TUNA DIP

1 (3-ounce) package cream cheese, softened
1 cup sour cream
1 (6-ounce) can tuna, drained and flaked
1 tablespoon chopped chives
1 teaspoon Worcestershire sauce
Salt and pepper to taste

Combine cream cheese and sour cream, mixing until smooth. Gently fold in remaining ingredients. Makes about 2 cups.

SMOKED TUNA DIP

1 (3-ounce) package cream cheese, softened
1 cup sour cream
1 (6-ounce) package smoked tuna, chopped
1 tablespoon chopped green onions
1 teaspoon Worcestershire sauce
Salt and pepper to taste

Combine cream cheese and sour cream, mixing until smooth. Gently fold in remaining ingredients. Makes about 2 cups.

MUSHROOM CHEESE MOLD

2 (8-ounce) packages cream cheese, softened
2 cups shredded Cheddar cheese, softened
1 teaspoon minced garlic
2 teaspoons spicy mustard
Salt and pepper to taste
1 (4-ounce) can mushrooms, drained and finely chopped
¼ cup finely chopped onion

Combine cream cheese, Cheddar cheese, garlic, mustard, and salt and pepper, mixing until smooth. Carefully fold in mushrooms and onions. Spread into a greased 3-cup bowl or mold. Chill until firm.

BLEU CHEESE DIP

1 (4-ounce) package crumbled bleu cheese
½ cup sour cream
½ cup mayonnaise
½ cup finely chopped celery
Salt and pepper to taste

Combine all ingredients, mixing well. Makes about 2 cups.

CORN AND BLACK BEAN SALSA

1 (14-ounce) can corn, drained
1 (14-ounce) can black beans, drained and rinsed
1 (10-ounce) can diced tomatoes with chiles, drained
1 bunch green onion, chopped
1 red bell pepper, seeded and chopped
1 teaspoon cumin
1 teaspoon garlic salt

Combine all ingredients, mixing well. Makes about 4 cups.

BLACK OLIVE SALSA

2 tomatoes, seeded and chopped
1 bunch chopped green onions
1 (4½-ounce) can jalapeño peppers, drained and chopped
1 (4½-ounce) can chopped black olives, drained
3 tablespoons olive oil
1½ tablespoons white vinegar
1 teaspoon minced garlic
½ teaspoon dried oregano
Salt to taste

Combine all ingredients; chill. Serve with tortilla chips. Makes about 6 servings.

VEGETARIAN RANCH DIP

1 (10-ounce) block soft tofu
1 (1-ounce) package dry vegetarian ranch dip mix
3 tablespoons soymilk (optional – add to make suitable for drizzling)

Combine all ingredients. Makes about 4 servings.

TEXAS CAVIAR

1 (16-ounce) can black-eyed peas, drained and rinsed
1 (15-ounce) can black beans, drained and rinsed
1 (15-ounce) can corn, drained
1 (8-ounce) bottle Italian dressing
1 red bell pepper, seeded and chopped
3 chopped green onions
1 jalapeño pepper, seeded and finely chopped

Combine all ingredients; chill before serving. Makes about 4 cups.

SUPER-QUICK CREAM CHEESE SPREAD

1 (8-ounce) package cream cheese, softened
½ cup chopped walnuts
½ cup chopped green olives

Mix together all ingredients. Serve on crackers or bread. Makes about 2 cups.

PIMENTO CHEESE

1½ cups mayonnaise
1 (4-ounce) jar pimentos, drained
1 teaspoon grated onion
½ teaspoon salt
¼ teaspoon cayenne pepper
2 cups shredded sharp Cheddar cheese

In a large bowl, combine mayonnaise, pimentos, onion, salt, and cayenne pepper; mix thoroughly. Add Cheddar cheese and stir to combine. Makes about 4 cups.

Sour Cream Pesto Dip

1 cup sour cream
½ cup pesto
3 tablespoons grated Parmesan cheese

In a medium bowl, combine all ingredients and mix well to blend. Chill. Serve with crudités and chips for dipping, or as a sandwich spread. Makes about 1½ cups.

Hot Chipped Beef Dip

2 (8-ounce) packages cream cheese, softened
1 cup sour cream
1 (5-ounce) jar chipped beef, chopped
3 chopped green onions
1 tablespoon horseradish
1 cup pecans, chopped

Combine cream cheese, sour cream, chipped beef, green onions, and horseradish, mixing well. Spread into a small greased baking dish, and sprinkle with pecans. Bake at 350° for about 20 minutes. Makes about 3 cups.

Hot Bean Dip

1 (15-ounce) can chili beans, undrained
1 (10-ounce) can diced tomatoes with chiles, drained
1 cup sour cream
1 cup shredded Monterey Jack cheese

Partially mash chili beans with a fork. Combine all ingredients, cooking over very low heat until thoroughly heated. Do not boil. Makes about 3 cups.

Cheese, Chile, and Bean Dip

1 (16-ounce) can refried beans
1 (8-ounce) package cream cheese, cubed
1 (4-ounce) can diced green chiles, drained
Hot sauce (optional)
1 cup shredded Cheddar cheese, divided

Mix refried beans, cubed cream cheese, green chiles, and ½ cup cheese in slow cooker and cook on high for 1 to 1½ hours; stir frequently until melted. Add pepper sauce to taste, if desired. Sprinkle rest of cheese on top. Serve with tortilla chips. Makes about 4 cups.

Hot Tamale Dip

1 (15-ounce) can tamales, finely chopped
1 cup salsa
1 (8-ounce) block processed cheese, cubed

Combine all ingredients, cooking over low heat until cheese is thoroughly melted. Makes about 3 cups.

CHILI CORN DIP

1 (15-ounce) can chili with beans
1 (14-ounce) can corn, drained
1 cup salsa

Combine all ingredients, cooking over low heat until heated through.
Makes about 3 cups.

WHITE CHEESE DIP

1½ cups grated Parmesan cheese
1 cup shredded Monterey Jack cheese
2 (4½-ounce) cans chopped green chiles, undrained
½ cup mayonnaise
½ teaspoon cumin

Combine all ingredients. Bake at 350° for about 20 minutes. Makes
about 3 cups.

PEPPERONI PIZZA DIP

1 (8-ounce) package cream cheese, softened
1 cup sour cream
1 (3½-ounce) package pepperoni, finely chopped
½ cup pizza sauce
½ cup shredded mozzarella cheese
3 chopped green onions

Combine all ingredients, mixing well. Bake at 350° for about 20
minutes. Makes about 3 cups.

Almost Instant Fondue

1 (8-ounce) wedge Brie, Camembert, or Cambozola cheese
2 tablespoons chopped pistachio nuts or cashews

Place cheese on a round shallow baking dish. Sprinkle with nuts. Bake at 450° for 5 to 8 minutes until cheese begins to melt. Makes 2 servings.

Brie and Garlic Dip

2 heads garlic
1 tablespoon olive oil
1 (8-ounce) round Brie cheese
Seasoned salt and pepper, to taste

Cut top ½-inch off the top of the garlic heads. Remove some of the loose papery skin, leaving the heads intact. Place each on a square of foil, drizzle with the olive oil, and wrap well. Bake at 350° for 50 to 60 minutes, until the garlic is very soft and begins to brown. Cool until easy to handle. Squeeze each head to remove the soft roasted cloves.

In a food processor, cream Brie cheese with the seasoned salt, pepper, and garlic cloves. (You can also cream these ingredients together using the back of a spoon.) Refrigerate several hours to blend flavors. Serve with crackers, crostini, or sliced French bread. Makes about 2 cups.

BAKED BRIE WITH PEACHES AND RASPBERRY PRESERVES

1 (8-ounce) round Brie cheese
2 tablespoons raspberry preserves
1 cup peaches, peeled and diced
1 tablespoon brown sugar

Place Brie in a small shallow baking dish. Spread preserves evenly over cheese and top with peaches. Sprinkle with brown sugar. Bake at 450° for 10 to 12 minutes or until cheese softens. Serve with crackers and French bread slices. Makes 2 servings.

ANTIPASTO PLATTER

1 (3½-ounce) package sliced pepperoni
1 (4-ounce) jar pepperoncini peppers, drained
½ pound provolone, cubed
¼ pound salami, sliced
3 Roma tomatoes, sliced
Romaine lettuce leaves
Italian dressing

Arrange pepperoni, pepperoncini, provolone, salami, and tomatoes on lettuce-lined platter. Drizzle Italian dressing over all. Makes about 6 servings.

BACON-WRAPPED SCALLOPS

1 pound bacon
12 to 16 scallops

Wrap one slice of bacon around each scallop. Bake at 375° for about 20 minutes. Makes 12 to 16 servings.

BACON-WRAPPED WATER CHESTNUTS

1 pound bacon
2 (8-ounce) cans whole water chestnuts, drained
½ cup soy sauce

Cut each strip of bacon crosswise into thirds. Wrap one segment of bacon around each water chestnut, securing with a toothpick. Toss with soy sauce. Bake at 375° for about 20 minutes. Makes about 3 dozen.

BACON-WRAPPED PARMESAN CRACKERS

1 pound bacon
24 to 32 rectangular, buttery crackers (such as Club)
⅔ cup grated Parmesan cheese

Cut each strip of bacon crosswise in half. Sprinkle each cracker with about 1 teaspoon Parmesan cheese, and then wrap with bacon. Place seam-side down on baking sheet. Bake at 250° for about 1 hour. Makes 2 to 2½ dozen.

PESTO CHEESE

¼ pound mozzarella cheese, cubed
½ cup basil pesto
¼ cup grated Parmesan cheese
Crackers

Bake mozzarella cheese at 400° for 4 to 6 minutes or until cheese begins to melt. Remove from oven and drop pesto by teaspoonfuls over cheese. Top with Parmesan cheese and return to oven for 1 minute. Serve with crackers. Makes 4 servings.

Hot Broccoli Dip

1 (8-ounce) package cream cheese
1 (8-ounce) package processed cheese
1 (16-ounce) bag frozen chopped broccoli, thawed and drained

Combine all ingredients, heating over low heat until thoroughly melted and smooth. Makes about 4 cups.

Hot Broccoli Dip with Bacon

1 (8-ounce) package cream cheese
1 (8-ounce) package processed cheese
1 (16-ounce) bag frozen chopped broccoli, thawed and drained
½ pound bacon, cooked and crumbled

Combine cream cheese, processed cheese, and broccoli, cooking over low heat until thoroughly melted and smooth. Remove from heat and stir in bacon. Makes about 4 cups.

Artichoke Dip

1 (14-ounce) can artichoke hearts, drained
1½ cups mozzarella cheese
1 cup grated Parmesan cheese
1 cup mayonnaise

Chop artichoke into small pieces. Combine with the rest of the ingredients. Heat in oven at 350° for 30 minutes or until brown. Makes about 4 cups.

HOT ARTICHOKE DIP WITH BACON

2 cups mayonnaise
2 (14-ounce) cans artichoke hearts, drained and chopped
2 cups shredded Parmesan cheese
1 pound bacon, cooked and crumbled
Corn chips or crackers

Combine all ingredients. Bake at 350° for 30 minutes, or until heated through. Serve with corn chips or crackers. Makes about 6 cups.

HOT SPINACH AND ARTICHOKE DIP

1 cup mayonnaise
1 cup sour cream
1 (10-ounce) package frozen spinach, thawed and drained
1 (14-ounce) can marinated artichoke hearts, drained and chopped
1 (1-ounce) envelope vegetable soup mix
½ cup grated Parmesan cheese

Combine all ingredients, mixing well. Bake at 350° for about 20 minutes. Makes about 4 cups.

CHILI CHEESE DIP

1 (15-ounce) can chili without beans
½ to ¾ cup shredded Cheddar cheese
Corn chips

Combine chili and cheese in medium saucepan. Cook over medium heat, stirring frequently, until cheese is melted. Serve with corn chips. Makes about 2 cups.

CRAB DIP

1 pound lump crabmeat, picked over to remove bits of shell
1 cup mayonnaise
½ cup onions, finely chopped
2 garlic cloves, minced
1 cup shredded Cheddar cheese
2 tablespoons Worcestershire sauce
2 tablespoons lemon juice
1 teaspoon salt
1 teaspoon pepper
Crackers

In a shallow baking dish, combine all ingredients. Bake at 325° for about 40 minutes. Serve with crackers. Makes about 4 cups.

HOT CRAB DIP WITH FRESH HERBS

2 (8-ounce) packages cream cheese, softened
½ cup milk
2 tablespoons chopped chives
2 tablespoons chopped fresh parsley
2 tablespoons horseradish
1 pound lump crabmeat, picked over to remove bits of shell

Combine cream cheese, milk, chives, parsley, and horseradish. Gently stir in crabmeat. Bake at 350° for 30 minutes or until heated through. Serve with crackers. Makes about 4 cups.

ROQUEFORT SHRIMP

2 pounds shrimp, peeled and deveined
1 (3-ounce) bag crab boil
1 onion, chopped
1 (4-ounce) package Roquefort cheese, crumbled
2 tablespoons olive oil
Salt and pepper to taste
Crackers

Combine shrimp, crab boil, and onion; cover with water and bring just to a boil. Remove from heat and let sit 1 to 2 minutes, or until shrimp are just cooked through. Drain and toss with Roquefort cheese, olive oil, salt, and pepper. Serve immediately with crackers. Makes about 8 servings.

BEEFY PECAN SPREAD

1 (8-ounce) package cream cheese, softened
½ cup sour cream
2 tablespoons milk
1 (2½-ounce) jar dried beef, finely chopped
¼ cup finely chopped red bell pepper
2 tablespoons finely chopped onion
Salt and pepper to taste
½ cup chopped pecans
2 tablespoons butter, melted

Combine cream cheese, sour cream, and milk, mixing until smooth. Stir in chopped dried beef, bell pepper, onion, and salt and pepper to taste. Spread in a small baking dish. Combine pecans and melted butter; sprinkle over top. Bake at 350° for about 15 minutes. Makes about 2 cups.

CHILI CON QUESO

1 onion, finely chopped
2 tablespoons butter
1 (10½-ounce) can diced tomatoes with chiles, drained
1 cup shredded Cheddar cheese
1 cup shredded Monterey Jack cheese
1 teaspoon cornstarch
Corn chips

Cook onion in butter until soft. Add tomatoes and simmer 2 or 3 minutes. Toss cheeses in cornstarch and gradually add to hot tomatoes, stirring each batch until melted. Serve with corn chips. Makes about 2 cups.

SPICY CHEESE NACHOS

1 (6-ounce) bag tortilla chips
2 cups shredded Monterey Jack cheese
4 jalapeño peppers, sliced

Layer half tortilla chips, half cheese, and half sliced peppers in a large baking dish. Repeat layers. Bake at 400° for about 5 minutes. Makes about 6 servings.

SPICY BLACK BEAN NACHOS

1 (6-ounce) bag tortilla chips
1 (14-ounce) can black beans, drained
2 cups shredded Cheddar cheese
4 jalapeño peppers, sliced

Layer half tortilla chips, half beans, half cheese, and half sliced peppers in a large baking dish. Repeat layers. Bake at 400° for about 5 minutes. Makes about 8 servings.

BUTTERED CROSTINI

1 baguette, sliced
¼ cup butter, melted

Brush baguette slices with melted butter. Bake at 400° for about 10 minutes. Makes about 3 dozen.

GARLIC CROSTINI

1 baguette, sliced
¼ cup butter, melted
2 teaspoons garlic salt

Brush baguette slices with melted butter, and sprinkle with garlic salt. Bake at 400° for about 10 minutes. Makes about 3 dozen.

HERBED GARLIC CROSTINI

1 baguette, sliced
¼ cup butter, melted
2 teaspoons garlic salt
2 teaspoons Italian seasoning

Brush baguette slices with melted butter, and sprinkle with garlic salt and Italian seasoning. Bake at 400° for about 10 minutes. Makes about 3 dozen.

HERBED TOAST POINTS

½ cup butter, softened
1 teaspoon dried basil
1 teaspoon dried oregano
1 teaspoon dried thyme
1 loaf thin-sliced bread

Combine first 4 ingredients, beating until smooth. Spread evenly over bread. Trim crusts from bread, and then cut into quarters. Bake at 300° for 15 minutes or until crisp and golden. Serve with dips and spreads. Makes about 8 dozen.

WONTON DIPPERS

12 square wonton wrappers

Cut wonton wrappers into quarters, and place on cookie sheet coated with nonstick cooking spray. Bake at 350° for about 8 minutes or until golden brown. Use instead of crackers with dips. Makes 48.

HOMEMADE FAT-FREE TORTILLA CHIPS

8 corn tortillas
¼ teaspoon cumin
¼ teaspoon pepper
¼ teaspoon salt

Cut a stack of tortillas into 8 wedges each. Spread wedges in a single layer on a baking sheet. Sprinkle with cumin, pepper, and salt (optional). Bake at 375° for about 10 minutes, or until crisp and dry. Monitor chips; do not overbrown. Turn after 5 minutes. Store in airtight container. When serving, freshen up in microwave about 1 minute. Let sit 5 minutes before serving. Makes 64 chips.

FRUIT DIP

½ cup peanut butter
¼ cup chocolate syrup or honey
Fresh fruit

Combine the peanut butter and chocolate syrup or honey in a mixing bowl, and stir until well mixed. Dip in pieces of fresh fruit. Makes ¾ cup.

PIÑA COLADA DIP

1 (8-ounce) can crushed pineapple, undrained
1 (3-ounce) package instant coconut pudding and pie filling mix
¾ cup whole milk
½ cup sour cream

In a food processor or blender, combine all ingredients. Blend or process for 30 seconds. Cover and refrigerate several hours to blend flavors. Serve with fresh fruit for dipping. Makes about 2 cups.

SPINACH QUESADILLAS

1 (16-ounce) bag frozen chopped spinach, thawed and well
** drained**
2 cups shredded mozzarella cheese
8 flour tortillas, flavored or plain

Sprinkle half of the cheese on the tortillas. Add spinach, and then top with remaining cheese. Top each with another tortilla and press gently. Warm nonstick skillet for 1 minute over medium heat. Cook each quesadilla for 2 to 3 minutes on each side, until cheese melts and tortillas are crisp, pressing gently with spatula as they cook. Cut each into 6 wedges to serve. Makes 24 servings.

MINI PIZZAS

1 (10-ounce) can refrigerated biscuits
½ cup shredded mozzarella cheese
48 pepperoni slices
½ cup pizza sauce

Dip a pair of scissors in flour, and cut 5 to 6 biscuits into quarters. Place on a greased cookie sheet. Flatten each piece with bottom of a glass that has been greased and dipped into flour. Spread sauce onto dough, and top with slices of pepperoni and cheese. Bake at 350° for 7 to 10 minutes. Makes 24 pizzas.

PARMESAN CRACKERS WITH FIGS

2 cups freshly grated Parmesan or pecorino cheese
2 ripe figs, sliced
2 tablespoons honey

Spray a nonstick skillet with cooking spray, and warm over medium heat. Make two circles of Parmesan cheese on the skillet, each about 4 inches across, just thick enough so you can't see the bottom through it. This should take about 2 tablespoons of the cheese. Cook on first side for 2 minutes, watching carefully, until the edges are golden. Carefully turn wafers, and cook 1 minute longer. Gently flatten with spatula if they begin to curl or fold. Remove from pan, and drain on paper towels. Repeat until all the cheese is used. To serve, top each cheese wafer with some fig or date slices, and drizzle with honey. Figs may be substituted with 8 Medjool dates. Makes about 8 servings.

EASY DEVILED EGGS

3 hard-boiled eggs, peeled and cut into halves
1 tablespoon mayonnaise
¼ tablespoon spicy mustard
1 tablespoon pickle relish

Remove yolks from eggs, leaving the whites intact. In a bowl, combine the yolks with the rest of the ingredients, and mix well. Spoon the mixture into the hole of each egg half. Makes 6 servings.

CURRIED DEVILED EGGS

6 hard-boiled eggs, peeled and cut in halves
3 tablespoons mayonnaise
1 tablespoon sweet pickle relish
1 tablespoon mustard
½ teaspoon curry powder
Salt and pepper to taste
Paprika

Remove yolks from eggs, leaving the whites intact. In a bowl, combine yolks and mayonnaise; mix until smooth. Add relish, mustard, curry powder, salt, and pepper; stir to combine. Spoon yolk mixture into the egg whites, and sprinkle with paprika. Makes 12 servings.

CHEESY DEVILED EGGS

6 hard-boiled eggs, peeled and cut into halves
1 (3-ounce) package cream cheese, softened
1 (4-ounce) package bleu cheese, softened
¼ cup mayonnaise
Salt and pepper to taste

Remove yolks from eggs, leaving the whites intact. In a bowl, combine yolks and mayonnaise; mix until smooth. Spoon yolk mixture into egg whites. Makes 12 servings.

BRIE BRUSCHETTA

1 loaf crusty French bread, sliced 1-inch thick
6 to 8 ripe tomatoes, chopped
1 (8-ounce) round Brie cheese, thinly sliced
Salt and pepper to taste

Under broiler or on grill, toast one side of the French bread slices. Turn slices over. Brush the untoasted side with some of the juices from the chopped tomatoes. Layer slices of Brie on the bread. Return to broiler or grill, and toast 2 to 3 minutes, until cheese is melted. Top with the chopped tomatoes, and sprinkle with salt and pepper.

SOUTHERN CHEESE STRAWS

½ cup butter, softened
2 cups sharp shredded Cheddar cheese
2 cups flour
Salt to taste
1 teaspoon cayenne pepper

Combine all ingredients in a bowl; mix well. Spoon into a pastry bag. Press straws onto a nonstick baking sheet. Bake at 350° for 7 minutes. Makes 100 servings.

Onion and Pecan Cheese Straws

1 cup butter, softened
2 cups shredded sharp Cheddar cheese, softened
3 to 4 cups flour
1 (1½-ounce) package dry onion soup mix
1 cup finely chopped pecans
2 tablespoons chopped green onion

Combine all ingredients, adding flour until dough is no longer sticky. Roll into logs, wrap, and chill. Slice about ¼-inch thick. Bake at 300° for about 20 minutes. Makes 8 to 10 dozen.

Southwestern Tortilla Strips

¼ cup butter, melted
2 teaspoons chili powder
½ teaspoon cumin
½ teaspoon garlic powder
½ teaspoon onion powder
12 (6-inch) corn tortillas

Combine butter, chili powder, cumin, garlic powder, and onion powder; brush over tortillas. Cut each tortilla into strips. Bake at 350° for about 15 minutes. Makes about 10 servings.

Spicy Popcorn

2 tablespoons butter, melted
½ teaspoon chili powder
½ teaspoon garlic salt
½ teaspoon onion powder
6 cups popcorn

Combine butter, chili powder, garlic salt, and onion powder; toss with popcorn. Makes 6 cups.

SNACK MIX

6 cups popcorn
4 cups pretzel rings
1 (4-ounce) can shoestring potatoes
¼ cup butter, melted
1 tablespoon dry onion soup mix

Combine popcorn, pretzel rings, and shoestring potatoes. Combine melted butter and onion soup mix, and pour over popcorn mixture. Spread out on a large baking sheet. Bake at 325° for about 10 minutes, stirring once. Makes about 10 cups.

CHEESY DILL SNACK MIX

1 (12-ounce) box rice cereal squares
½ cup butter, melted
½ cup grated Parmesan cheese
2 teaspoons dried dill

Combine all ingredients. Spread out on a large baking sheet. Bake at 325° for about 10 minutes, stirring once. Makes 4 servings.

EVERYBODY'S FAVORITE SAUSAGE BALLS

3 cups all-purpose baking mix
1 pound spicy sausage
2¼ cups shredded sharp Cheddar cheese

Combine all ingredients, stirring until well blended. Form mixture into 1-inch balls. Bake at 350° for about 15 minutes, or until sausage is thoroughly cooked. Makes about 4 dozen.

SOUTHWESTERN SNACK MIX

6 cups popcorn
4 cups pretzel sticks
1 (12-ounce) can peanuts
1 (4-ounce) can shoestring potatoes
1 (3-ounce) can french-fried onions
½ cup butter, melted
1 (1-ounce) package taco seasoning mix

Combine popcorn, pretzel sticks, peanuts, shoestring potatoes, and french-fried onions. Combine melted butter and taco seasoning mix; pour over popcorn mixture. Spread out on a large baking sheet. Bake at 325° for about 10 minutes, stirring once. Makes 12 cups.

SAUSAGE BALLS

1 pound pork sausage
⅓ cup breadcrumbs
½ teaspoon dried sage
1 egg, beaten
½ cup ketchup
2 tablespoons brown sugar
1 tablespoon soy sauce
1 tablespoon vinegar

Combine sausage, breadcrumbs, sage, and egg in a bowl; mix well. Shape into 1-inch balls. Cook in nonstick skillet over low heat until brown on all sides; drain. Pour mixture of ketchup, brown sugar, soy sauce, and vinegar over sausage balls; mix well. Simmer for 15 to 20 minutes, or until sausage balls are tender. Serve in a chafing dish. Makes 32 servings.

SALMON-STUFFED TOMATOES

1 pint cherry tomatoes, cored and drained
1 (6-ounce) can salmon, drained and flaked
¼ cup mayonnaise
1 tablespoon onion salt
Pepper to taste

Cut a thin slice from the bottoms of the tomatoes, so they will sit up evenly. Combine salmon, mayonnaise, onion salt, and pepper to taste. Fill tomatoes with salmon mixture. Chill before serving. Makes about 24.

PECAN CHICKEN TENDERS

½ cup butter
1 cup flour
1 teaspoon baking powder
2 teaspoons garlic salt
2 teaspoons paprika
½ teaspoon pepper
½ cup chopped pecans
1 tablespoon sesame seeds
1 egg, beaten
½ cup milk
6 boneless, skinless chicken breasts, cut into strips

Melt butter in a large glass baking dish at 375°; set aside. Combine flour, baking powder, garlic salt, paprika, pepper, pecans, and sesame seeds in a large shallow dish. Combine egg and milk in a separate dish. Dip each chicken breast strip in egg mixture, and then dredge in flour mixture. Place in prepared baking dish. Bake about 25 minutes or until cooked through. Makes 12 servings.

TOASTED CHEESE ROLL-UPS

1 cup shredded Cheddar cheese, softened
¼ cup butter, softened
Dash cayenne pepper
8 slices thin white bread

Combine cheese, butter, and cayenne pepper, beating until smooth.
Spread evenly over bread slices. Remove crusts, roll up, and place
seam-side down on baking sheet. Bake at 400° for about 10 minutes.
Cut in half before serving. Makes 8 servings.

SAUCY COCKTAIL WEENIES

3 (5-ounce) packages cocktail wieners
1 (10¾-ounce) can condensed tomato soup
¼ cup brown sugar
¼ cup water
2 tablespoons apple cider vinegar
1 tablespoon Worcestershire sauce
1 small onion, chopped

Combine all ingredients; bring to boil. Reduce heat, and simmer
about 10 minutes. Makes about 12 servings.

SWEET AND TANGY COCKTAIL WEENIES

3 (5-ounce) packages cocktail wieners
1 cup ketchup
1 cup grape jelly
¼ cup Dijon mustard

Combine all ingredients; bring to a boil. Reduce heat, and simmer
about 10 minutes. Makes about 12 servings.

BRAIDED PIZZA LOAF

2 (9-ounce) packages refrigerated crescent roll dough
¼ cup pizza sauce
Pepperoni slices
1 cup shredded mozzarella cheese
1 egg, beaten
¼ cup grated Parmesan cheese

Unroll 1 package of crescent roll dough; pinch seams together to seal. Place on greased baking sheet. Spread with pizza sauce and layer with pepperoni slices and mozzarella cheese.

Unroll second package of crescent roll dough; pinch seams together to seal; cut dough into 3 long strips. Place one strip on each side of layered dough, pinching to seal. Cut remaining strip into 3 long strips; braid and lay across center of loaf, pressing at top and bottom to seal. Brush with beaten egg, and sprinkle with Parmesan cheese. Bake at 375° for about 15 minutes. Makes 8 servings.

BLEU CHEESE-STUFFED CELERY

6 celery stalks
1 (3-ounce) package cream cheese, softened
2 tablespoons butter, softened
2 ounces bleu cheese, softened
1 tablespoon green onion, chopped
¼ cup chopped roasted pecans

Trim celery to 3-inch pieces. Combine cream cheese, butter, bleu cheese, and green onions, blending well. Spoon into celery pieces. Sprinkle with pecans. Makes about 18 pieces.

OLIVE CHEESE BITES

1 (5-ounce) jar cheese spread with bacon
¼ cup butter or margarine
Dash hot sauce
Dash Worcestershire sauce
¾ cup flour, sifted
30 stuffed olives

Blend cheese spread, butter, hot sauce, and Worcestershire sauce until light and fluffy. Stir in flour until dough forms. Shape about 1 teaspoon dough around each olive. Bake at 400° for 12 to 15 minutes. Makes 30 pieces.

HAM AND OLIVE BITES

1 cup finely chopped ham
½ cup chopped pecans
½ cup chopped olives
½ cup mayonnaise
Rye bread rounds
Capers, drained

Combine ham, pecans, olives, and enough mayonnaise to hold mixture together. Spread over rye bread rounds and top with capers. Makes about 3 dozen.

SWEET AND SALTY PECANS

3 tablespoons butter
2 cups pecan halves
⅔ cup sugar
1 tablespoon salt

Melt butter in a medium skillet over medium heat. Add remaining ingredients. Cook, stirring constantly, about 8 minutes. Spread over a greased baking sheet and cool. Makes 2 cups.

SPICED WALNUTS

1 pound walnut halves
1 cup butter, melted
3 cups powdered sugar
2 tablespoons cinnamon
2 teaspoons ground cloves
2 teaspoons nutmeg

Combine walnuts and butter; spread out on a large baking sheet. Bake at 300° for about 20 minutes, stirring once. Combine sugar and spices, and toss with hot walnuts. Makes about 4 cups.

MAKE-AHEAD ARTICHOKE BITES

2 (14-ounce) cans artichoke hearts, drained and chopped
2 eggs, lightly beaten
½ cup grated Parmesan cheese
½ cup Italian-seasoned breadcrumbs
½ teaspoon garlic salt

Combine all ingredients. Roll into ½-inch balls, and freeze on cookie sheet. Bake frozen balls at 350° for about 15 minutes or until golden brown. Makes about 3 dozen.

CRAB AND AVOCADO TOASTS

15 slices white bread, toasted
1 avocado, peeled and chopped
2 (3-ounce) packages cream cheese, softened
3 tablespoons mayonnaise
1½ teaspoons lemon juice
½ teaspoon onion powder
Dash hot sauce
1 cup fresh lump crabmeat, picked over to remove bits of shell

Trim crusts from bread, and cut each slice into 4 triangles. In a food processor, combine avocado, cream cheese, mayonnaise, lemon juice, onion powder, and hot sauce; process until smooth. Spread toasts with avocado mixture, and top with crabmeat. Makes 60 appetizers.

MEXICAN OLIVE PINWHEELS

1 (8-ounce) carton sour cream
1 (8-ounce) package cream cheese, softened
1 (4½-ounce) can chopped black olives, drained
1 cup shredded Monterey Jack cheese
½ cup green olives, chopped
½ cup chopped green onions
2 jalapeño peppers, seeded and minced
6 (8-inch) flour tortillas

Combine all ingredients except tortillas. Spread mixture evenly over tortillas, and roll uplyroll-style. Wrap in plastic, and chill overnight. Slice to serve. Makes about 3 dozen pinwheels.

Stuffed Mushrooms

16 large mushrooms, stems removed and chopped
½ cup butter, melted and divided
3 tablespoons chopped red bell pepper
3 tablespoons chopped green onions
1 teaspoon minced garlic
1 cup fresh breadcrumbs
Salt and pepper to taste

Cook mushroom caps in 3 tablespoons melted butter for 3 minutes; remove from pan. Cook chopped mushroom stems, red bell pepper, green onions, and garlic in remaining butter for about 5 minutes; stir in breadcrumbs and salt and pepper to taste. Fill mushrooms with stuffing mixture. Bake at 350° for about 10 minutes. Makes 8 servings.

Sausage-Stuffed Mushrooms

24 large mushrooms, stems removed
2 tablespoons butter or margarine, melted
½ pound bulk sausage
¼ cup chopped onion
½ teaspoon minced garlic
2 tablespoons picante sauce
1 (8-ounce) package processed cheese, thinly sliced

Brush mushroom caps with melted butter. Cook sausage, onion, and garlic in large skillet over medium heat until sausage is fully cooked. Add picante sauce. Spoon sausage mixture into mushroom caps. Cut each slice of cheese into quarters. Top each mushroom with a slice of cheese. Bake at 400° for 8 minutes. Makes 24.

PEPPERONI-STUFFED MUSHROOMS

16 large mushrooms, stems removed and chopped
5 tablespoons butter, melted and divided
½ cup chopped onion
½ cup chopped pepperoni
2 teaspoons Italian seasoning
¼ cup shredded mozzarella cheese

Toss mushroom caps with 3 tablespoons melted butter. Sauté chopped mushroom stems, onion, pepperoni, and Italian seasoning in remaining 2 tablespoons butter until onion is soft. Spoon mixture into mushroom caps and top with shredded cheese. Bake at 350° for about 10 minutes. Makes 16 servings.

CRAB-STUFFED MUSHROOMS

16 large mushrooms, stems removed
2 tablespoons butter, melted
1 (6-ounce) can crabmeat, drained and picked over to remove bits
of shell
½ cup breadcrumbs
2 teaspoons mayonnaise
1 teaspoon lemon juice
½ teaspoon garlic salt

Toss mushroom caps with butter. Combine crabmeat, breadcrumbs, mayonnaise, lemon juice, and garlic salt. Stuff mushroom caps with crab mixture, and drizzle with any remaining butter. Bake at 350° for about 10 minutes. Makes 16 servings.

MARINATED MUSHROOMS

⅓ cup olive oil
2 tablespoons red vinegar
1 teaspoon minced garlic
2 teaspoons Italian seasoning
Salt and pepper to taste
8 ounces small whole mushrooms
1 small red bell pepper, chopped

Combine olive oil, vinegar, garlic, Italian seasoning, and salt and pepper to taste, mixing well. Combine mushrooms and red bell pepper; toss with olive oil mixture and chill overnight. Makes about 8 servings.

MARINATED SUN-DRIED TOMATOES

1 (3-ounce) package sun-dried tomatoes, chopped
½ cup red vinegar
½ cup olive oil
2 teaspoons garlic, minced
1 teaspoon dried rosemary
1 teaspoon dried basil
Salt and pepper to taste
1 (8-ounce) package cream cheese

Combine sun-dried tomatoes, vinegar, olive oil, garlic, rosemary, basil, and salt and pepper to taste. Chill overnight. Pour over cream cheese, and serve with crackers. Makes about 16 servings.

Prosciutto-Wrapped Asparagus

1 bunch asparagus
1 (6-ounce) package garlic-and-herb-flavored Boursin cheese
6 to 8 ounces prosciutto, sliced paper-thin

Snap ends off asparagus, and steam or boil just until crisp and tender, about 3 to 5 minutes, depending on thickness. Plunge into a bowl of ice water; drain and lay on paper towels to dry. Spread cheese in a thin layer over each slice of prosciutto. Place one stalk of asparagus in the center of each piece of prosciutto; roll and place seam-side down on serving platter. Chill until ready to serve. Makes 16 servings.

Pepperoni-Parmesan Bites

1 cup flour
1 teaspoon baking powder
½ teaspoon dried basil
⅓ cup grated Parmesan cheese
1 cup milk
1 egg
½ cup finely chopped pepperoni

Coat 2 (12-muffin) mini muffin tins with cooking spray. Whisk flour, baking powder, and basil together in a large bowl. Stir in cheese, milk, egg, and pepperoni. Spoon into mini muffin tins. Bake at 350° for about 20 minutes. Makes 24 appetizers.

AVOCADO AND CRABMEAT COCKTAIL

1 cup ketchup
1 tablespoon mango chutney
1 teaspoon Worcestershire sauce
½ teaspoon salt
Juice of 1 lemon
1 avocado, peeled and diced
½ pound lump crabmeat, picked over

Combine ketchup, chutney, Worcestershire sauce, salt, and lemon juice for sauce. Lightly toss avocado and crabmeat together; serve with sauce. Makes 4 to 6 servings.

DEVILED HAM AND CHEESE DIP

1 (4½-ounce) can deviled ham
¼ cup Swiss cheese, shredded
1 tablespoon mayonnaise
2 teaspoons pickle relish
¼ teaspoon hot sauce
Crackers

Combine all ingredients and chill thoroughly. Serve with crackers. Makes about 1 cup.

DEVILED HAM AND CHEESE ROLLS

1 (16-count) pan frozen dinner rolls, thawed
1 recipe Deviled Ham and Cheese Dip (above)

Remove rolls from pan. Slice each roll in half; fill with dip. Replace rolls in pan. Bake at 350° for 10 to 12 minutes or according to package directions. Makes 16 rolls.

Apple-Orange Cooler

1 (6-ounce) can frozen orange juice concentrate, thawed
1 (6-ounce) can frozen lemonade concentrate, thawed
1 (32-ounce) bottle apple juice
1 (2-liter) bottle ginger ale, chilled

Combine all ingredients. Makes about 1 gallon.

Aloha Punch

1 (46-ounce) can pineapple juice
1 (46-ounce) can orange juice
½ cup lemon juice
1 (2-liter) bottle ginger ale, chilled

Combine pineapple juice, orange juice, and lemon juice; chill. Add ginger ale just before serving. Makes about 12 servings.

Aloha Sherbet Punch

1 recipe Aloha Punch
1 pint pineapple sherbet, softened

Combine punch and pineapple sherbet just before serving. Makes about 16 servings.

Mock Sangría

1 (46-ounce) can cranberry juice
1 (46-ounce) can orange juice
1 (46-ounce) can grape juice
Apples and oranges, sliced

Combine all ingredients; chill before serving. Makes about 18 servings.

Mock White Sangría

1 (46-ounce) can apple juice
1 (6-ounce) can frozen lemonade concentrate, thawed
1 (6-ounce) can frozen limeade concentrate, thawed
Green apples, limes, and lemons, sliced
1 (2-liter) bottle ginger ale, chilled

Combine apple juice, lemonade concentrate, limeade concentrate, and fruit; chill. Add ginger ale just before serving. Makes about 1 gallon.

Minted Lemonade

1 (2-quart) package lemonade mix
2 quarts water
½ cup fresh mint leaves, crushed

Combine lemonade mix and water; bring to a boil. Pour over mint leaves, and let sit until cool. Strain before serving. Makes 2 quarts.

Apricot-Ginger Lemonade

1 (2-quart) package lemonade mix
2 quarts water
2 cups apricot nectar
1 (2-liter) bottle ginger ale, chilled

Combine lemonade mix, water, and apricot nectar; chill thoroughly. Add ginger ale just before serving. Makes about 1 gallon.

Minted Iced Tea

2 quarts water
2 (1-quart) tea bags
½ cup fresh mint leaves, crushed

Bring water to a boil; remove from heat. Add tea bags and mint leaves; let sit until cool. Strain before serving, adding more water if too strong. Makes about 2 quarts.

Wassail

2 (46-ounce) cans apple juice
1 cup orange juice
1 cup lemon juice
1 cup brown sugar
6 whole cinnamon sticks
6 whole cloves
6 whole allspice berries

Combine all ingredients, and bring to a boil. Reduce heat, and simmer for about an hour. Remove whole spices before serving. Makes about 12 servings.

OLD-FASHIONED PARTY PUNCH

1 (16-ounce) carton lime sherbet
2 (2-liter) bottles ginger ale

Scoop lime sherbet into punch bowl; pour ginger ale over, and stir gently. Makes about 20 servings.

WARM CRANBERRY APPLE CIDER

1 quart apple cider
1 quart cranberry juice
2 cups orange juice
½ cup lemon juice
¾ cup sugar
3 sticks cinnamon
1½ teaspoons whole cloves
1½ teaspoons whole allspice
1 vanilla bean

Combine all ingredients in a large saucepan. Heat over low burner, stirring occasionally, until warm and fragrant. Makes about 10 servings.

COFFEE SLUSH PUNCH

1 cup sugar
1 cup water
⅓ cup instant coffee
3 (13-ounce) cans evaporated milk, chilled
1 quart vanilla ice cream, slightly softened
1 (2-liter) bottle club soda, chilled

Combine sugar, water, and coffee in small saucepan. Heat, stirring constantly, until sugar and coffee are dissolved. In a pitcher, combine coffee mixture with remaining ingredients, and stir until slushy. Makes about 32 servings.

PINEAPPLE PUNCH

1 (46-ounce) can pineapple juice
2 cups cranberry juice
1 cup lemon juice
1 cup sugar
1 (2-liter) bottle ginger ale

Combine juices with sugar, stirring until sugar is dissolved. Add ginger ale just before serving. Makes about 32 servings.

FRUITED ICE RING FOR PUNCH

Assorted fresh fruit (sliced lemons, limes, bunches of grapes, etc.)

Fill a ring mold halfway full with water; freeze until firm. Arrange fruit on top of ice; add water to come about halfway up fruit. Freeze until firm. Float in punch bowl. Makes 1 ring.

STRAWBERRY PUNCH

1 (46-ounce) can pineapple juice
1 cup lemon juice
2 (16-ounce) bags frozen strawberries in syrup, thawed and
  chopped
1 quart ginger ale, chilled

Combine pineapple juice, lemon juice, and strawberries with syrup;
chill. Just before serving, stir in ginger ale. Makes about 3 quarts.

CRANBERRY-ORANGE SLUSH PUNCH

½ cup sugar
1 cup water
1 (46-ounce) can cranberry juice
1 cup orange juice
½ cup lemon juice
1 liter ginger ale

Combine sugar and water; bring to a boil, and boil for 5 minutes. Add
cranberry juice, orange juice, and lemon juice to sugar mixture. Pour
into a 3-quart freezer-safe dish and freeze, stirring several times
during freezing process. Scrape into serving bowl, and add ginger ale,
breaking up into a slushy punch. Makes about 2½ quarts.

RUSSIAN TEA MIX

1 (9-ounce) jar instant orange beverage mix
1 cup instant tea mix
1 cup sugar
1 teaspoon ground cinnamon
1 teaspoon ground cloves

Combine all ingredients, mixing well. Use 1 tablespoon mix for each cup of boiling water. Makes about 4 cups mix.

APPLE SLUSH PUNCH

½ cup sugar
1 cup water
1 (46-ounce) can apple juice
1 cup orange juice
½ cup lemon juice
1 liter ginger ale

Combine sugar and water; bring to a boil, and boil for 5 minutes. Add apple juice, orange juice, and lemon juice to sugar mixture. Pour into a 3-quart freezer-safe dish, and freeze, stirring several times during freezing process. Scrape into serving bowl and add ginger ale, breaking up into a slushy punch. Makes about 2½ quarts.

HONEST-TO-GOODNESS HOT CHOCOLATE

2 (1-ounce) squares unsweetened baking chocolate
¾ cup water
¼ cup sugar
Dash salt
3½ cups milk
1 teaspoon vanilla extract

Combine chocolate, water, sugar, and salt in a medium saucepan over low heat; stir until chocolate is melted. Increase heat, and bring to a boil; boil 3 minutes, stirring constantly. Reduce heat, and gradually add milk; do not boil. Add vanilla extract. Makes 6 servings.

FRENCH HOT CHOCOLATE

2 (1-ounce) squares unsweetened baking chocolate
½ cup water
⅔ cup sugar
Dash salt
½ cup heavy whipping cream, stiffly whipped
4 cups hot milk

Combine chocolate, water, sugar, and salt in a medium saucepan over low heat; cook, stirring constantly, about 10 minutes. Cool. Fold in whipped cream. Put a dollop of chocolate cream inside each cup and pour hot milk over. Makes 6 servings.

WATERMELON ICE CUBES

4¼ cups watermelon puree

Puree seedless watermelon and pour into ice cube trays. Freeze and enjoy in your favorite beverages. Adds a light, fruity flavor to beverages, from sparkling water to sodas.

SALADS, DRESSINGS, AND SAUCES

BLACK BEAN AND CORN SALAD

2 (15-ounce) cans black beans, drained and rinsed
2 (15-ounce) cans corn, drained
1 red bell pepper, chopped
3 celery stalks, chopped
1 small red onion, chopped
1 teaspoon minced garlic
½ cup sugar
½ cup vinegar
½ cup olive oil
1 teaspoon cumin
1 teaspoon dried oregano
Salt and pepper to taste

Combine beans, corn, bell pepper, celery, onion, and garlic. Combine sugar, vinegar, olive oil, cumin, oregano, and salt and pepper. Pour over bean and corn mixture, and toss to combine. Makes 8 to 10 servings.

CHICKEN, BLACK BEAN, AND CORN SALAD

4 cups chicken, cooked and chopped
1 recipe Black Bean and Corn Salad (above)

Combine chicken with Black Bean and Corn Salad. Makes 8 to 10 servings.

TABBOULEH CHEESE SALAD

1 cup bulgur wheat
2 cups Cheddar cheese, cubed
3 tomatoes, chopped
⅓ cup Italian salad dressing

Rinse bulgur, and soak in cold water to cover for at least 30 minutes, or until bulgur is soft but still chewy. Drain well. Combine with remaining ingredients, and toss to coat. Cover and chill 30 minutes. Makes 4 servings.

GREEK PASTA SALAD

1 (16-ounce) package orzo pasta, cooked and drained
⅔ cup olive oil
⅓ cup lemon juice
2 tablespoons vinegar
2 chopped green onions
2 tablespoons chopped fresh parsley
1 (4-ounce) package feta cheese
1 (4-ounce) can sliced black olives, drained
¼ cup pine nuts, toasted
Salt and pepper to taste

Combine all ingredients, tossing well to coat. Makes 4 servings.

Italian Pasta Salad

1 (16-ounce) package frozen cheese tortellini, prepared according
  to package directions
1 (14-ounce) can artichoke heart quarters, drained
1 red bell pepper, chopped
1 small red onion, chopped
1 (4-ounce) can sliced black olives, drained
½ pint grape tomatoes, halved
¼ cup shredded Parmesan cheese
1 (8-ounce) bottle Italian dressing

Combine all ingredients. Makes 8 servings.

Italian Shrimp and Pasta Salad

4 cups shrimp, cooked and peeled
1 recipe Italian Pasta Salad (above)

Combine shrimp with pasta salad. Makes 8 servings.

Macaroni Salad

1 pound dried elbow macaroni
1 bell pepper, finely chopped
1 onion, finely chopped
4 carrots, grated
1 (14-ounce) can sweetened condensed milk
½ cup vinegar
½ cup sugar
1 cup mayonnaise

Cook macaroni and drain. Mix remaining ingredients together.
Marinate overnight. Makes 8 servings.

CHICKEN SALAD

1 (2½- to 3-pound) chicken, cooked and coarsely chopped
2 cups chopped celery
¼ cup chopped green bell pepper
1 cup sweet pickle relish
6 hard-boiled eggs, chopped
1½ cups mayonnaise
1 teaspoon fresh lemon juice

Combine chicken, celery, green bell pepper, relish, and eggs in a bowl. Add mayonnaise and lemon juice; mix gently. Chill until ready to serve. Makes 8 servings.

CURRIED CHICKEN SALAD

6 boneless, skinless chicken breasts, cooked and chopped
1 cup chopped celery
1 (15-ounce) can pineapple tidbits
1 cup red seedless grapes, halved
⅓ cup fresh parsley, chopped
1 to 1½ cups mayonnaise
2 tablespoons mango chutney
2 tablespoons curry powder
Salt and pepper to taste

Combine chicken, celery, pineapple, grapes, and parsley in a large bowl. Combine mayonnaise, chutney, curry powder, and salt and pepper. Add to chicken mixture. Makes about 12 servings.

BLEU CHEESE CHICKEN SALAD

2½ cups cooked and chopped chicken
⅔ cup chopped walnuts, toasted
3 celery stalks, finely chopped
3 green onions, thinly sliced
1 cup seedless grapes, halved
1 (8-ounce) can pineapple tidbits, well drained
Bleu Cheese Dressing (p. 94)

Combine all ingredients except dressing in a large bowl. Toss lightly with Bleu Cheese Dressing. Makes 8 servings.

BALSAMIC CHICKEN SALAD

1 (10-ounce) package baby salad greens
2 (5-ounce) packages sliced grilled chicken breast
½ pound Havarti cheese, cubed
½ cup balsamic vinaigrette dressing

Slice chicken breasts into strips. Toss with salad greens, Havarti cheese, and vinaigrette dressing. Makes 4 servings.

BERRY CHICKEN SALAD

1 pound boneless, skinless chicken breasts, cut into strips
1 cup Catalina or French salad dressing
1 (10-ounce) package mixed salad greens
2 cups sliced strawberries, blueberries, or raspberries

In a large skillet, simmer chicken in ¼ cup of the salad dressing over medium heat until thoroughly cooked. Toss greens, berries, and chicken in a large bowl with remaining dressing. Makes 4 servings.

Chicken and Bacon Macaroni Salad

1 cup sour cream
½ cup Italian dressing
Salt and pepper to taste
8 ounces dried elbow macaroni, cooked and drained
2 cups cooked and chopped chicken
½ pound bacon, cooked and crumbled
2 hard-boiled eggs, chopped
1 large tomato, seeded and chopped

Combine sour cream, Italian dressing, and salt and pepper to taste. Combine with remaining ingredients, tossing lightly to coat. Makes 6 servings.

Pickle Chicken Salad

2 cups cooked and chopped chicken
2 cups hard-boiled and chopped eggs
1½ cups diced celery
½ cup sweet pickles
½ cup mayonnaise
1 teaspoon salt
⅛ teaspoon pepper

Combine chicken, eggs, celery, and pickles; mix well. Add mayonnaise, salt, and pepper. Mix together thoroughly. Chill. Makes 6 servings.

Hot Chicken Salad

2 cups cooked and cubed chicken
1½ cups celery, diced
½ cups nuts, chopped
1 cup mayonnaise
2 tablespoons lemon juice
½ teaspoon salt
½ cup American cheese, grated
1 cup potato chips, finely crushed

Combine chicken, celery, nuts, mayonnaise, lemon juice, and salt.
Heat thoroughly. Pile into 6 small casseroles. Sprinkle with grated
cheese, and top with crushed potato chips. Bake at 400° for 10
minutes or until brown. Makes 6 servings.

Chicken Fruit Salad

1 orange
15 large grapes
1 banana
½ cup crushed pineapple, drained
1 apple, cored and diced
3 cups cooked and diced white chicken meat
1 cup mayonnaise
Lettuce

Remove seeds and membrane from orange pieces, and cut into halves.
Cut grapes into halves, removing seeds. Slice banana. Mix all
ingredients lightly but thoroughly. Chill and serve on lettuce. Makes 4
servings.

POLYNESIAN CHICKEN SALAD

3 cups cooked and chopped chicken
1 cup celery, chopped
1 (10-ounce) can mandarin oranges, drained
1 (8-ounce) can crushed pineapple, drained
1 (8-ounce) bottle French vinaigrette
⅓ cup chopped almonds, toasted
¼ cup mayonnaise
¼ cup shredded coconut
Salt and pepper to taste

Combine all ingredients, tossing lightly to coat. Makes 6 servings.

SEAFOOD SALAD

¼ cup mayonnaise
1 tablespoon pickle juice
2 tablespoons sweet pickle, diced
1 cup canned tuna or shrimp
½ cup sliced celery
½ cup canned peas, chilled
1 cup coarsely crushed potato chips
Lettuce

Mix mayonnaise with pickle juice. Toss with pickles, tuna or shrimp, celery, and peas. Toss gently with potato chips. Serve on lettuce. Makes 4 servings.

TUNA SALAD

1 (7-ounce) can tuna, drained
⅓ cup chopped dill pickle
¼ teaspoon celery seeds
Seasoning salt to taste
¼ teaspoon mustard
2 tablespoons mayonnaise

Combine tuna, pickle, celery seeds, seasoning salt, and mustard in a bowl. Add mayonnaise; mix with fork. Makes 4 servings.

SHRIMP SALAD

1 pound shrimp, cooked, peeled, and minced
3 hard-boiled eggs, finely chopped
2 cups minced celery
½ cup mayonnaise
Salt and pepper to taste

In a large bowl combine shrimp, eggs, celery, and mayonnaise; mix well. Add salt and pepper, and stir to combine. Makes 4 servings.

PIQUANT SHRIMP SALAD

1 pound shrimp, cooked, peeled, and minced
1 cup minced celery
½ cup mayonnaise
2 tablespoons capers, drained and chopped
Salt and pepper to taste

In a large bowl combine shrimp, celery, mayonnaise, and capers; mix well. Add salt and pepper, and stir to combine. Makes 4 servings.

SALMON SALAD

1 (1-pound) can salmon, drained and broken into small pieces
1 cup chopped celery
2 cups lettuce, torn into coarse threads
¼ cup chopped pickles
Salt and pepper to taste
French dressing
3 hard-boiled eggs, cut into wedges

Combine salmon, celery, lettuce, pickles, salt, and pepper; toss lightly. Dribble with French dressing. Moud into cupped lettuce leaves. Garnish with egg wedges. Makes 4 servings.

ASIAN SHRIMP SALAD

1 pound shrimp, cooked and peeled
1 (10-ounce) package frozen green peas, thawed
2 celery stalks, finely chopped
3 chopped green onions
½ cup mayonnaise
1 tablespoon lemon juice
½ teaspoon minced garlic
½ teaspoon curry powder
¼ teaspoon ground ginger
Salt and pepper to taste
1 (3-ounce) can chow mein noodles
½ cup cashews, coarsely chopped

Combine all ingredients except noodles and cashews. Chill until serving time. Gently toss chow mein noodles and cashews with shrimp mixture. Makes 4 servings.

QUICK ORIENTAL SALAD

1 (1-pounce) package spinach salad mix
1 cup sliced water chestnuts
½ pound mandarin orange segments, undrained

Serve spinach sprinkled with water chestnuts and tossed with orange segments and their juice. Makes 4 to 6 servings.

GREEN SALAD WITH RAISINS, PINE NUTS, AND FETA

¼ cup olive oil
2 tablespoons balsamic vinegar
½ teaspoon minced garlic
Salt and pepper to taste
1 head romaine lettuce, cleaned and chopped
½ cup raisins
¼ cup pine nuts, toasted
3 green onions, thinly sliced
1 (4-ounce) package crumbled feta cheese

Combine olive oil, vinegar, garlic, and salt and pepper for dressing. Gently toss with remaining ingredients. Makes 8 servings.

CANADIAN BACON PEACH SALAD

1 (10-ounce) bag mixed salad greens
1 (12-ounce) package cooked Canadian bacon, slices quartered
2 peaches, sliced
½ cup honey mustard salad dressing

Toss ingredients in a large bowl and serve. Makes 4 servings.

LAYERED OVERNIGHT SALAD

1 head lettuce, chopped
½ cup chopped onion
½ cup chopped celery
1 (5-ounce) can sliced water chestnuts, drained
1 (10-ounce) package frozen green peas, thawed
2 cups mayonnaise
1 tablespoon sugar
2 tomatoes, seeded and chopped
6 hard-boiled eggs, chopped
½ pound bacon, cooked and crumbled
1 cup shredded Cheddar cheese

Place lettuce in bottom of a 9-inch x 13-inch baking dish. Combine onions and celery and sprinkle over lettuce. Combine water chestnuts and peas; sprinkle over onion mixture. Combine mayonnaise and sugar; spread over pea mixture. Refrigerate overnight. Before serving, layer tomatoes, eggs, bacon, and cheese over mayonnaise. Makes 12 servings.

CHILLED PEA AND MUSHROOM SALAD

2 (10-ounces) packages frozen green peas, thawed
8 ounces sliced mushrooms
⅓ cup olive oil
2 tablespoons cocktail onions, thinly sliced
1 teaspoon dried oregano
Salt and pepper to taste

Combine all ingredients; cover and chill. Makes about 12 servings.

Artichoke-Green Bean Salad

½ pound fresh green beans, trimmed
1 (8-ounce) jar marinated artichoke hearts
½ cup chopped walnuts, toasted
Salt and pepper

Cover green beans with boiling water and cook, uncovered, for about 4 to 5 minutes until crisp and tender. Drain and coarsely chop artichoke hearts, reserving liquid. Combine beans in a bowl with artichoke hearts and their liquid and salt and pepper to taste. Top salad with walnuts. Makes 4 servings.

Green Pea Salad

1 (16-ounce) can green peas, drained
3 hard-boiled eggs, chopped
¾ cup chopped celery
1 large apple, chopped
2 sweet pickles, chopped
1 dill pickle, chopped
1 tablespoon chopped pimento,
2 tablespoons mayonnaise
Salt and pepper to taste
Lettuce leaf

Mix first 7 ingredients together and chill for two hours. Toss with mayonnaise, salt, and pepper; serve on lettuce leaf. Makes 6 servings.

Vegetable Salad

1 head lettuce, chopped
2 green bell peppers, sliced
3 tomatoes, seeded and chopped
2 cucumbers, peeled, seeded, and chopped
½ teaspoon salt
1 cup olive oil

Toss vegetables together, and add salt and olive oil. Makes 6 servings.

Mixed Vegetable Salad

3 tomatoes, cut into wedges
1 green bell pepper, cut into rings
6 green onions, sliced
6 radishes, sliced
1 head lettuce, chopped
French dressing

Toss vegetables with dressing. Makes 6 servings.

Broccoli Salad

1 bunch broccoli, chopped
1 head cauliflower, chopped
1 cup shredded Cheddar cheese
1 Vidalia onion, sliced
4 slices bacon, cooked and crumbled
1 cup mayonnaise
¼ cup sugar
¼ cup apple cider vinegar

Combine broccoli, cauliflower, cheese, onion, and bacon in a large bowl. Blend mayonnaise and sugar in a small bowl. Stir in vinegar. Add to salad; mix well. Makes 12 servings.

BROCCOLI RAISIN SALAD

2 bunches fresh broccoli, cut into florets
1 cup chopped pecans
1 small onion, chopped
½ cup raisins
1 pound bacon, fried and crumbled
1 cup mayonnaise
½ cup sugar
1 tablespoon apple cider vinegar

Cook broccoli in a small amount of boiling water for 1 to 2 minutes; broccoli should still be very crisp. Drain, and rinse with cold water. Drain well, and add pecans, onion, raisins, and bacon.

Combine mayonnaise, sugar, and apple cider vinegar; stir until sugar is dissolved. Pour over broccoli mixture, and toss to combine. Makes about 10 servings.

CABBAGE SALAD

1 teaspoon sugar
1 teaspoon salt
1 egg
¼ cup evaporated milk
¼ cup water
1 tablespoon margarine
½ cup hot vinegar
3 cups finely chopped cabbage

Mix sugar, salt, and egg. Heat milk and combine with water. Add sugar, salt, egg, and margarine; stir over medium heat until thick. Stir in vinegar and cabbage mixture, and let cool. Makes 4 to 6 servings.

COLESLAW

1 large head cabbage, shredded
1 large green bell pepper, chopped
1 large red onion, thinly sliced into rings
⅔ cup chopped celery
1 (4-ounce) jar chopped pimentos, drained
1 cup sugar
1 cup white vinegar
1 teaspoon dry mustard
2 teaspoons sugar
2 teaspoons dried dill
2 teaspoons dried parsley
Paprika to taste
1 tablespoon salt
¾ cup oil

Combine cabbage, green bell pepper, onion, celery, and pimentos in a large bowl. Sprinkle with 1 cup sugar. Combine vinegar, dry mustard, 2 teaspoons sugar, dill, parsley, paprika, and salt in a saucepan. Bring to a rolling boil. Pour over cabbage mixture. Chill, covered, for 4 hours to overnight. Toss before serving. Makes 16 servings.

NECTARINE COLESLAW

4 cups creamy coleslaw
2 nectarines, peaches, or peeled mangoes, chopped
½ cup honey roasted peanuts or cashews

Combine all ingredients in a medium bowl, and toss gently to blend. Makes 4 to 6 servings.

CONFETTI SLAW

¼ head green cabbage, shredded
¼ head red cabbage, shredded
1 red bell pepper, julienned
1 carrot, shredded
¼ cup mayonnaise
1 teaspoon honey
Juice of half an orange
Juice of half a lemon
Salt and pepper to taste

Combine green cabbage, red cabbage, red bell pepper, and carrot in a
large bowl. Combine remaining ingredients, and pour over vegetable
mixture. Chill. Makes 4 servings.

ALMOND AND GRAPE COLESLAW

1 small head cabbage, shredded
2 cups white seedless grapes
1 cup sliced almonds, toasted
1 cup mayonnaise
2 tablespoons apple cider vinegar
1 tablespoon dry mustard
Salt and pepper to taste

Combine cabbage, grapes, and almonds in a large bowl. Combine
mayonnaise, apple cider vinegar, dry mustard, and salt and pepper to
taste. Pour over cabbage mixture, and toss lightly to coat. Makes 8
servings.

APPLE COLESLAW

3 large tart apples, cored and shredded
1 small head cabbage, shredded
⅔ cup mayonnaise
⅓ cup sugar
1 tablespoon apple cider vinegar
¼ teaspoon celery seed
Juice of 1 lemon
Salt and pepper to taste

Combine all ingredients; chill before serving. Makes about 8 servings.

OLD-FASHIONED POTATO SALAD

4 potatoes, peeled and cooked
Salt and pepper to taste
1 cup mayonnaise
½ cup finely chopped dill pickle
½ cup finely chopped onion
3 hard-boiled eggs, finely chopped
2 tablespoons mustard
2 tablespoons Thousand Island salad dressing
Sliced hard-boiled egg
Paprika

Mash potatoes with salt, pepper, and mayonnaise in a mixer bowl until smooth. Add pickle, onion, eggs, mustard, and Thousand Island dressing; mix well. Spoon into serving bowl; garnish with additional slices of boiled egg and paprika. Makes 8 servings.

TANGY NEW POTATO SALAD

½ cup butter, melted
1 bunch chopped green onions
¼ cup mayonnaise
2 tablespoons Dijon mustard
1 tablespoon horseradish
1 tablespoon lemon juice
1 teaspoon dried dill
1 teaspoon celery seed
Salt and pepper to taste
1½ pounds new potatoes, cooked and quartered

Combine butter, green onions, mayonnaise, mustard, horseradish, lemon juice, dill, celery seed, and salt and pepper. Add potatoes, and toss lightly to coat. Makes about 10 servings.

HOT POTATO SALAD

1 pound bacon, chopped
2 cups chopped onion
1 cup apple cider vinegar
1½ tablespoons sugar
Salt and pepper to taste
3 pounds potatoes, cooked, peeled, and sliced

Cook bacon in a large skillet over medium heat until crisp; remove to paper towels to drain. Pour off all but 3 tablespoons bacon grease; add onion and cook until tender. Add vinegar, sugar, and salt and pepper to taste. Bring to a boil. Pour over potato slices, add cooked bacon, and toss lightly to coat. Makes 12 servings.

Pesto Potato Salad

5 cups creamy deli potato salad
1 (10-ounce) container basil pesto
2 red bell peppers, chopped

Mix all ingredients in medium bowl. Cover and chill for 1 to 2 hours to blend flavors. Makes about 8 servings.

Tex-Mex Potato Salad

5 cups potato salad
2 (11-ounce) cans corn with red and green peppers, drained
⅓ cup ranch salad dressing
1 teaspoon chili powder

Mix all ingredients gently in large bowl; cover and refrigerate. Makes about 8 servings.

Three-Bean and Pasta Salad

16 ounces mostaccioli or mafalda pasta
1 (15-ounce) can three bean salad, chilled
2 cups grape tomatoes

Cook pasta in boiling salted water until desired doneness or as directed on package. Drain. Combine with undrained three-bean salad and tomatoes in medium bowl. Mix gently, cover, and chill. Makes 4 servings.

THREE-BEAN SALAD

1 (1-pound) can cut green beans, drained and rinsed
1 (1-pound) can cut yellow wax beans, drained and rinsed
1 (1-pound) can red kidney beans, drained and rinsed
¼ cup chopped green bell pepper
1 medium onion, sliced very thin
½ cup cider vinegar
⅓ cup cooking oil
½ cup sugar
1 teaspoon salt
1 teaspoon pepper

Combine beans, bell pepper, and onion. Mix together the rest of the ingredients and pour over beans. Makes 8 to 10 servings.

GRAPE AND MELON SALAD

1 cantaloupe, peeled, seeded, and cut into cubes or balls
2 cups red grapes
½ cup mayonnaise
¼ cup pineapple-orange juice

Combine cantaloupe cubes and grapes in a large bowl. In a small bowl, mix together mayonnaise and juice and stir to blend. Pour over fruit, and refrigerate for 1 to 2 hours before serving. Makes 4 servings.

TANGY APPLE SALAD

1 cup diced tart apple
1 cup diced celery
½ cup raisins
½ cup French dressing

Combine all ingredients; chill. Makes about 4 servings.

MANDARIN SALAD

2 tomatoes, peeled and sliced
2 (11-ounce) cans mandarin oranges, drained
1 cup onion thinly sliced
3 cups lettuce leaves, torn into bite-sized pieces

Combine ingredients. Good served with Orange Juice Dressing
(p. 90). Makes 4 servings.

FRUIT SALAD

2 large Delicious apples, cored and chopped
2 cups white grapes
2 cups peeled and seeded oranges or tangerines
2 cups red grapes, seeds removed

Mix together and serve chilled. Makes 8 cups.

FRUIT SALAD №2

3 apples, cored
3 bananas
3 oranges
1 (8-ounce) can pineapple chunks
1 cup pecans
3 tablespoons mayonnaise

Peel apples, oranges, and bananas. Cut all fruit and pecans into small
pieces; mix with mayonnaise. Makes about 4 servings.

OLD-FASHIONED FRUIT SALAD

1 (15-ounce) can pineapple chunks
½ cup sugar
3 apples, cored and chopped
3 oranges, peeled and seeded
3 bananas, sliced
1 cup grapes, halved
1 cup miniature marshmallows

Drain pineapple, reserving ¼ cup juice. Combine reserved juice with sugar in a bowl; mix well. Combine pineapple, apples, oranges, bananas, grapes, and marshmallows in another bowl; mix well. Add pineapple juice mixture; toss gently to mix. Chill for 1 hour. Makes 12 servings.

MINTED FRUIT SALAD

3 cups cantaloupe balls
3 cups honeydew balls
3 cups blueberries
½ cup honey
½ cup water
½ cup ginger ale
1 tablespoon fresh mint, chopped
1 tablespoon lemon juice
½ teaspoon cardamom

Combine cantaloupe, honeydew, and blueberries; set aside. Combine remaining ingredients in a small saucepan, and warm over low heat for about 5 minutes. Pour over fruit, and toss lightly. Makes 8 servings.

WALDORF SALAD

1 (3-ounce) package cream cheese, softened
1 teaspoon sugar
2 teaspoons orange or pineapple juice
3 large apples, cored and diced
1 (8-ounce) can pineapple tidbits, drained
2 tablespoons chopped celery
2 tablespoons chopped pecans
2 tablespoons raisins

Combine cream cheese, sugar, and orange or pineapple juice.
Combine apples, pineapple, celery, pecans, and raisins; gently fold in
cream cheese mixture. Chill until serving time. Makes about 8
servings.

EASTER SALAD

6 pear halves, cored
5 tablespoons cream cheese, softened
6 lettuce leafs
12 almonds, blanched
12 whole cloves
6 teaspoons mayonnaise

Fill pears with cream cheese. Place on a lettuce leaf, round side of
pear up. Watch Easter bunny evolve as cloves are stuck in each side
of pear at the small end for eyes and the long almonds slightly back
of the cloves for ears. Complete with a teaspoon of mayonnaise at the
rough end for tail. Makes 6 servings.

PISTACHIO PUDDING SALAD

1 (8-ounce) can crushed pineapple, drained
1 package instant pistachio pudding mix
½ cup whipped cream topping
1½ cups miniature marshmallows

In a large bowl, combine the pineapple and pudding mix. Stir in the whipped cream toppingand marshmallows, and mix well. Makes 4 servings.

FAST COTTAGE CHEESE SALAD

1 (3-ounce) box gelatin, any flavor
1 (8-ounce) small carton cottage cheese
1 (8-ounce) can crushed pineapple, drained
1 (4½-ounce) package whipped cream topping

Combine the dry gelatin with the cottage cheese and mix well. Add the whipped cream toppingand pineapple; mix well and refrigerate. Makes 4 servings.

FAST AND FROSTY ORANGE SALAD

1 (3-ounce) package orange gelatin
1 (3-ounce) package regular vanilla pudding
2 cups water
1 (8-ounce) can crushed pineapple
1 (4½-ounce) container whipped cream topping

Mix together and bring to a boil. Cool. Stir in pineapple and whipped topping. Chill for 2 hours. Makes 4 servings.

Golden Glow Salad

1 (3-ounce) package orange gelatin
1 cup hot water
1 cup pineapple juice
1 tablespoon vinegar
½ teaspoon salt
1 cup diced canned pineapple, drained
1 cup carrot, grated
Lettuce
Mayonnaise

Dissolve gelatin in hot water. Add pineapple juice, vinegar, and salt; chill. When slightly thickened add pineapple and carrot; chill until firm. Unmold on lettuce; garnish with mayonnaise. Makes 4 servings.

Sweet Carrot Salad

1 pound carrots, shredded
1 (8-ounce) can crushed pineapple, drained
½ cup miniature marshmallows
½ cup shredded coconut
2 tablespoons sour cream
2 tablespoons lemon juice
2 tablespoons honey

Combine all ingredients; chill before serving. Makes 8 to 10 servings.

SIX-CUP SALAD

1 cup mandarin orange slices, drained
1 cup shredded coconut
1 cup pineapple tidbits, drained
1 cup miniature marshmallows
1 cup green seedless grapes, halved
1 cup sour cream

Combine all ingredients. Chill. Makes 12 servings.

WINTER SALAD

2 tablespoons gelatin
½ cup water
2 cups cranberries
¾ cup sugar
½ teaspoon salt
¾ cup diced celery
¾ cup diced apple
Lettuce
Salad dressing

Soak the gelatin in water for 5 minutes. Cook the cranberries in 2½ cups of water until tender, add sugar, and cook for 5 minutes, stirring occasionally. Add salt, and strain. Add softened gelatin, and stir until dissolved. When the mixture begins to thicken, add celery and apples, and pour into a shallow pan. Chill. When firm, cut into pieces for serving. Serve on lettuce and garnish with salad dressing. Makes 4 servings.

OVERNIGHT CHERRY SALAD

2 cups sour cream
2 cups cottage cheese
2 cups whipped cream topping
1 (6-ounce) package cherry-flavored gelatin
1 (17-ounce) can dark sweet pitted cherries, drained
1 cup chopped pecans

Combine all ingredients. Chill overnight. Makes 12 to 16 servings.

TOMATO ASPIC SALAD CUBES

1 (3-ounce) package plain gelatin
1 cup chicken stock
1½ cups diced tomato
½ cup diced celery
½ cup shredded cabbage
1 carrot, grated
1 green bell pepper, chopped
2 tablespoons minced onion
2 tablespoons vinegar
½ teaspoon salt
¼ teaspoon cayenne pepper
Lettuce
Mayonnaise

Soak gelatin in stock; dissolve over hot water. Add other ingredients and seasonings. Chill thoroughly in ice tray with cube grid. Pile a few jellied cubes lightly on lettuce leaf; top with mayonnaise. Makes 6 to 8 servings.

Frozen Fruit Salad

1 teaspoon gelatin
3 tablespoons syrup from canned fruit
½ cup mayonnaise
⅔ cup whipping cream
2 cups canned fruit cocktail
Marshmallows, dates, and nuts (optional)
Powdered sugar
Salt
Paprika

Soak gelatin in syrup; dissolve over hot water. Add slowly to mayonnaise. Beat cream, and gradually beat into first mixture. Add drained fruit, and season to taste with sugar, salt, and paprika. Makes 4 servings.

Frozen Nougat Cream Salad

½ teaspoon gelatin
1 tablespoon water
3 tablespoons cherry syrup
⅓ cup mayonnaise
1 cup whipping cream
⅓ cup powdered sugar
¼ teaspoon salt
6 marshmallows, diced
6 ounces maraschino cherries, minced
⅓ cup chopped pecans
Lettuce cups

Soak gelatin in cold water; dissolve over hot water. Add to cherry syrup, and then stir into mayonnaise. Fold in cream that has been beaten, adding confectioner's sugar and salt. Add remaining ingredients; freeze. Serve in squares in lettuce cups. Makes 4 servings.

MOLDED RAW CRANBERRY SALAD

2 cups water
1 (3-ounce) package orange gelatin
Juice of 1 lemon
½ cup granulated sugar
2 cups raw cranberries
1 cup chopped nuts
1 cup chopped celery
Lettuce cups

Pour ½ cup cold water in bowl. Add gelatin on top of water. Add 1½ cups hot water and stir until dissolved. Add lemon juice and sugar. Set aside to cool. Grind raw cranberries; chop nuts and celery fine. Add these ingredients to gelatin. Place salad in individual molds and let congeal in the refrigerator. Serve in lettuce cups. Makes 4 servings.

ASPARAGUS BAVARIAN SALAD

1 tablespoon gelatin
¼ cups cold water
Reserved asparagus liquid plus enough water to equal 1½ cups
1 can green asparagus
1 cup evaporated milk, whipped
¼ teaspoon salt
¼ teaspoon white pepper
Dash mace
½ pimento, chopped

Soak gelatin in cold water; dissolve in hot asparagus liquid. Chill. Arrange stalks of asparagus around the sides of a dampened mold. When the jelly begins to congeal, add ½ cup of asparagus that has been put through a sieve, salt, pepper, mace, the chopped pimento, and the whipped evaporated milk. Turn into the mold, and set in the refrigerator to congeal. Makes 4 servings.

FROZEN CRANBERRY SALAD

1 (8-ounce) package cream cheese, softened
2 tablespoons sugar
2 tablespoons mayonnaise
1 (15-ounce) can whole berry cranberry sauce, undrained
1 (4-ounce) can crushed pineapple, undrained
½ cup chopped pecans
1 cup whipping cream

Combine first three ingredients, blending well. Stir in cranberry sauce
and pineapple. Gently fold in pecans and whipped cream. Coat a
3-quart baking dish with cooking spray and spread fruit mixture in.
Cover and freeze until firm. Makes about 12 servings.

PINEAPPLE-CARROT SALAD RING

1 cup water
1 (3-ounce) package lemon gelatin
1 cup pineapple juice
1 cup sliced pineapple
4 or 5 carrots, grated
Lettuce
Mayonnaise or French dressing

Heat 1 cup water, and pour over gelatin. Add 1 cup cold pineapple
juice. Set aside to cook. Add grated carrot and pineapple that has
been cut in small tidbits. Place in individual molds or in a large ring
mold. Place in refrigerator to congeal. Turn out on a bed of lettuce,
and garnish with French dressing or mayonnaise. Makes 4 servings.

Avocado and Grapefruit Salad

2 large pink grapefruit
2 ripe avocados
12 large Bibb lettuce leaves
Sweet Celery Seed Dressing (below)

Cut peel and pith away from grapefruit, and cut into segments, reserving any grapefruit juice; set aside. Peel and slice avocados; toss in reserved grapefruit juice. Arrange grapefruit segments and avocado slices on Bibb lettuce leaves; serve with Celery Seed Dressing. Makes 6 servings.

Sweet Celery Seed Dressing

⅓ cup light corn syrup
¼ cup sugar
¼ cup apple cider vinegar
2 teaspoons celery seed
1 teaspoon dry mustard
1 teaspoon onion salt
Pepper to taste
1 cup olive oil

Combine corn syrup, sugar, apple cider vinegar, celery seed, dry mustard, onion salt, and pepper to taste, mixing well. Slowly add olive oil, whisking constantly. Makes about 1¾ cups.

CREAMY CELERY SEED DRESSING

1½ cups mayonnaise
¼ cup pineapple juice
Juice and zest of 1 lemon
½ teaspoon celery seed
Salt and pepper to taste

Combine all ingredients, whisking well. Makes about 1¼ cups.

BETTER THAN THOUSAND ISLAND DRESSING

1 cup mayonnaise
½ cup chili sauce
½ cup sour cream
1 hard-boiled egg, peeled and finely chopped
2 tablespoons green bell pepper, finely chopped
2 tablespoons horseradish
2 tablespoons chopped green olives
1 teaspoon onion juice

Combine all ingredients. Makes 2½ cups.

ORANGE JUICE DRESSING

¼ cup orange juice
2 teaspoons vinegar
2 teaspoons honey
1 tablespoon canola oil

Combine juice, vinegar, and honey. Slowly add oil, whisking constantly. Makes about ⅓ cup.

FRENCH VINAIGRETTE

¼ cup apple cider vinegar
1 tablespoon sugar
¼ teaspoon paprika
¼ teaspoon dry mustard
Salt and pepper to taste
¾ cup olive oil

Combine first 5 ingredients. Slowly add oil, whisking constantly.
Makes 1 cup.

CREAMY FRENCH VINAIGRETTE

¼ cup apple cider vinegar
¼ cup sour cream
1 tablespoon sugar
¼ teaspoon paprika
¼ teaspoon dry mustard
Salt and pepper to taste
¾ cup olive oil

Combine all ingredients. Slowly add oil, whisking constantly. Makes
1¼ cups.

CURRIED FRENCH VINAIGRETTE

¼ cup apple cider vinegar
1 tablespoon sugar
¼ teaspoon curry powder
¼ teaspoon paprika
¼ teaspoon dry mustard
Salt and pepper to taste
¾ cup olive oil

Combine first 6 ingredients. Slowly add oil, whisking constantly.
Makes 1 cup.

HONEY FRENCH VINAIGRETTE

½ cup honey
¼ cup lemon juice
1 tablespoon sugar
½ teaspoon celery seed
¼ teaspoon grated lemon zest
¼ teaspoon paprika
¼ teaspoon dry mustard
Salt and pepper to taste
¾ cup olive oil

Combine first 8 ingredients. Slowly add oil, whisking constantly. Makes 1½ cups.

HONEY-LIME FRENCH VINAIGRETTE

½ cup honey
¼ cup lime juice
1 tablespoon sugar
¼ teaspoon grated lime zest
¼ teaspoon paprika
¼ teaspoon dry mustard
Salt and pepper to taste
¾ cup olive oil

Combine first 7 ingredients. Slowly add oil, whisking constantly. Makes 1½ cups.

TANGY FRENCH VINAIGRETTE

¼ **cup apple cider vinegar**
¼ **cup horseradish**
1 tablespoon sugar
¼ **teaspoon paprika**
¼ **teaspoon dry mustard**
Salt and pepper to taste
¾ **cup olive oil**

Combine first 6 ingredients. Slowly add oil, whisking constantly.
Makes 1¼ cups.

TOMATO FRENCH VINAIGRETTE

½ **(10¾-ounce) can tomato soup**
¼ **cup apple cider vinegar**
1 tablespoon sugar
1 tablespoon chopped onion
½ **teaspoon dried basil**
¼ **teaspoon paprika**
¼ **teaspoon dry mustard**
Salt and pepper to taste
¾ **cup olive oil**

Combine first 8 ingredients. Slowly add oil, whisking constantly.
Makes 1⅔ cups.

GREEK SALAD DRESSING

⅓ to ½ cup vinegar
1 tablespoon minced garlic
1 tablespoon sugar
½ teaspoon oregano
Salt and pepper to taste
1 cup olive oil

Combine first 5 ingredients. Slowly add oil, whisking constantly.
Makes about 1½ cups.

OREGANO-GARLIC VINAIGRETTE

⅓ cup vinegar
1 teaspoon salt
1 teaspoon sugar
1 teaspoon minced garlic
½ teaspoon oregano
Pepper to taste
⅔ cup olive oil

Combine first 6 ingredients. Slowly add oil, whisking constantly.
Makes about 1 cup.

BLEU CHEESE DRESSING

1 cup mayonnaise
¼ cup crumbled bleu cheese
1 tablespoon lemon juice
Salt and pepper to taste
Milk to thin, optional

Combine mayonnaise, bleu cheese, lemon juice, and salt and pepper.
Add milk, little by little, until dressing is thinned to desired
consistency. Makes about 1¼ cups.

BARBECUE SAUCE

¼ cup water
3 tablespoons brown sugar
2 tablespoons ketchup
2 tablespoons lemon juice
2 tablespoons apple cider vinegar
2 tablespoons Worcestershire sauce
2 tablespoons butter, melted
2 teaspoons dry mustard
2 teaspoons paprika
2 teaspoons chili powder
Salt and pepper to taste

Combine all ingredients in small saucepan, and cook over low heat until heated through. Makes about 1¼ cups.

COCKTAIL SAUCE

1 cup ketchup
2 tablespoons lemon juice
2 tablespoons chili sauce
1 tablespoon Worcestershire sauce
2 teaspoons horseradish
Salt to taste
Dash hot sauce

Combine all ingredients; serve with cold cooked shrimp. Makes about 1 cup.

APPLE-MUSTARD SAUCE FOR PORK

1 cup apple cider
1 cup chicken broth, divided
½ cup chopped dried apples
½ cup cider vinegar
⅓ cup packed brown sugar
1 tablespoon cornstarch
2 tablespoons Dijon mustard
Salt and pepper to taste

Combine apple cider, ¾ cup chicken broth, apples, vinegar, and brown sugar in a small saucepan over medium-high heat. Bring to a boil, stirring occasionally. Reduce heat and simmer about 5 minutes. Whisk together cornstarch and remaining ¼ cup chicken broth; whisk into apple mixture. Simmer 2 minutes. Remove from heat and add mustard and salt and pepper to taste. Makes about 3 cups.

TARTAR SAUCE

1 cup mayonnaise
2 tablespoons capers, drained and chopped
2 tablespoons dill pickle relish
2 tablespoons minced olives
2 tablespoons minced onion
2 tablespoons chopped fresh parsley

Combine all ingredients; chill before serving. Makes about 1⅔ cups.

QUICK AND EASY PASTA SAUCE

1 (28-ounce) can tomato purée
1 (16-ounce) can tomato sauce
2 tablespoons Italian seasoning
3 tablespoons garlic powder with parsley

Put all the ingredients in a saucepan, and simmer for 15 minutes. Serve over your favorite pasta. Makes about 6 cups.

QUICK FRESH TOMATO SAUCE

1 tablespoon olive oil
1 pound tomatoes, coarsely chopped
1 handful basil leaves, coarsely chopped

Heat olive oil in large saucepan. Add tomatoes and cook for 5 minutes. Add basil and cook for another minute. Makes about 6 cups.

FAST CREAMY PASTA SAUCE

4 tablespoons butter
3 garlic cloves, pressed
⅓ cup grated Parmesan cheese
½ teaspoon dried basil
¾ cup whipping cream

In a small saucepan, melt butter. Add garlic, cheese, and basil, stirring to blend over medium-low heat. Stir in cream. Makes about 1 cup.

QUICK CHEESE SAUCE

½ **pound Velveeta cheese**
2 tablespoons butter
1 cup milk
1 tablespoon cornstarch

Cut up cheese, and place in a saucepan. Add butter and milk. Heat slowly until cheese melts. Dissolve cornstarch in ½ cup water; stir in a little at a time until sauce is the desired consistency. Makes 4 servings.

CAPER SAUCE

1 cup sour cream
1 cup mayonnaise
¼ **cup capers**
1 teaspoon lemon juice

Mix together all ingredients; refrigerate. Makes 2¼ cups.

HORSERADISH SAUCE

½ **cup mayonnaise**
½ **cup sour cream**
¼ **cup horseradish**
2 teaspoons paprika

Combine all ingredients, mixing well. Makes about 1¼ cups.

RÉMOULADE SAUCE

½ **cup mayonnaise**
½ **cup sour cream**
½ **cup Creole mustard**
2 **chopped green onions**
2 **tablespoons capers, drained and chopped**

Combine all ingredients, mixing well. Makes about 1½ cups.

PESTO

2 **cloves garlic, peeled**
2 **cups fresh basil leaves**
1 **tablespoon pine nuts, toasted**
¼ **cup extra virgin olive oil**
⅛ **teaspoon salt**

Chop garlic in food processor or blender until minced. Add next 2 ingredients and purée until smooth. With food processor running, slowly drizzle in olive oil. Season with salt. Makes about 2½ cups.

LEMON-BASIL AÏOLI

1 **cup mayonnaise**
½ **cup sour cream**
¼ **cup chopped fresh basil**
2 **teaspoons minced garlic**
Juice and zest from 1 lemon

Combine all ingredients, mixing well. Makes about 1¾ cups.

Plum Sauce for Baked Ham

1 (8-ounce) jar plum jam
1 tablespoon dry mustard
¼ teaspoon vinegar

Combine all ingredients, mixing well. Spread over ham before baking. Makes 1 cup.

Tarragon Sauce

½ cup mayonnaise
2 tablespoons olive oil
2 tablespoons Dijon mustard
1 tablespoon vinegar
2 teaspoons dried tarragon
½ teaspoon sugar
Salt and pepper to taste

Combine all ingredients, mixing well. Makes about 1 cup.

Lemon Grilling Sauce

½ cup lemon juice
¼ cup olive oil
2 tablespoons chopped onion
1 teaspoon minced garlic
½ teaspoon dried thyme
Salt and pepper to taste

Combine all ingredients. Use as marinade or basting sauce. Makes about ¾ cup.

HERBED GRILLING SAUCE

1 small onion, chopped
1 tablespoon minced garlic
2 sprigs fresh rosemary
12 fresh mint leaves
½ cup vinegar
½ cup water

Combine all ingredients in a small saucepan, and bring just to a boil. Chill and use as a marinade or basting sauce. Makes about 1 cup.

BUTTER SAUCE

1 cup butter
Juice and zest of 1 lemon
¼ cup chopped fresh parsley
¼ teaspoon paprika
Salt and pepper to taste

Combine all ingredients in a small saucepan; cook over low heat until smooth. Makes 1 cup.

ORANGE BUTTER SAUCE

1 (6-ounce) can frozen orange juice concentrate, thawed
½ cup butter
¼ cup lemon juice
½ teaspoon dry mustard
½ teaspoon celery salt
½ teaspoon onion salt
¼ teaspoon rosemary
Dash black pepper

Combine all ingredients in a small saucepan; cook over low heat until smooth. Makes 1½ cups.

SWEET-AND-SOUR APRICOT SAUCE

2 (28-ounce) cans apricot halves, drained
1 (4-ounce) can crushed pineapple, drained
½ cup honey
½ cup brown sugar
2 tablespoons apple cider vinegar
½ teaspoon minced garlic
Salt and pepper to taste

Purée apricots in a food processor or blender until smooth. Combine with remaining ingredients in a medium saucepan; cook over medium heat about 10 minutes. Makes about 2½ cups.

White Sauce Mix

2 cups instant nonfat dry milk
1 cup unbleached flour
1 cup butter or margarine
2 teaspoons salt

Combine dry milk, flour, and salt. Mix well. With a pastry blender, cut in butter or margarine until mixture resembles fine crumbs. Lightly pack in a large airtight container. Makes about 1 quart.

White Sauce

½ cup White Sauce Mix (above)
1 cup cool water, milk, tomato juice, or chicken or beef broth

Combine in a small saucepan (for thinner white sauce decrease the mix to ¼ cup or for thicker white sauce increase mix to ¾ cup). Cook over low heat until smooth, stirring constantly. Season with pepper, herbs, and spices. Makes about 1½ cups of sauce.

Variations: To make a cheese sauce, add ½ to 1 cup shredded Cheddar cheese after mixture thickens. Stir until cheese is melted. To make a curry sauce, add 1 teaspoon curry powder to thickened mixture.

Quick Beef Gravy

¼ cup water
2 teaspoons butter, melted
¼ cup flour
2 cups beef broth

Thoroughly mix first 3 ingredients in a bowl. Add mixture and beef stock to a saucepan. Cook over medium heat for about 5 to 10 minutes. Makes about 2½ cups.

SOUPS AND SANDWICHES

CHEESY HAM AND CORN SOUP

3 quarts water
2 pounds cooked ham, chopped
2 onions, chopped
1 (14-ounce) can diced tomatoes
1 red bell pepper, chopped
1 (10-ounce) package frozen corn
½ teaspoon garlic salt
Pepper to taste
½ cup shredded Monterey Jack cheese

Combine all ingredients except cheese in a large stockpot; simmer about 1 hour. Stir in cheese just before serving. Makes 6 servings.

HAMBURGER SOUP

1 pound ground chuck
1 onion, chopped
1 garlic clove, minced
8 cups beef broth
1 cup green beans, trimmed
1 cup green peas
1 cup carrots, sliced
1 (10-ounce) can cream-style corn
2 (10-ounce) cans diced tomatoes
Salt and pepper to taste

In a large skillet, sauté ground chuck, onion, and garlic until meat is brown. Drain and transfer to a large stockpot. Add remaining ingredients. Bring to a boil; reduce heat and simmer for 45 minutes, or until vegetables are tender. Makes 6 servings.

PEANUT BUTTER SOUP

1 (8-ounce) can evaporated milk
4 tablespoons shortening
1 tablespoon flour
Salt
½ cup peanut butter

Dilute the milk with an equal quantity of water. Make a white sauce of fat, flour, milk, and salt. Stir in the peanut butter, and cook for a few minutes longer. Makes 2 servings.

POTATO SOUP

4 tablespoons butter
½ cup finely chopped onion
2 tablespoons flour
4 cups peeled and cubed potatoes
3 cups milk
½ cup chicken broth
Salt and pepper to taste

In a large saucepan, melt the butter over medium heat. Add the onion, and cook until soft, about 5 minutes. Whisk in the flour, and cook for 1 minute. Add the potatoes, milk, and chicken broth. Cook until potatoes are tender, about 15 minutes. Season with salt and pepper. Makes 4 to 6 servings.

Quick Egg Soup

1 vegetable bouillon cube
1½ cups boiling water
1 egg

Dissolve bouillon cube in boiling water; remove from heat. Beat egg, and blend it into vegetable broth. Reheat slowly. Do not boil. Makes 1 serving.

Quick Cabbage Soup

2 cups Chinese cabbage or green cabbage, shredded
2 teaspoons oil
3 cups water
1 vegetable bouillon cube

Sauté cabbage in oil for 2 minutes over medium-high heat. Add water and bouillon cube. Continue cooking over medium heat for 8 minutes. Serve hot. Sautéing in vegetable stock or white grape juice will significantly reduce fat. Makes 2 servings.

Pasta Fagioli Soup

1 (14-ounce) can chicken or vegetable broth
1 cup pasta
1 (12-ounce) can diced tomatoes
1 (15-ounce) can white beans

Cook all together for about 20 minutes. Makes 4 servings.

CORN CHOWDER

2 cups cooked and chopped chicken
1 (10¾-ounce) can potato soup
1 (10¾-ounce) can cream of chicken soup
1 (10-ounce) can corn
1½ cups milk
1 cup chicken broth
⅓ cup sliced green onions
1½ cups shredded Cheddar cheese

Combine all ingredients except cheese in saucepan; mix well. Cook over medium heat for 5 to 8 minutes, or until heated through, stirring constantly. Remove from heat. Stir in cheese until melted. Makes 8 servings.

FRENCH ONION SOUP

6 sweet onions, chopped
¼ cup olive oil
1 teaspoon dried thyme
1 bay leaf
5 (10½-ounce) cans beef consommé
5 cups water
10 (1½-inch thick) slices French bread
2½ cups shredded Swiss cheese

Cook onion in oil in large stockpot until tender. Add thyme, bay leaf, consommé, and water. Bring to a boil; reduce heat and simmer for 20 minutes. While soup simmers, top each bread slice with ¼ cup shredded Swiss cheese. Place under preheated broiler for 2 to 3 minutes, or until cheese melts. Ladle soup into bowls, and top each serving with a slice broiled cheese toast. Makes 10 servings.

BLACK BEAN AND SAUSAGE SOUP

3 (15-ounce) cans black beans
2 tablespoons olive oil
1 cup chopped onion
2 teaspoons minced garlic
2 (15-ounce) cans vegetable broth
1 (28-ounce) can diced tomatoes
1 (10-ounce) can tomatoes with green chiles
2 teaspoons cumin
1½ teaspoons dried oregano
1 pound smoked sausage, sliced

Drain 2 cans black beans, leaving 1 undrained. Heat oil over medium heat; add onion and garlic, and sauté until onion is soft, about 5 minutes. Add remaining ingredients, including drained and undrained beans. Simmer about 20 minutes, stirring occasionally and mashing beans with a fork. Makes 8 servings.

CREAM OF TOMATO SOUP WITH BASIL

1 (10¾-ounce) can condensed tomato soup
1¼ cups milk
½ teaspoon dried basil

Combine all ingredients in small saucepan, and whisk until smooth. Warm over low heat until heated through. Makes 2 servings.

SENEGALESE SOUP

2 egg yolks, beaten
1 cup half-and-half
1 teaspoon curry powder
Dash cayenne pepper
Salt to taste
3 cups hot chicken broth
1 cup cooked and chopped chicken
Juice and zest of 1 lemon
¼ cup chopped fresh parsley

Combine beaten egg yolks, half-and-half, curry powder, cayenne pepper, and salt in a saucepan; mix well. Slowly add hot chicken broth, stirring constantly. Cook and stir over low heat until soup thickens. Add chicken, lemon juice, lemon zest, and parsley. Cook until just heated through. Makes 4 servings.

LEMON-ROSEMARY CHICKEN CROISSANTS

½ cup mayonnaise
¼ cup pesto
¼ cup grated Parmesan cheese
8 (2-ounce) croissants, sliced
1 recipe Lemon-Rosemary Chicken (p. 277)
Lettuce and tomato

Combine mayonnaise, pesto, and Parmesan cheese. Spread evenly over cut sides of croissants. Top 8 halves with chicken, lettuce, tomato, and remaining croissant halves. Makes 8 servings.

SPICY ASIAN DUCK WRAPS

1 tablespoon dark sesame oil
1 pound boneless duck breast
⅓ cup hoisin sauce
2 teaspoons grated orange rind
2 tablespoons orange juice
2 teaspoons hot chili sauce
4 (6-inch) flour tortillas, warmed
½ cucumber, peeled, seeded, and chopped
¼ cup bean sprouts
2 chopped green onions
2 teaspoons sesame seeds

Warm oil over medium-high heat. Add duck; cook 2 minutes on each side. Reduce heat to medium; cover and cook an additional 3 minutes on each side or until done. Slice thinly and set aside.

Combine hoisin sauce, orange rind, orange juice, and hot chili sauce. Spread about 2 tablespoons hoisin mixture down center of each tortilla. Divide sliced duck, cucumber, bean sprouts, green onions, and sesame seeds evenly over each tortilla. Roll up and serve. Makes 4 servings.

PINEAPPLE SANDWICHES

1 fresh pineapple, peeled, cored, and cut into 8 slices
¾ cup mayonnaise
¼ cup honey
8 slices thick white bread, toasted (if desired)

Lay pineapple slices between layers of paper towels to drain. Combine mayonnaise and honey. Spread over bread slices. Place 2 slices of pineapple between 2 pieces bread. Makes 4 servings.

WALDORF CHICKEN SALAD SANDWICHES

4 Kaiser rolls, cut in half
1 cup chicken salad
12 very thin apple slices
4 slices Cheddar cheese

Layer bottom half of each roll with salad, 3 apple slices, and 1 cheese slice. Top with remaining halves. Makes 4 servings.

BREADS

HOMEMADE BAKING MIX

1¼ cups flour
1½ teaspoons sugar
1 teaspoon baking powder
3 tablespoons vegetable oil

Combine flour, sugar, and baking powder, whisking well. Slowly add oil, cutting in with pastry blender (or 2 knives), until mix is consistency of cornmeal. Store in tightly covered container. Use for pancakes, waffles, biscuits, or coffeecake. Makes about 1⅓ cups.

FAST AND EASY PEPPERONI ROLLS

1 (9-ounce) can refrigerated crescent roll dough
Pepperoni slices
Cheese cubes

Separate each crescent roll, and add about 4 pieces of pepperoni and 4 pieces of cheese to each section. Press all the edges closed so that you can't see anything inside. Place on a cookie sheet, and bake according to the crescent roll directions (about 11 to 15 minutes or until golden brown.) Serve warm. Makes 4 servings.

CHEESE TWISTS

1 (10-ounce) can refrigerated buttermilk biscuits
1 egg, beaten
1 cup cheese, grated

Separate biscuits; roll each into a 10-inch strip and twist. Bring around in a circle and seal ends by pinching dough. Brush with beaten egg, and sprinkle with cheese. Bake at temperature and time indicated on can of biscuits. Cool slightly before serving. Makes 4 servings.

CHILI-CORN TWISTS

⅓ cup cornmeal
1½ teaspoons chili powder
1 (11-ounce) can refrigerated breadstick dough
¼ cup butter, melted

Combine cornmeal and chili powder; roll each piece of breadstick dough in melted butter and then in cornmeal mixture. Bake according to package directions. Makes 8 servings.

QUICK SOFT PRETZELS

1 (10-ounce) can refrigerated pizza dough
1 egg, beaten
1 tablespoon water
2 tablespoons coarse salt

Place pizza dough on lightly floured waxed paper and roll into a 10 inch x 10-inch rectangle. Cut dough lengthwise into 10 1-inch-wide strips. Shape each strip into a circle, overlapping about 4 inches from each end and leaving ends free. Taking one end of the dough in each hand, twist at the point where the dough overlaps. Lift each end across to the edge of the circle opposite it. Tuck ends under to seal.

Place pretzels 1 inch apart on an ungreased baking sheet. Beat egg and water in a bowl. Brush pretzels with egg mixture, and sprinkle with salt. Bake at 350° for 15 to 17 minutes or until golden. Serve warm. Makes 4 servings.

MINI FOCACCIA

1 (11-ounce) can refrigerated soft breadstick dough
2 tablespoons olive oil
¼ cup grated Parmesan cheese
2 teaspoons dried Italian seasoning

Lightly grease cookie sheets, or line with parchment paper. Remove dough from can, and separate into 8 coils, but do not unroll. Place on prepared pans, and press each coil of dough into a 5-inch circle. Drizzle with olive oil. Combine cheese and seasoning; mix well. Sprinkle over each coil. Bake at 375° for 8 to 14 minutes until golden brown. Remove from cookie sheets immediately. Makes 4 servings.

CHEESY CRESCENT ROLLS

1 (9-ounce) can refrigerated crescent roll dough
1 cup shredded Cheddar cheese

Unroll crescent roll dough pieces; place 2 tablespoons cheese in center of each. Roll up and bake according to package directions. Makes 8 servings.

CHEESY GARLIC CRESCENT ROLLS

1 (9-ounce) can refrigerated crescent roll dough
1 cup shredded Cheddar cheese
¼ cup butter, melted
1 teaspoon garlic salt

Unroll crescent roll dough pieces; place 2 tablespoons cheese in center of each. Roll up and bake according to package directions. Brush with melted butter, and sprinkle with garlic salt. Makes 8 servings.

PARMESAN BREAD RING

1 (13-ounce) can refrigerated Italian bread dough
2 tablespoons butter, melted
½ cup grated Parmesan cheese
1½ teaspoons dried Italian seasoning
½ teaspoon garlic salt

Roll bread dough into a rectangle, approximately 16 inches x 6 inches. Spread butter evenly over dough. Combine Parmesan, Italian seasoning, and garlic salt; sprinkle down middle of bread dough. Fold dough over lengthwise, and pinch edges well to seal. Bring ends together to meet in a circle; pinch well to seal. Place on greased cookie sheet, and cut ¼-inch-deep slits in dough every 2 inches. Bake at 350° for about 20 minutes. Makes 8 servings.

HOT SAUSAGE CHEESE BREAD

2 loaves frozen bread dough, thawed
1 pound sausage
½ bell pepper, chopped
½ onion, chopped
½ cup shredded Cheddar cheese
½ cup mozzarella cheese, shredded

Roll each loaf of thawed bread dough to ¼-inch thickness and let rest. Brown sausage with bell pepper and onion until fully cooked. Drain well. Roll dough again to ¼-inch thickness. Spread sausage mixture evenly down centers of dough. Fold dough over sausage filling, and pinch well to seal. Bake seam-side down on a greased baking sheet at 375° for about 30 minutes. Slice to serve. Makes about 10 servings.

Spicy Cheese Bread

2 cups pepper jack cheese, shredded and softened
½ cup butter, softened
½ cup mayonnaise
1 (16-ounce) loaf French bread, sliced

Combine cheese, butter, and mayonnaise; beat until of a spreadable consistency. Spread evenly over bread slices. Bake at 400° for about 10 minutes. Makes about 16 servings.

Parmesan Pita Crisps

4 pita bread pockets
Butter, melted
Parmesan cheese, grated

Pull pita pockets apart and cut each half into quarters. Brush with melted butter, and sprinkle with Parmesan cheese. Broil until crisp. Makes 32 pieces.

Rosemary Garlic Focaccia

1 (10-ounce) can refrigerated pizza dough
2 tablespoons olive oil
1 tablespoon rosemary, crumbled
1 teaspoon garlic salt

Unroll pizza dough, and flatten with fingertips. Let sit for 15 minutes. Flatten again. Brush with olive oil, and sprinkle with rosemary and garlic salt. Bake according to package directions. Makes 8 servings.

CAESAR PARMESAN BREAD

1 (16-ounce) loaf French bread, sliced
Caesar dressing
Grated Parmesan cheese

Brush each slice of bread with dressing, and then sprinkle with Parmesan cheese. Broil until toasted. Makes about 20 servings.

CHEESY BACON BREAD

1 (16-ounce) loaf French bread, sliced
2 cups shredded Cheddar cheese
½ pound bacon, cooked and crumbled

Sprinkle each slice of bread with shredded cheese, and then sprinkle with bacon. Broil until cheese is melted. Makes about 20 servings.

CRISP BISCUITS

2 cups flour
2 teaspoons sugar
1 teaspoon baking powder
1 teaspoon salt
⅓ cup shortening
⅔ cup milk

Whisk together dry ingredients. Cut shortening in until mixture resembles cornmeal. Stir in enough milk to make a soft dough; knead lightly. Roll to ¼-inch thickness, and cut with biscuit cutter. Bake on ungreased baking sheet at 425° for about 10 minutes. Makes about 2 dozen.

BUTTERMILK BISCUITS

1 cup self-rising flour
1 teaspoon sugar
¼ cup shortening
½ cup buttermilk
1 to 2 tablespoons margarine, softened

Sift flour into a bowl; add sugar. Cut in shortening until crumbly. Add buttermilk; mix well. Roll or pat to ½-inch thickness on floured surface. Cut with biscuit cutter. Arrange on a greased baking sheet. Brush with margarine. Let stand for 5 to 10 minutes. Bake at 450° for 10 minutes or until golden brown. Serve hot. Makes 7 servings.

POTATO BISCUITS

1 (2-ounce) package instant mashed potatoes
2 teaspoons sugar
¼ cup butter, melted
1 cup hot water
3 cups biscuit mix

Combine all ingredients. Add more water if necessary. Pat out to about ½-inch thick, and cut with a biscuit cutter. Bake at 425° for about 8 minutes. Makes about 10 servings.

SWEET CREAM BISCUITS

1¼ cups self-rising flour
¼ cup sugar
1 cup whipping cream

Combine all ingredients, stirring just until moistened. Pat out about ½-inch thick and cut with a biscuit cutter. Bake at 400° for about 10 minutes. Makes about 8 servings.

HERBED BISCUITS

1¾ cups biscuit mix
2 tablespoons green onion, thinly sliced
½ teaspoon dried basil, crushed
½ cup skim milk

In a mixing bowl, stir together biscuit mix, green onions, and basil. Add milk; stir just until dough clings together. On a floured surface knead dough 10 to 12 strokes. Roll out to a ½-inch thickness. Using a 2-inch biscuit cutter, cut dough into 12 biscuits. Reroll the trimmings as necessary. Bake biscuits on an ungreased baking sheet in a 425° oven for about 12 minutes. Makes 1 dozen biscuits.

SOUR CREAM BISCUITS

2 cups biscuit mix
½ cup butter, melted
1 (8-ounce) carton sour cream

Combine all ingredients, mixing well. Spoon into greased mini-muffin pans, filling half-full. Bake at 450° for 10 to 12 minutes. Makes 4 dozen.

CHEESY SOUR CREAM BISCUITS

2 cups biscuit mix
½ cup butter, melted
1 (8-ounce) carton sour cream
½ cup shredded Cheddar cheese

Combine all ingredients, mixing well. Spoon into greased mini-muffin pans, filling half-full. Bake at 450° for 10 to 12 minutes. Makes 4 dozen.

FAST BISCUITS

1 teaspoon sugar
1¼ cups self-rising flour
2 tablespoons mayonnaise
½ cup milk

Mix all ingredients, and drop by spoonfuls on a greased baking sheet. Bake at 425° until brown. Makes 6 servings.

QUICK CHEESE BISCUITS

2 cups buttermilk baking mix
⅔ cup milk
½ cup shredded Cheddar cheese
2 tablespoons butter or margarine, melted
½ teaspoon garlic powder

In a bowl, stir the biscuit mix, milk, and cheese just until moistened. Drop onto an ungreased baking sheet. Mix butter and garlic powder; brush over biscuits. Bake at 475° for 8 to 10 minutes or until golden brown. Serve warm. Makes 12 servings.

BISCUIT BEIGNETS

1 (10-count) can refrigerated biscuit dough
4 cups oil
Powdered sugar

Cut each piece of biscuit dough into quarters; fry in hot oil, turning once, until golden brown. Drain on paper towels and toss in powdered sugar. Makes about 40.

QUICK FEATHERY SOUTHERN BISCUITS

2 cups self-rising flour
¼ cup shortening or margarine
½ to ¾ cup milk or buttermilk

Place flour in a medium bowl. Add shortening, and using pastry blender or two knives, cut in until consistency of coarse crumbs. With a fork, blend in just enough milk until dough leaves sides of bowl. Turn out onto lightly floured surface, and knead 10 to 12 strokes. Roll dough out to ½-inch thick. Shape with 2-inch cutter. Bake on ungreased baking sheet at 500° (place biscuits 1 inch apart for crusty sides or almost touching for soft sides) for 8 to 10 minutes until golden. Makes 12 servings.

Sweet Potato Biscuits

1 cup mashed sweet potatoes
⅔ cup milk
4 tablespoons butter, melted
1¼ cups flour
3½ tablespoons baking powder
2 tablespoons sugar
½ teaspoon salt

Combine sweet potatoes, milk, and melted butter, stirring until well mixed. Sift together flour, baking powder, sugar, and salt. Combine potato mixture with flour mixture, stirring to make a soft dough. Turn out onto floured surface, and knead several times. Pat or roll out to ½-inch thick. Cut out rounds with a 2-inch cutter. Bake on greased baking sheet at 450° for about 15 minutes. Makes about 1 dozen biscuits.

Cinnamon Biscuit Doughnuts

1 (10-count) can refrigerated biscuit dough
4 cups oil
Sugar
Cinnamon

Cut each piece of biscuit dough into quarters. Fry in hot oil, turning once, until golden brown. Drain on paper towels and toss in a mixture of sugar and cinnamon. Makes about 40.

CINNAMON RING

1 cup pecans, chopped and divided
¾ cup brown sugar
1 tablespoon cinnamon
3 (10-count) cans refrigerated biscuit dough
½ cup butter, melted
1 cup powdered sugar
Milk

Sprinkle ½ cup pecans in greased Bundt pan; set aside. Combine brown sugar and cinnamon. Dip each biscuit in melted butter, then roll in sugar mixture. Stand biscuits on end around pan. Sprinkle remaining nuts over and around biscuits. Bake at 325° for about 45 minutes. Mix powdered sugar with just enough milk to make a glaze; drizzle over warm ring. Makes about 15 servings.

RAISIN BRAN MUFFINS

2 cups whole wheat flour
1½ cups bran
¼ cup brown sugar
1¼ teaspoons baking soda
¼ teaspoon salt
2 cups buttermilk
1 cup raisins
1 egg
½ cup molasses
2 tablespoons butter, melted

Combine whole wheat flour, bran, brown sugar, baking soda, and salt, whisking until smooth. Stir in buttermilk, raisins, egg, molasses, and butter. Spoon into greased or lined muffin cups, filling about ⅔ full. Bake at 350° for about 20 minutes. Makes about 2 dozen.

QUICK AND EASY CHERRY BREAD

1 loaf frozen bread dough
1 (21-ounce) can tart cherry pie filling

Let the frozen bread loaf rise once. Knead, reshape, and place in a
greased loaf pan. Let rise again. Make 2 slits in the top of the loaf to
a depth equal to one-third of the loaf. Divide and place the cherry pie
filling in the slits. Let rise again to full size and brush the top of the
loaf with melted butter and sprinkle with cinnamon sugar. Bake at
350° for 35 to 40 minutes. Remove the loaf from the pan and cool.
May be served either warm or cold. Makes 1 loaf.

BLUEBERRY SOUR CREAM CORN MUFFINS

1 cup all-purpose flour
¾ cup cornmeal
2 teaspoons baking powder
½ teaspoon baking soda
¼ teaspoon salt
1 egg, beaten
1 cup sour cream
⅓ cup frozen unsweetened apple juice concentrate, thawed
1½ cups fresh or frozen (not thawed) blueberries
⅔ cup cream cheese
2 tablespoons no-sugar-added blueberry fruit spread

Grease or line 12 medium-sized muffin cups; set aside. Combine dry
ingredients in medium bowl. Add combined egg, sour cream, and
apple juice concentrate; mix just until dry ingredients are moistened.
Gently stir in blueberries. Spoon batter into prepared cups, filling
each cup ¾ full. Bake at 400° for 8 to 20 minutes or until golden
brown. Let stand in pan on wire rack 5 minutes. Remove from pan;
cool slightly. Combine cream cheese and fruit spread; serve with
warm muffins. Makes 1 dozen muffins.

QUICK PUMPKIN BREAD

1 (18-ounce) box pound cake mix
1 cup canned pumpkin
2 eggs
⅓ cup milk
1 teaspoon cinnamon
½ teaspoon allspice

Combine all ingredients, mixing well. Pour into a greased loaf pan.
Bake at 350° for about 1 hour. Makes about 10 servings.

MONKEY BREAD

4 (10-ounce) cans refrigerated buttermilk biscuits, quartered
Cinnamon and sugar mixture
Walnuts
1½ cup butter
1 cup brown sugar

Divide biscuit dough into 16 biscuits. Place in a bag with cinnamon
sugar mixture and shake. Place in a well-greased and floured Bundt
pan, throwing in walnuts. In a saucepan, melt the butter. Add the
brown sugar, and cook until melted, stirring frequently. Pour over
biscuits in pan. Bake at 350° for 35 minutes. Cool for 10 minutes,
then remove. Makes 12 servings.

GINGER MUFFINS

½ cup shortening
½ cup sugar
1 egg
1 cup molasses
3 cups flour
1½ teaspoons baking soda
1 teaspoon cinnamon
1 teaspoon ground ginger
½ teaspoon ground cloves
½ teaspoon salt
1 cup hot water

Cream shortening and sugar until light and fluffy; add egg and molasses, beating well. Combine dry ingredients; stir into creamed mixture. Gradually add hot water. Spoon into greased or lined muffin cups, filling about ⅔ full. Bake at 375° for about 20 minutes. Makes about 2 dozen.

CINNAMON TOAST

2 slices white bread
Butter
1 teaspoon cinnamon
1 teaspoon sugar

Lightly toast the bread in a toaster. Butter the bread, and sprinkle cinnamon and sugar on top. Makes 2 servings.

CHOCOLATE CHERRY BREAD

1¾ cups flour
⅓ cup cocoa
1 teaspoon baking soda
½ teaspoon salt
½ cup butter, softened
1 cup sugar
1 egg
1 teaspoon vanilla
1 cup buttermilk
1 cup dried cherries
1½ cup pecans, chopped

Combine flour, cocoa, baking soda, and salt, whisking well; set aside. Cream butter and sugar until light and fluffy; add egg and vanilla, beating well. Alternately add buttermilk and dry ingredients, mixing until just combined after each addition; gently fold in cherries and pecans. Pour into a greased loaf pan. Bake at 350° for about 1 hour and 15 minutes. Makes 1 loaf.

QUICK GRAHAM BREAD

½ cup brown sugar
¾ cup cold water
½ cup shortening, melted
¾ cup milk
1 cup white flour
1⅓ teaspoon salt
1 teaspoon baking soda
2 cups graham flour

Dissolve sugar in water; add shortening and milk. Sift white flour, measure out 1 cup, and sift again with salt and baking soda. Add to first mixture. Add graham flour. Mix thoroughly. Bake in well-oiled bread pan at 375° for 1 hour. Makes 1 loaf.

CRANBERRY BANANA BREAD

¾ **cup butter, softened**
1½ **cups sugar**
3 **eggs**
1 **teaspoon vanilla extract**
2 **drops orange extract**
4 **large ripe bananas**
3½ **cups self-rising flour**
1 **cup pecans, chopped**
1 **(14-ounce) can whole-berry cranberry sauce**

Beat butter and sugar until light and fluffy. Add eggs, vanilla, and orange extract, beating well. Add bananas and beat until smooth. Gradually stir in flour. Add pecans and cranberry sauce, stirring until just combined. Pour into 3 greased loaf pans. Bake at 325° for about 45 minutes. Makes 3 loaves.

STRAWBERRY BREAD

3 **cups flour**
2 **cups sugar**
2 **teaspoons cinnamon**
1 **teaspoon salt**
1 **teaspoon baking soda**
1 **(16-ounce) bag frozen strawberries, thawed and chopped**
1¼ **cups vegetable oil**
3 **eggs, beaten**
1 **teaspoon vanilla extract**
¼ **teaspoon almond extract**

Combine flour, sugar, cinnamon, salt, and baking soda. Add remaining ingredients, mixing just until combined. Pour into 2 greased loaf pans. Bake at 350° for 1 hour. Makes 2 loaves.

Carrot Raisin Bread

1 (8-ounce) package cream cheese, softened
1½ cups sugar
2 eggs
2 tablespoons milk
1 teaspoon vanilla
2 cups flour
1 teaspoon baking powder
1 teaspoon baking soda
1 teaspoon cinnamon
¼ teaspoon nutmeg
1½ cups carrots, shredded
1 cup pecans or walnuts, chopped
½ cup raisins

Beat cream cheese and sugar until smooth. Blend in eggs, milk, and vanilla. Combine flour, baking powder, baking soda, cinnamon, and nutmeg; add to cream cheese mixture, stirring just until moistened. Fold in carrots, nuts, and raisins. Pour into a greased loaf pan. Bake at 350° for 1 hour. Makes 1 loaf.

BANANA NUT BREAD

2½ cups flour, divided
¾ cup walnuts or pecans, chopped
1½ teaspoons baking powder
¾ teaspoon baking soda
1 teaspoon salt
1½ cups sugar
¾ cup vegetable oil
½ cup brown sugar
⅓ cup buttermilk
3 large ripe bananas
3 eggs
1 teaspoon vanilla

Toss ¼ cup flour with nuts; set aside. Combine remaining 1¼ cups flour, baking powder, baking soda, salt, and sugar, whisking to combine. Add oil, brown sugar, buttermilk, and bananas. Beat for 2 minutes. Add eggs and vanilla; beat 1 minute more. Fold in floured nuts. Pour into a greased Bundt pan. Bake at 350° for 1 hour. Makes about 16 servings.

JOHNNY CAKE

3 cups cornmeal
1 cup flour
Dash salt
1 teaspoon baking soda
1 cup buttermilk
⅓ cup molasses

In a large bowl, combine cornmeal, flour, and salt. In a small bowl, mix baking soda with buttermilk and molasses; add to dry ingredients. Mix thoroughly. Pour into a greased iron skillet. Bake at 400° for 25 to 30 minutes or until brown. Makes 12 servings.

PUMPKIN BREAD

3 cups sugar
1 cup vegetable oil
4 eggs
1 (16-ounce) can mashed pumpkin
3½ cups flour
2 teaspoons baking soda
1 teaspoon salt
1 teaspoon baking powder
1 teaspoon nutmeg
1 teaspoon allspice
1 teaspoon cinnamon
¼ teaspoon ground cloves
⅔ cup buttermilk

Cream sugar and oil until fluffy; add eggs and pumpkin, mixing well.
Combine flour, baking soda, salt, baking powder, nutmeg, allspice,
cinnamon, and cloves; add alternately with buttermilk to creamed
mixture. Pour into 2 greased loaf pans. Bake at 350° for about 45
minutes. Makes 2 loaves.

SOUR CREAM CORN MUFFINS

1 cup sour cream
1 cup self-rising cornmeal
1 cup creamed corn
2 eggs
½ cup vegetable oil
1 teaspoon salt

Combine all ingredients. Spoon batter into 12 lined muffin cups. Bake
at 400° for about 30 minutes. Makes 12 muffins.

Pineapple Zucchini Bread

1 cup vegetable oil
3 eggs
3½ teaspoons sugar
1 teaspoon vanilla
2 cups zucchini, shredded
1 (8½-ounce) can unsweetened crushed pineapple in juice, drained
3 cups all-purpose flour
1½ teaspoons cinnamon
1 teaspoon baking soda
¾ teaspoon nutmeg
¾ teaspoon salt
1 cup raisins
½ cup walnuts, chopped (optional)

Mix oil, eggs, sugar, and vanilla in a large bowl; stir in zucchini and pineapple. Combine flour, cinnamon, baking soda, nutmeg, and salt in a medium bowl; stir into oil mixture. Stir in raisins and walnuts, if desired. Spread batter evenly into 2 greased and floured loaf pans. Bake at 350°, until breads are golden and toothpick inserted in centers comes out clean, 50 to 60 minutes. Cool in pans on wire racks 10 minutes; remove from pans and cool completely on wire rack. Makes 2 loaves.

ZUCCHINI RAISIN BREAD

2½ cups sugar
1 cup vegetable oil
3 eggs
2 teaspoons vanilla
2 cups zucchini, peeled and shredded
3 cups flour
2 teaspoons cinnamon
1 teaspoon salt
1 teaspoon baking soda
1 teaspoon baking powder
½ cup golden raisins

Cream sugar with oil until fluffy; beat in eggs and vanilla. Lightly fold in zucchini. Combine flour, cinnamon, salt, baking soda, and baking powder. Add to zucchini mixture, mixing until just combined. Fold in raisins. Pour into 2 greased loaf pans. Bake at 325° for about 1 hour. Makes 2 loaves.

HUSH PUPPIES

1½ cups cornmeal
½ cup flour
½ teaspoon baking soda
1 teaspoon salt
½ onion, chopped
1 cup buttermilk
1 egg
Vegetable oil

In a large bowl, combine the cornmeal, flour, baking soda, salt, and onion; mix well. In another bowl, whisk together buttermilk and egg; add to dry ingredients. Heat oil in a large pot with deep sides. Drop batter by teaspoonfuls into the hot oil. Fry in batches until golden brown, about 2 minutes. Drain. Makes about 12 servings.

CITRUS-GLAZED MUFFINS

2 cups flour
1 teaspoon baking powder
½ cup butter or margarine, softened
1 cup sugar
2 eggs
¾ cup buttermilk
1 cup raisins
1 cup pecans, chopped
1 cup powdered sugar
Juice and zest of 2 oranges
Juice and zest of 1 lemon

Whisk flour and baking powder together; set aside. Cream butter and sugar until light and fluffy; add eggs and beat until well combined. Add flour mixture alternately with buttermilk to butter mixture, stirring just until ingredients are incorporated. Fold in raisins and pecans. Fill muffin cups half-full. Bake at 350° for about 20 minutes. Combine powdered sugar with juices and zests; pour over muffins while still warm. Makes about 24 muffins.

CRACKLIN' BREAD

2 cups cornmeal
1 teaspoon salt
1 teaspoon baking soda
½ teaspoon baking powder
1 cup buttermilk
1 egg, beaten
1 cup pork cracklings

In a large bowl, combine cornmeal, salt, baking soda, and baking powder. Add buttermilk, egg, and cracklings; mix well. Pour into a greased iron skillet. Bake at 400° for 25 to 30 minutes or until brown. Makes about 12 servings.

CORNPONES

2 cups cornmeal
2 teaspoons salt
1 tablespoon sugar
¼ cup shortening, melted and hot
1½ cups boiling water

Whisk together cornmeal, salt, and sugar; stir in shortening. Add boiling water and mix well. Drop by tablespoonfuls onto large greased baking sheet. Bake at 425° for about 25 minutes. Makes about 2 dozen.

SOUTHERN CORNBREAD

¼ cup bacon grease
2 cups cornmeal
1 teaspoon baking soda
1 teaspoon salt
2 eggs, beaten
2 cups buttermilk

Heat bacon grease in a large iron skillet at 450°. While skillet is heating, combine cornmeal, baking soda, and salt; add eggs and buttermilk. Pour into hot skillet. Bake at 450° about 25 minutes. Makes 8 servings.

Jalapeño Cornbread

1 tablespoon oil or shortening
1½ cups cornmeal
1 tablespoon baking powder
½ teaspoon salt
1 cup shredded sharp Cheddar cheese
3 jalapeño peppers, seeded and minced
3 eggs
½ cup oil
1 cup sour cream
1 (8-ounce) can creamed corn

Heat oil in a large cast-iron skillet at 400°. While skillet is heating, whisk cornmeal, baking powder, and salt together; add cheese and peppers. Add eggs, oil, sour cream, and corn, mixing well. Pour into hot skillet. Bake at 400° about 25 minutes.

Cheesy Onion Cornbread

1 large onion, finely chopped
¼ cup butter
1½ cups self-rising cornmeal
2 tablespoons sugar
1 cup shredded sharp Cheddar cheese, divided
2 eggs, beaten
1 cup sour cream
1 cup creamed corn
¼ cup buttermilk
¼ cup vegetable oil

Cook onion in butter until soft; remove from heat. Add cornmeal, sugar, ½ cup shredded cheese, eggs, sour cream, corn, buttermilk, and vegetable oil. Pour into a greased pan. Bake at 400° for 20 minutes. Top with remaining ½ cup cheese. Bake 10 minutes more. Makes about 12 servings.

VEGETABLES AND
SIDE DISHES

Shoepeg Corn and Green Bean Casserole

1 (14-ounce) can shoepeg corn, drained
1 (14-ounce) can French-style green beans, drained
1 (4-ounce) can sliced water chestnuts, drained and coarsely
  chopped
1 (10¾-ounce) can cream of celery soup
1 cup sour cream
2 tablespoons milk
1 cup shredded Cheddar cheese
2 cups buttery cracker crumbs
¼ cup butter, melted

Combine corn, green beans, water chestnuts, soup, sour cream, milk, and shredded cheese; mix well. Pour into a greased 2-quart baking dish. Combine cracker crumbs and melted butter, and sprinkle over top. Bake at 350° for about 30 minutes. Makes 6 to 8 servings.

Buttered Ginger Carrots

6 tablespoons butter
1 teaspoon fresh ginger, peeled and minced
2 pounds carrots, peeled and sliced

Melt butter in a large skillet over medium-high heat; add ginger and cook until tender. Add carrots; toss until well coated. Reduce heat, cover, and cook until tender. Makes 8 servings.

CAULIFLOWER À LA POLONAISE

1 head cauliflower, chopped and steamed
¼ cup butter, divided
¼ cup fresh breadcrumbs
2 tablespoons fresh parsley
2 hard-boiled eggs, peeled and chopped

Place warm cauliflower in serving dish. Melt 2 tablespoons butter in skillet; add breadcrumbs and parsley and heat for 2 minutes. Sprinkle eggs and breadcrumb mixture on cauliflower. Melt remaining 2 tablespoons butter, and drizzle over all. Makes 6 servings.

CHEESY CAULIFLOWER

1 head cauliflower, chopped and steamed
¾ cup shredded sharp Cheddar cheese
½ cup mayonnaise
1 tablespoon Dijon mustard

Combine all ingredients, stirring well to blend. Bake at 350° for about 20 minutes. Makes 4 servings.

GREEN BEANS AMANDINE

3 (9-ounce) packages frozen French-style green beans, cooked and
** drained**
Salt and pepper to taste
½ cup sliced almonds
½ cup butter

Toss cooked green beans with salt and pepper to taste. Brown almonds in butter, and toss with green beans. Makes 8 servings.

BAKED EGGPLANT GRATIN

1 large eggplant, peeled and chopped
1 small onion, chopped
Salt and pepper to taste
1 cup water
3 tablespoons butter, melted
1 egg, beaten
¾ cup grated Parmesan cheeseand divided
½ cup Italian-seasoned breadcrumbs
2 tablespoons olive oil

Cook eggplant, onion, and salt and pepper to taste in water until tender; drain. Add butter, egg, and ½ cup Parmesan cheese. Spread in a small greased baking dish. Combine remaining ¼ cup Parmesan cheese and breadcrumbs; sprinkle over eggplant mixture, and drizzle with olive oil. Bake at 350° for about 25 minutes. Makes 4 servings.

BAKED POTATOES WITH SPINACH

1 (10-ounce) package frozen chopped spinach, thawed and
  drained
¼ cup butter, divided
1 tablespoon lemon juice
Salt and pepper to taste
2 large baked potatoes, warm

Cook spinach in 2 tablespoons butter until heated through. Add lemon juice and salt and pepper to taste. Cut potatoes in half, and scoop out pulp; mash with remaining 2 tablespoons butter and salt and pepper to taste. Return pulp to potato shells, and top with cooked spinach. Makes 4 servings.

Tortellini with Herbed Cheese Sauce

¾ cup milk
1½ cups cottage cheese
¼ cup grated Parmesan cheese
1 tablespoon Italian seasoning
Juice and zest of 1 lemon
1 (16-ounce) bag cheese tortellini, cooked and drained

Combine milk, cottage cheese, Parmesan cheese, Italian seasoning, and lemon juice and zest, mixing until smooth. Toss with hot cooked tortellini. Makes 8 servings.

Wild Rice Pilaf

1 (6-ounce) package long grain and wild rice mix, cooked
1 (14-ounce) can Mexican-style corn, drained
3 chopped green onions
1 tomato, seeded and chopped
2 tablespoons olive oil
1 tablespoon vinegar
Salt and pepper to taste

Combine all ingredients, tossing well to combine. Makes 4 to 6 servings.

PARMESAN POTATOES

¼ cup flour
½ cup grated Parmesan cheese
½ teaspoon garlic salt
Pepper to taste
1 pound new potatoes, quartered
¼ cup butter

Combine flour, Parmesan cheese, garlic salt, and pepper; pour over potatoes, tossing well to coat. Melt butter in 2-quart casserole at 375°; add coated potatoes and stir well. Bake about 45 minutes, stirring once. Makes 3 to 4 servings.

BAKED BREADED TOMATOES

2 large tomatoes, halved
Salt and pepper to taste
1 tablespoon Dijon mustard
¼ cup Italian-seasoned breadcrumbs
¼ cup grated Parmesan cheese
1 tablespoon olive oil

Sprinkle tomatoes with salt and pepper; spread with Dijon mustard. Combine breadcrumbs and Parmesan cheese; sprinkle over mustard. Drizzle with olive oil. Bake at 400° for about 15 minutes. Makes 4 servings.

ROASTED GREEN BEANS AND SHALLOTS

2 (14-ounce) cans whole green beans, drained
2 shallots, thinly sliced
2 teaspoons garlic, minced
1 tablespoon olive oil
½ teaspoon dried basil
Salt and pepper to taste

Combine all ingredients, tossing well. Bake at 400° for about 15 minutes. Makes about 6 servings.

CURRIED VEGETABLE COUSCOUS

2 tablespoons butter
1 squash, sliced
1 zucchini, sliced
1 red bell pepper, chopped
2 chopped green onions
2 teaspoons garlic, minced
1 large tomato, seeded and chopped
1 teaspoon curry powder
Salt and pepper to taste
1 (10-ounce) package couscous, cooked and kept warm

Melt butter in a large skillet over medium-high heat. Add squash, zucchini, red bell pepper, green onions, and garlic. Cook and stir until vegetables are crisp-tender. Add tomato, curry powder, and salt and pepper, cooking 1 to 2 minutes more. Stir in couscous. Makes about 6 servings.

QUICK ROASTED POTATOES

2 tablespoons butter
2 tablespoons olive oil
3 cups potatoes, chopped
1 onion, chopped
2 teaspoons garlic, minced
Salt and pepper to taste

Heat butter and olive oil in large ovenproof skillet over medium-high heat; add potatoes, onion, garlic, and salt and pepper. Cook and stir about 10 minutes. Bake at 400° for about 20 minutes more. Makes 4 servings.

STUFFED POTATOES

2 large baked potatoes, still warm
½ cup sour cream
2 chopped green onions
2 tablespoons butter, melted
1 teaspoon garlic salt
Pepper to taste

Cut potatoes in half lengthwise; scoop out pulp and mash. Add sour cream, green onions, butter, garlic salt, and pepper, stirring well. Fill potato skins with mashed potato mixture. Bake at 425° for about 10 minutes. Makes 4 servings.

LOADED BAKED POTATOES

2 large baked potatoes, still warm
½ cup sour cream
½ cup shredded Cheddar cheese
2 chopped green onions
2 slices bacon, cooked and crumbled
2 tablespoons butter, melted
1 teaspoon garlic salt
Pepper to taste

Cut potatoes in half lengthwise; scoop out pulp and mash. Add sour cream, cheese, green onions, bacon, butter, garlic salt, and pepper, stirring well. Fill potato skins with mashed potato mixture. Bake at 425° for about 10 minutes. Makes 4 servings.

CREAMY ROTINI WITH PEAS

1 (8-ounce) bag rotini, cooked and drained
1 (10¾-ounce) can cream of mushroom soup
1 (14-ounce) can green peas, drained
½ cup milk
Salt and pepper to taste

Combine all ingredients, tossing well to coat. Serve hot or cold. Makes 4 to 6 servings.

SAUTÉED SUMMER VEGETABLE BLEND

1 tablespoon olive oil
1 small onion, chopped
1 small red bell pepper, chopped
2 large squash, sliced
1 teaspoon dried basil
4 Roma tomatoes, sliced
Salt and pepper to taste

Warm olive oil in large skillet over medium-high heat; add onion, red bell pepper, squash, and basil. Cook and stir about 5 minutes, until crisp-tender. Add Roma tomatoes and salt and pepper to taste, stirring about 2 minutes. Makes about 4 servings.

BALSAMIC ROASTED VEGETABLE BLEND

2 large squash, sliced
2 large zucchini, sliced
1 medium eggplant, peeled and cubed
1 red onion, chopped
1 red bell pepper, chopped
2 tablespoons olive oil
2 tablespoons balsamic vinegar
Salt and pepper to taste

Combine all ingredients, tossing well to coat. Spread on large baking sheet. Bake at 425° for about 20 minutes, stirring once. Makes about 6 servings.

GREEN PEA CASSEROLE

3 tablespoons butter
1 small onion, chopped
2 celery stalks, chopped
2 (15-ounce) cans English peas, drained
1 (4-ounce) can sliced mushrooms, drained
1 (2-ounce) jar diced pimento, drained
1 (10¾-ounce) can cream of mushroom soup
¼ cup milk
1 cup cracker crumbs

Melt butter in medium saucepan; add onion and celery, and cook until tender. Add peas, mushrooms, pimento, soup, and milk, stirring well. Pour into a greased 2-quart casserole, and top with cracker crumbs. Bake at 350° for about 20 minutes. Makes about 6 servings.

QUICK WHITE RICE

⅔ cup chicken stock
1⅓ cups water
1⅓ cups quick-cooking rice

Bring stock and water to a boil in a saucepan over high heat. Stir in rice, cover pan, and remove from heat. Let stand 5 minutes. Fluff with a fork before serving. Makes 4 servings.

QUICK WHITE RICE WITH GREEN BEANS

⅔ cup chicken stock
1⅓ cups water
1⅓ cups quick-cooking rice
1 (8-ounce) can green beans, drained

Bring stock and water to a boil in a saucepan over high heat. Stir in rice, cover pan, and remove from heat. Let stand 5 minutes. Stir in green beans. Fluff with a fork before serving. Makes 4 servings.

QUICK CREAMY POLENTA

4¼ cups water
2 cups cornmeal
1 teaspoon salt
⅛ teaspoon pepper, optional

Boil water in a large saucepan; gradually whisk in cornmeal and salt. Reduce heat and simmer, whisking constantly, until thickened, about 10 minutes. Season to taste with pepper. Makes 4 servings.

CHICKPEAS

1 pound dried chickpeas, picked over
1 small onion, halved
2 sprigs fresh thyme
1 tablespoon salt

Cover chickpeas with water by 2 inches in a 3-quart saucepan. Boil, covered, 2 minutes. Remove from heat, and let chickpeas stand covered 1 hour. Drain chickpeas and return to pan. Add water to cover by 4 inches, onion, and thyme. Simmer uncovered until chickpeas are tender, about 1¼ hours, adding salt during last 10 minutes of cooking. Drain chickpeas and transfer to a bowl of cold water. Slip skins from chickpeas by rubbing them with fingers, and then drain well. Makes 6 to 8 servings.

BAKED YELLOW SQUASH

1 medium yellow squash
2 slices onion (¼-inch thick)
Salt and pepper to taste

Wash squash and cut stem and blossom ends. Wrap squash and onion in aluminum foil. Bake at 350° for 30 to 35 minutes, depending on size of squash. Season with salt and pepper as desired. Makes 2 servings.

QUICK, SOUTHERN-STYLE RED BEANS AND RICE

6 slices of bacon
2 onions, cut into ½-inch wedges
1 garlic clove, minced
1 cup beef broth
1 cup rice, uncooked
1 teaspoon dried thyme
1 teaspoon salt
1 green bell pepper, diced
2 cups kidney beans

Cut bacon into 1-inch pieces, and cook in a 10-inch skillet over medium heat until browned but not crisp, about 5 minutes. Remove bacon from skillet; drain off all but 1 tablespoon of drippings. Add onion and garlic to skillet; cook until onion is tender but not brown, about 5 minutes. Add enough water to beef broth to make 2½ cups. Add to skillet and bring to a boil. Stir in rice, bacon, thyme, and salt. Cover tightly and simmer 15 minutes. Add bell pepper, cover, and continue cooking 5 minutes. Remove from heat. Stir in beans. Let stand covered until all liquid is absorbed, about 5 minutes. Makes 4 to 6 servings.

QUICK POTATOES

2 cans small whole potatoes
2 tablespoons oil
Paprika

Pat potatoes dry with paper towels. Pour oil into a 10-inch x 6-inch baking dish. Add potatoes; stir to coat potatoes evenly with oil. Sprinkle with paprika. Bake at 375° for 30 minutes or until lightly browned and thoroughly heated. Makes 4 servings.

MASHED POTATOES

6 potatoes, peeled, cubed, and boiled
⅔ cup milk
2 tablespoons butter
Salt to taste
Paprika

Combine potatoes, milk, butter, and salt in a bowl of electric mixer. Whip on high for 2 minutes, or until potatoes are fluffy. Season with paprika. Makes 6 to 8 servings.

POTATO PUFF

3 eggs, separated
2 cups mashed potatoes
½ cup sour cream
½ cup grated Parmesan cheese

In a large bowl, beat egg whites until stiff. In a medium bowl, beat egg yolks until smooth, and add warm potatoes. Fold in sour cream and cheese; fold in the beaten egg whites. Pour into a 2-quart glass casserole. Bake at 350° for 40 to 45 minutes until puffed and brown. Makes 4 servings.

Potato Casserole

4 potatoes, sliced
1 large onion, sliced
1 (10¾-ounce) can cream of chicken soup
1 soup can milk
Cheddar cheese, grated

In casserole bowl put a layer of potatoes and then a layer of onions until dish is about half full. Combine soup and milk; mix well. Add soup mixture to casserole. Bake at 300° approximately 40 minutes, or until potatoes are tender. Top with grated cheese. Return to oven until cheese is melted. Makes 6 to 8 servings.

Quick Cherry Tomatoes

2 pints cherry tomatoes
2 teaspoons margarine
2 tablespoons fresh basil, chopped

In a nonstick skillet over medium-high heat, sauté tomatoes in melted margarine just until heated through, about 3 minutes. Sprinkle with basil. Cook and stir until basil is wilted, about 1 minute. Serve hot. Makes 6 to 8 servings.

Variation: Instead of basil, use a combination of basil, parsley, oregano, thyme, or a combination of parsley.

Seasoned Roasted Vegetables

1 pound asparagus, trimmed
2 red bell peppers, seeded and sliced
1 (1-ounce) package savory herb soup mix
3 tablespoons olive oil

Place vegetables on a baking sheet. In a small bowl, combine soup mix and olive oil; drizzle over vegetables, and toss to coat. Bake at 400° for 15 to 20 minutes, until vegetables are crisp and tender. Makes 4 to 6 servings.

Asparagus Casserole

3 (15-ounce) cans asparagus spears, drained, liquid from 1 can
  reserved
1 (10¾-ounce) can golden mushroom soup
1 (10¾-ounce) can cream of mushroom soup
Salt and pepper to taste
1½ cups shredded mozzarella cheese
1 cup breadcrumbs
¼ cup butter, melted

Place asparagus in greased 3-quart casserole. Combine reserved asparagus liquid, soups, and salt and pepper to taste, mixing until smooth; pour over asparagus. Top with mozzarella cheese, and sprinkle with breadcrumbs. Drizzle butter over all. Bake at 325° for about 30 minutes.

CAESAR ASPARAGUS

1 pound fresh asparagus, trimmed
¼ cup olive oil
3 tablespoons lemon juice
Salt and pepper
⅓ cup Parmesan cheese, freshly grated

Place asparagus on baking sheet and drizzle with olive oil, lemon juice, salt, and pepper. Sprinkle with Parmesan cheese. Bake at 400° for 15 to 18 minutes, until asparagus is crisp and tender. Makes 4 servings.

BRUSSELS SPROUTS

½ cup butter
1 small onion, chopped
2 pints fresh Brussels sprouts, washed, outer leaves removed
2 tablespoons water

Melt the butter in a saucepan. Sauté the onion for 2 to 3 minutes, until it is soft but not brown. Add Brussels sprouts and water. Cover and cook until the Brussels sprouts are done but not mushy. Makes 4 to 6 servings.

VEGETABLE MEDLEY

1 (1-pound) bag fresh mixed vegetables
1 (10¾-ounce) can cream of mushroom soup

Combine all ingredients. Simmer for 5 to 10 minutes until heated through. Makes 4 servings.

MICRO-FAST POTATOES

4 to 5 potatoes, sliced
Butter
Powdered American cheese
Garlic salt and pepper

Place in a glass pie plate or shallow glass dish. Spread butter across top of potatoes. Sprinkle with powdered American cheese. Sprinkle garlic salt and pepper over the top. Cover with plastic wrap, and microwave 3 minutes on high. Cautiously lift plastic wrap, and stir around. Cover again and microwave 3 more minutes. Check for tenderness. Cook until tender adding minutes as necessary for your microwave. Makes 6 to 8 servings.

DELICIOUS FAST-BAKED POTATOES

4 potatoes
¼ cup butter
Garlic salt to taste

Scrub baking potatoes, and cut in half lengthwise. Melt ¼ cup butter in baking dish. Dip potato into melted butter. Sprinkle with garlic salt. Bake in hot oven until done. Makes 4 servings

BROCCOLI CASSEROLE

3 (10-ounce) packages frozen broccoli, cooked and drained
¼ cup butter, cubed
1 pound American cheese
Breadcrumbs

On low heat, combine broccoli, butter, and cheese. After cheese has melted, place in casserole dish and sprinkle top with breadcrumbs. Bake at 350° for 30 minutes. Makes 8 servings.

FAST AND FANCY SWEET POTATOES

3 tablespoons butter
½ cup liquid brown sugar
6 medium sweet potatoes, cooked and sliced

Combine butter and brown sugar in 1-cup glass measuring cup.
Microwave on high for 2 minutes or until hot. Stir. Place sweet
potatoes in 1½-quart glass casserole. Pour sugar mixture over top.
Microwave on high for 6 to 8 minutes, stirring occasionally. Makes 6
to 8 servings.

FAST ARMENIAN PILAF

1 (8-ounce) package vermicelli or angel hair pasta, broken up
2 to 3 tablespoons butter
1 cup rice
1 to 2 bouillon cubes (chicken or beef)
2½ cups hot water

Melt butter in a 2-quart saucepan. Sauté vermicelli in melted butter
until light brown. Add rice, and continue to sauté until it darkens
slightly. Dissolve bouillon in water, and add to saucepan. Bring to
rolling boil, reduce heat, and simmer for 25 minutes covered. Slightly
open the pot lid, and cook for 5 minutes more. Makes 4 servings.

QUICK PASTA

1 pound zucchini, finely chopped
4 cups pasta sauce
¾ pound fresh angel hair pasta
2 tablespoons Parmesan cheese, shredded

Place zucchini in a steamer basket over boiling water. Cover pan, and steam 3 minutes or until tender. Drain, and return zucchini to same pan. Add pasta sauce, and simmer over medium low heat until just heated through. Cook pasta in a large pan of boiling water about 3 minutes, or until al dente. Drain. Serve pasta with sauce and sprinkled with Parmesan. Makes 6 to 8 servings.

QUICK RAVIOLI

9 ounces fresh spinach ravioli, cooked according to package
2 cups pasta sauce, hot
¼ cup fresh parsley, chopped
¼ cup grated Parmesan cheese

Drain ravioli, and toss with remaining ingredients. Makes 4 servings.

PESTO PASTA

1 pound dried linguine
1 (12-ounce) container pesto
2 cups grape tomatoes
½ cup grated Parmesan cheese

Cook pasta as directed on package; drain and return to pot. Stir in basil pesto, tossing gently over low heat until pasta is coated. Add grape tomatoes and toss for 1 minute. Sprinkle with cheese. Makes 6 to 8 servings.

SPINACH AND TOMATO PASTA

2 tomatoes, chopped
1 garlic clove, minced
1 tablespoon olive oil
Salt
½ pound fresh spinach
9 ounces dried pasta, cooked
Feta or Parmesan cheese

Sauté tomatoes with garlic and olive oil, and cook down to desired consistency (add salt to taste). Add spinach and stir until wilted. Toss all with hot cooked pasta. Add feta or Parmesan cheese, if desired. Makes 4 servings.

PESTO PEPPERS WITH PENNE

2 cups dried penne or mostaccioli pasta
1 (16-ounce) package frozen mixed bell peppers and onions
1 (10-ounce) package pesto
Parmesan cheese, grated

Cook pasta in boiling salted water to desired doneness or as directed on package. Drain. Meanwhile, stir-fry bell pepper in heavy nonstick skillet with 1 tablespoon water until heated through and tender. Stir in cooked, drained pasta and pesto. Cook over low heat, stirring carefully, until thoroughly heated. Sprinkle with Parmesan cheese, if desired. Makes 4 servings.

QUICK TORTELLINI

9 ounces fresh cheese tortellini
2 cups tomato sauce, hot
¼ cup fresh parsley, chopped
¼ cup Parmesan cheese, shredded

Cook tortellini in a large pan of boiling water 6 to 7 minutes or until just cooked through. Drain well, and toss with remaining ingredients. Makes 4 servings.

QUICK SPAGHETTI

9 ounces fresh spaghetti
2 cups tomato sauce, hot
¼ cup fresh parsley, chopped
¼ cup Parmesan cheese, shredded

Cook spaghetti in a large pan of boiling water 3 to 4 minutes or until just cooked through. Drain well, and toss with remaining ingredients. Makes 4 servings.

TOMATO PESTO SPAGHETTI

1 pound dried spaghetti
1 (10-ounce) container pesto
4 ripe tomatoes, chopped

Cook spaghetti according to package directions until al dente. Drain, reserving 2 tablespoons cooking liquid. Return to pot along with reserved cooking liquid. Stir in pesto over low heat until spaghetti is evenly coated. Add tomatoes at last minute before servings. Makes 6 to 8 servings.

BAKED BEANS

1 medium onion, chopped
1 green bell pepper, chopped
⅓ cup sweet pickle relish
¼ cup vinegar
1 cup chili sauce
½ cup molasses
1 tablespoon mustard
¼ teaspoon hot sauce
4 (16-ounce) cans baked beans

Combine all ingredients except beans in a saucepan. Simmer 10 minutes. Stir in beans. Makes 8 servings.

SPANISH RICE

3 tablespoons olive oil
1 medium onion, minced
¼ cup green bell pepper, chopped
1 garlic clove, minced
2½ cups canned tomatoes or tomato juice
1 teaspoon salt
3 cups rice, cooked

Heat the olive oil in a frying pan. Add the onion, pepper, and garlic, and cook 2 or 3 minutes. Add the tomatoes and salt, and blend well. Stir in the rice. Cover the pan, and cook on low until the tomato juice is absorbed, about 15 minutes. Makes 6 servings.

SAVORY RED CABBAGE

4 cups red cabbage, shredded
¼ cup vinegar
¾ cup water
¼ cup brown sugar
¼ teaspoon ground cloves, or 5 whole ones
2 tart apples, cored and diced
1 teaspoon salt

Combine all the ingredients and cook at low temperature until the cabbage and apples are tender, about 20 minutes. Makes 4 servings.

CREAMY CABBAGE

6 cups cabbage, shredded
⅓ cup water
Salt and pepper to taste
1 (3-ounce) package cream cheese, softened
½ teaspoon celery seed
2 tablespoons butter

Cook cabbage in water with salt and pepper to taste until tender. Drain and add remaining ingredients, tossing until well combined. Makes 6 servings.

GREEN ONION AND CORNBREAD STUFFING

1 (10¾-ounce) can French onion soup
1 soup can water
¼ cup margarine
1 cup celery, cut into ¼-inch cubes
1 cup green onions, thinly sliced
1½ teaspoons poultry seasoning
2 (8-ounce) packages cornbread stuffing mix
Vegetable cooking spray

In a saucepan, combine soup, water, margarine, celery, onions, and poultry seasoning. Bring to a boil, and remove from heat. Stir in cornbread stuffing mix. Bake stuffing in 1½-quart casserole lightly coated with nonstick vegetable cooking spray. Cover. Bake at 350° for 45 minutes or until set. Makes about 8 servings.

(This recipe used by permission of the National Turkey Federation)

APRICOT TURKEY DRESSING

1 cup dried apricots, chopped
1½ cups water or chicken stock
1 cup celery, chopped
¼ cup walnuts or pine nuts, chopped
12 slices bread, cut in small cubes

Bring the apricots and water (or chicken stock) just to a boil in a saucepan. Let stand for 10 minutes. Add the celery, nuts, and bread. Toss lightly to moisten the bread and blend the ingredients. Spoon into an oiled baking dish with a cover. Bake at 350° for about 40 minutes. Remove the cover the last 10 minutes of baking to brown the top of the dressing. Makes 12 servings.

Velvety Dumplings

3 (10¾-ounce) cans cream of chicken soup
1 soup can of water
1 soup can of milk
2 (10-count) cans refrigerated biscuits

Place soup, water, and milk in a large pot. Beat 1 minute with hand mixer until smooth. Bring to a boil. Cut biscuits into 4 pieces each. Drop 1 at a time, stirring frequently, so as not to scorch. Turn heat down to simmer. Cook on low until all biscuit pieces are fluffy, stirring frequently. Makes 8 servings.

Cornbread Dressing

1 cup chopped onion
½ cup celery, chopped
¼ cup margarine
3 to 4 cups chicken broth
6 cups day-old cornbread, crumbled
3 cups white bread, torn
2 to 3 eggs, beaten
¼ cup unsweetened applesauce
1 teaspoon dried sage
2 teaspoons salt
1 teaspoon pepper

Cook onion and celery in margarine and 3 cups chicken broth in saucepan until tender. Combine crumbled cornbread with torn white bread, eggs, applesauce, sage, salt, and pepper in a large bowl. Add onion mixture and chicken broth; mix well, adding additional chicken broth if needed for desired consistency. Spoon into 2 greased baking dishes. Bake at 450° for 30 minutes. Makes 12 servings.

GREEN BEANS

2 slices bacon, chopped
1 onion, chopped
2 garlic cloves, minced
1½ pounds green beans, trimmed, cooked, and drained
Salt and pepper to taste

In a skillet, brown bacon over medium-high heat. Add onion and garlic to the skillet and cook until onion is tender. Add green beans to the skillet; stir well. Add salt and pepper. Makes 4 to 6 servings.

MACARONI AND CHEESE

2 tablespoons flour
¼ teaspoon salt
3 tablespoons margarine, melted
2½ cups milk
1 cup Cheddar cheese, cubed
½ cup Swiss cheese, cubed
½ cup American cheese, cubed
1½ cups cooked elbow macaroni

Blend flour and salt into melted margarine in a large saucepan. Add milk all at once. Cook until thickened, stirring constantly. Stir in cheeses until melted. Fold in macaroni. Spoon into a greased baking 9-inch x 13-inch dish. Bake at 350° for 25 minutes. Makes 8 servings.

CHEESE GRITS

6 cups chicken broth
2 cups grits
2 eggs, beaten
⅓ cup milk
1 teaspoon salt
1 teaspoon garlic powder
1 cup Cheddar cheese, grated
¼ cup butter, softened

In a large saucepan, bring chicken broth to a boil. Stir in grits and whisk until all water is absorbed. Add the eggs, milk, salt, and garlic powder to the saucepan; mix well. Add cheese and butter; stir until melted. Pour mixture into a greased 9-inch x 13-inch casserole. Bake at 350° for 30 to 35 minutes, or until set. Makes 6 to 8 servings.

FRESH BROCCOLI CASSEROLE

1 bunch fresh broccoli, chopped and steamed
1 (10¾-ounce) can cream of chicken soup
2 cups sour cream
½ cup Parmesan cheese, grated

Combine broccoli, cream of chicken soup, and sour cream, mixing well. Pour into greased 9-inch x 13-inch baking dish, and top with Parmesan cheese. Bake at 350° for about 30 minutes. Makes about 6 servings.

DRESSING FROM THE HEARTLAND

1½ cups onion, chopped
1½ cups celery, diced
1½ cups green bell pepper, diced
½ cup margarine
12 slices dried bread, cubed
1 teaspoon poultry seasoning
1 teaspoon salt
¼ teaspoon dried sage
⅛ teaspoon black pepper
½ cup turkey broth

In a medium skillet, over medium-high heat, sauté onion, celery, and green pepper in margarine until tender. In a large bowl, combine onion mixture, bread cubes, poultry seasoning, salt, sage, pepper, and broth. Mix well. Spoon dressing into lightly greased 2-quart casserole dish. Bake covered at 325° for 45 to 50 minutes. Uncover last 5 minutes of baking time. Makes 12 servings.

(This recipe used by permission of the National Turkey Federation)

BROCCOLI CASSEROLE

1 (10-ounce) package frozen broccoli
1 (10¾-ounce) can cream of mushroom or chicken soup
2 eggs, beaten
1 cup mayonnaise
1½ cups Cheddar cheese, grated
2 cups crushed potato chips

Cook broccoli until tender; drain. Combine soup, eggs, mayonnaise, and cheese. Mix well. Add broccoli and pour into a buttered 9-inch x 13-inch casserole dish; top with potato chips. Bake at 350° for 30 minutes or until brown and firm. Makes 4 to 6 servings.

HOPPIN' JOHN

1 tablespoon olive oil
1 ham hock
1 onion, chopped
½ cup green bell pepper, chopped
2 garlic cloves, minced
1 pound dried black-eyed peas, soaked overnight and drained
6 cups chicken broth
1 bay leaf
2 sprigs fresh thyme
Salt and pepper to taste
3 cups rice, cooked and hot

In a large pot, brown the ham hock in olive oil. Add onion, green bell pepper, and garlic; sauté 2 minutes. Add the black-eyed peas, chicken broth, bay leaf, thyme, salt, and pepper; bring to a boil. Reduce heat, and simmer until peas are tender, about 45 minutes. Serve with rice. Makes 6 to 8 servings.

SPINACH CASSEROLE

1 (4½-ounce) carton cottage cheese
1 cup Cheddar cheese, grated
3 eggs
⅓ cup butter
3 tablespoons flour
1 (10-ounce) package frozen chopped spinach, thawed and
  drained
½ teaspoon salt

Combine all ingredients in a bowl, and stir well. Pour into a greased 9-inch x 13-inch casserole. Bake covered at 350° for 30 to 45 minutes. Makes 6 to 8 servings.

CORN CASSEROLE

1 (14-ounce) can corn
1 tablespoon minced onion
1 tablespoon pimento
1 tablespoon chopped bell pepper
1 (10¾-ounce) can cream of chicken soup
1 cup rice, cooked
Shredded Cheddar cheese

In a saucepan, combine corn, onion, pimento, and bell pepper. Cook over medium heat until vegetables are tender, about 5 minutes. Mix in cream of chicken soup and cooked rice. Pour into a buttered 9-inch x 13-inch casserole and cover with cheese. Bake at 350° for 20 minutes. Makes 4 to 6 servings.

POTATO AND CHEESE CASSEROLE

1 (2-pound) package frozen hash browns
½ cup butter, melted
1 teaspoon salt
½ teaspoon black pepper
½ cup chopped onion
1 cup milk
1 (10¾-ounce) can cream of chicken soup
2 cups shredded Cheddar cheese
1 cup sour cream
2 cups potato chips, crushed

In a large casserole, mix the first 5 ingredients together. In a saucepan, combine milk, soup, cheese, and cream. Cook over medium heat until cheese melts. Pour over potatoes and onion in casserole. Top with potato chip crumbs. Bake at 350° for 1 hour. Let stand 10 to 15 minutes before serving. Makes 8 servings.

GREEN BEAN CASSEROLE

3 (16-ounce) cans green beans, drained
3 slices bacon, chopped
6 tablespoons butter, melted
½ cup brown sugar, packed
Garlic powder to taste

Combine green beans, bacon, melted butter, and brown sugar in a bowl; mix gently. Spoon into a baking dish; sprinkle with garlic powder. Bake at 350° for 45 minutes. Makes 8 servings.

COPPER PENNY CARROTS

2 pounds carrots, cooked and sliced
1 medium onion, sliced
1 small green bell pepper, thinly sliced
1 (10¾-ounce) can condensed tomato soup
½ cup vegetable oil
1 cup sugar
¾ cup apple cider vinegar
Salt
1 teaspoon mustard
1 teaspoon Worcestershire sauce

Arrange vegetables in a bowl. Mix together with the rest of the ingredients in a saucepan. Bring to a boil, and stir until well blended. Pour over vegetables. Refrigerate for about 2 hours. Makes 8 servings.

GLAZED CARROTS

2 pounds carrots, peeled and sliced
½ cup water
3 tablespoons brown sugar
3 tablespoons honey
2 tablespoons margarine

Bring carrots to a boil in water in a saucepan; reduce heat. Simmer covered for 8 minutes. Add brown sugar, honey, and margarine; mix gently. Simmer over low heat until carrots are glazed. Makes 8 servings.

THREE-MEAT BAKED BEANS

8 ounces Polish sausage
8 ounces ground beef
3 tablespoons onion, chopped
5 slices bacon, fried and crumbled
2 (16-ounce) cans pork and beans
⅓ cup ketchup
¼ cup packed brown sugar
2 tablespoons molasses
1½ teaspoons Worcestershire sauce
1½ teaspoons mustard

Cut sausage into ¼-inch slices. Brown in skillet. Remove sausage with slotted spoon, and drain skillet. Add ground beef and onion to skillet. Cook until beef is brown and crumbly, stirring frequently; drain. Add sausage, bacon, pork and beans, ketchup, brown sugar, molasses, Worcestershire sauce, and mustard; mix well. Spoon into lightly greased 9-inch x 13-inch baking dish. Bake at 350° for 30 minutes. Makes 8 servings.

BUTTER BEANS

1 slice bacon
1 (16-ounce) can butter beans, drained
⅛ teaspoon black pepper
⅛ teaspoon salt
⅛ teaspoon garlic powder

In a medium saucepan, cook bacon over medium heat. When bacon is brown, remove from saucepan and discard. Add beans and seasonings to saucepan, and bring to a boil. Reduce heat, and simmer for 10 minutes. Makes 4 servings.

CREOLE OKRA

¼ cup chopped onion
1 green bell pepper, chopped
2 tablespoons butter
2 tablespoons olive oil
2 cups okra, sliced
1 (14-ounce) can diced tomatoes, drained
1 (14-ounce) can corn, drained
Salt and pepper to taste

Cook onion and bell pepper in butter and olive oil until tender. Add okra; cook 5 minutes. Add tomatoes, corn, and salt and pepper. Simmer about 15 minutes. Makes 8 servings.

CREAMED ONION GRATIN

1 (16-ounce) bag frozen pearl onions, thawed
1 (10¾-ounce) can cream of celery soup
¼ teaspoon nutmeg
Salt and pepper to taste
½ cup grated Parmesan cheese

Combine onions, soup, nutmeg, and salt and pepper to taste. Pour into a small greased baking dish. Top with Parmesan cheese. Cover. Bake at 350° for about 1 hour. Makes 4 servings.

BLACK-EYED PEPPERONI PEAS

3 (14-ounce) cans black-eyed peas, undrained
2 ounces pepperoni, chopped
1 green bell pepper, chopped
1 onion, chopped
¼ cup salsa
Salt and pepper to taste

Combine all ingredients. Simmer for about 1 hour. Makes 8 servings.

CRISPY BUTTERED POTATOES

6 medium white potatoes, peeled and thinly sliced
¼ cup butter, melted
Salt and pepper to taste

Blot potato slices with paper towels to dry. Toss with butter, salt, and pepper. Arrange in overlapping rows in a shallow baking dish. Pour any remaining butter over top. Bake at 350° for about 1 hour. Makes 6 servings.

SOUTHWESTERN OVEN FRIES

4 baking potatoes, cut into wedges
½ cup butter, melted
1 (1-ounce) package taco seasoning mix

Dip potato wedges in melted butter, then toss in taco seasoning. Roast on baking sheet at 350° for about 45 minutes. Makes 4 to 6 servings.

GRUYÈRE POTATOES AU GRATIN

1 cup sour cream
1½ cups Gruyère cheese, shredded
1 onion, diced
2 tablespoons chopped chives
5 potatoes, peeled and thinly sliced
1 cup breadcrumbs
¼ cup butter, melted

Combine sour cream, shredded Gruyère cheese, onion, and chives. Spread half of sour cream mixture in bottom of a greased 2-quart baking dish; top with half of sliced potatoes. Repeat layers. Top with breadcrumbs, and drizzle with melted butter. Cover. Bake at 350° for about 2 hours. Makes 6 servings.

BAKED POTATOES O'BRIEN

¼ cup butter
1 onion, chopped
½ green bell pepper, chopped
½ red bell pepper, chopped
3 tablespoons flour
2 cups milk
3 cups potatoes, cooked and cubed
Salt and pepper to taste
¾ cup sharp shredded Cheddar cheese

Melt butter in a large skillet; add onion, green bell pepper, and red bell pepper. Cook and stir until tender. Add flour, milk, potatoes, and salt and pepper. Pour into a greased 9-inch x 13-inch baking dish and top with shredded cheese. Bake at 350° for about 30 minutes. Makes 4 servings.

MICROWAVE POTATO CASSEROLE

½ cup butter, melted
1 cup chopped onion
1 (10¾-ounce) can cream of mushroom soup
1 cup sour cream
1 cup shredded Cheddar cheese
2 pounds frozen potato nuggets
Salt and pepper to taste

Combine butter and onion in large microwave-safe bowl; cook on high for 1 minute. Add remaining ingredients, stirring well. Cover and cook on high for about 10 minutes, stirring once. Makes 10 servings.

SPICY FRESH SPINACH

2 tablespoons water
1 tablespoon brown sugar
1 tablespoon Dijon mustard
½ teaspoon garlic salt
¼ teaspoon cayenne pepper
1 pound fresh spinach, trimmed

Combine water, brown sugar, Dijon mustard, garlic salt, and cayenne pepper in a large skillet; bring just to a boil. Add spinach, tossing to coat. Cook until wilted. Makes 2 servings.

SPINACH AND BACON AU GRATIN

1 (16-ounce) bag frozen chopped spinach, thawed and drained
½ pound bacon, cooked and crumbled
1 cup sour cream
½ cup shredded Cheddar cheese

Combine spinach, bacon, and sour cream; pour into small greased baking dish. Top with Cheddar cheese. Bake at 350° for about 30 minutes. Makes 4 servings.

MASHED POTATOES №2

4 potatoes, peeled and cut into ½-inch pieces
½ cup milk
¼ cup butter
Salt and pepper to taste

Cook potatoes in boiling water until tender, about 15 to 20 minutes. Drain water and mash potatoes. Stir in remaining ingredients. Makes 4 to 6 servings.

ONION SPINACH CASSEROLE

2 (10-ounce) packages frozen spinach, thawed and drained
1 (1½-ounce) package dry onion soup mix
1 cup sour cream
1 cup shredded Cheddar cheese

Combine all ingredients; pour into a small greased baking dish. Bake at 350° for about 30 minutes. Makes 4 servings.

OKRA CASSEROLE

1 medium onion, chopped
½ cup oil
1 tablespoon flour
Salt and pepper to taste
1 cup water
1¾ cups fresh or frozen okra, sliced
1 (15-ounce) can diced tomatoes, drained
1 cup shredded Cheddar cheese

Sauté onion in oil in a skillet. Stir in flour, salt, and pepper. Add water. Cook until thickened, stirring constantly. Layer okra, white sauce, tomatoes, and cheese in a 9-inch by 13-inch baking dish. Bake at 325° to 350° for about 30 minutes. Makes 4 servings.

PICKLED TARRAGON BEETS

2 (16-ounce) cans whole beets, drained, liquid reserved
½ cup apple cider vinegar
⅓ cup tarragon vinegar
½ cup cinnamon
8 whole cloves
¼ cup brown sugar
½ teaspoon salt

Combine reserved liquid from beets with remaining ingredients. Bring to a boil and simmer 15 minutes. Remove from heat, and add beets. Let chill overnight. Makes 8 servings.

FRIED GREEN TOMATOES

4 green tomatoes, sliced
½ cup flour
2½ teaspoons sugar
2 teaspoons salt
¼ teaspoon pepper
¾ cup evaporated milk
Oil

Drain tomato slices on a paper towel. Combine flour, sugar, salt, and pepper in a bowl. Coat tomatoes with flour mixture. Add evaporated milk to remaining flour mixture; mix until smooth. Dip tomato slices into batter, coating well. Fry tomatoes in ½-inch oil in a skillet until golden brown on both sides; drain. Makes 8 servings.

ZUCCHINI AND SQUASH CASSEROLE

4 cups yellow squash, diced
2 cups zucchini, diced
1 teaspoon salt
¼ cup butter
1 onion, chopped
2 garlic cloves, finely chopped
½ cup sour cream
½ teaspoon salt
½ teaspoon pepper
1 cup Cheddar cheese, grated
1 cup saltine cracker crumbs

Place squash and zucchini in a large saucepan. Add 1 teaspoon salt, and cover with water; bring to a boil. Cook until vegetables are soft, about 20 minutes.

In a skillet over medium-low heat, melt butter. Add onion and sauté until translucent, about 6 minutes. Add garlic and cook until fragrant, about 1 minute. Remove from heat.

In a large bowl, combine squash, zucchini, onion, garlic, butter, sour cream, ½ teaspoon salt, pepper, and Cheddar cheese. Mix well, then pour into a 9-inch x 13-inch casserole. Top with cracker crumbs. Bake at 350° for 25 to 30 minutes. Makes 8 to 10 servings.

FRESH CRANBERRY SAUCE

1 (16-ounce) bag fresh cranberries
1 cup water
2 cups sugar

Combine cranberries and water; bring to a boil, and mash berries as they begin to pop. Add sugar, and cook until dissolved. Sauce will congeal as it chills. Makes about 2 cups.

Potato Casserole №2

1 (2-pound) package frozen southern-style hash browns, thawed
1 (10½-ounce) can cream of chicken soup
½ cup butter, melted
½ cup chopped onion
1 pint sour cream
2 cups grated cheese
1 teaspoon salt
1 teaspoon black pepper
Cracker crumbs

Combine all ingredients except cracker crumbs; mix well. Pour into a lightly greased 9-inch by 13-inch baking dish. Top with crushed cracker crumbs. Bake at 350° for 45 minutes. Makes 8 servings.

Turnip Greens

4 strips bacon, sliced
1 onion, chopped
3 quarts water
1 teaspoon salt
1 teaspoon sugar
1 large bunch turnip greens, rinsed and patted dry

In a large pot, cook bacon until crispy. Add onion, and sauté until tender. Add water, salt, and sugar; cover and bring to a boil. Add turnip greens, and return to boil. Reduce heat, and cook until greens are tender, about 1 to 2 hours. Makes 8 servings.

COLLARD GREENS

2 ounces salt pork, sliced
3 Vidalia onions, finely chopped
8 garlic cloves, minced
1 large bunch collard greens, rinsed and patted dry
3 quarts chicken broth
1 teaspoon pepper
1 tablespoon seasoned salt
½ cup vinegar
4 teaspoons sugar

In a large pot, brown salt pork. Add onions and sauté until soft. Add garlic, and cook until fragrant, about 1 minute. Stir in collard greens, broth, pepper, seasoned salt, vinegar, and sugar. Bring to a boil; reduce heat, and simmer uncovered until greens are tender, about 1 to 2 hours. Makes 8 servings.

FRIED OKRA

1½ cups buttermilk
1 egg
2 cups cornmeal
1½ cups flour
1 teaspoon salt
½ teaspoon pepper
1 pound fresh okra, sliced into bite-sized pieces
Vegetable oil

In a large bowl, mix together buttermilk and egg. In another bowl, combine cornmeal, flour, salt, and pepper. Soak okra in buttermilk mixture, and then dredge in cornmeal mixture. Fry in preheated oil until crispy. Drain. Makes 4 servings.

VIDALIA ONION CASSEROLE

3 pounds Vidalia onions, thinly sliced
½ cup butter
1 cup rice, cooked
1½ cups milk
½ cup Swiss cheese, shredded
Salt to taste

Sauté onions in butter in a large skillet for 10 minutes or until tender. Add rice, milk, cheese, and salt; mix well. Spoon into a greased baking dish. Bake at 325° for 1 hour. Makes 6 servings.

SWEET-AND-SOUR GREEN BEANS

2 pounds fresh green beans, trimmed
6 slices bacon, chopped
1 medium onion, chopped
2 tablespoons vinegar
1 tablespoon brown sugar

Cook beans in salted water until tender; drain. Cook bacon over medium-heat until crisp; remove to paper towels; drain. Pour off all but 1 tablespoon bacon drippings; sauté onion in bacon drippings until tender. Add vinegar and sugar, and simmer about 5 minutes. Pour over green beans, tossing well to coat. Makes 8 servings.

TOMATO RELISH

3 large tomatoes, peeled, seeded, and finely chopped
1 bunch finely chopped green onions
1 green bell pepper, finely chopped
1 cucumber, peeled and finely chopped
2 celery stalks, finely chopped
3 tablespoons vinegar
2 tablespoons olive oil
1 tablespoon sugar
Salt and pepper to taste

Combine all ingredients, mixing well. Serve with roasted meat, greens, or beans. Makes about 2 cups.

SPICED CRANBERRY SAUCE

1 (16-ounce) bag fresh cranberries
1 cup water
2 cups sugar
1 teaspoon cinnamon
½ teaspoon ground cloves
Zest from 1 orange
Zest from 1 lemon

Combine cranberries and water; bring to a boil, and mash berries as they begin to pop. Add sugar, cinnamon, cloves, orange zest, and lemon zest; cook and stir until sugar dissolves. Sauce will congeal as it chills. Makes about 2 cups.

QUICK SPICED PEACHES

1 (14-ounce) can peach halves in syrup
½ cup light corn syrup
½ cup apple cider vinegar
1 tablespoon pickling spice

Drain peaches, reserving syrup. Combine reserved syrup, corn syrup, vinegar, and pickling spice; boil 10 minutes. Add peaches; reduce heat, and simmer about 10 minutes. Chill peaches in syrup overnight. Makes 4 servings.

BRUSSELS SPROUTS AND CARROTS WITH ROASTED CASHEWS

3 cups chicken broth
3 (10-ounce) packages frozen Brussels sprouts
3 large carrots, sliced diagonally
6 tablespoons butter
¾ cup roasted cashew halves
¼ teaspoon dried thyme
Salt and pepper to taste

Bring chicken broth to a boil in a medium saucepan; add Brussels sprouts and carrots, and cook until tender. Meanwhile, melt butter in a small saucepan over medium heat; add cashews, thyme, and salt and pepper. Cook and stir 3 to 4 minutes. Drain vegetables; pour sauce over drained vegetables, and toss lightly. Makes about 10 servings.

HOT CURRIED FRUIT

6 tablespoons butter or margarine
1 cup brown sugar
1 teaspoon curry powder
1 (14-ounce) can sliced peaches, drained
1 (14-ounce) can sliced pears, drained
1 (14-ounce) can pineapple chunks, drained
1 (6-ounce) jar maraschino cherries, drained

Combine butter, brown sugar, and curry powder in small saucepan; bring to a boil. Mix hot sugar mixture with drained fruits in a greased 2-quart casserole. Bake at 350° for about 20 minutes or until bubbly. Makes 8 to 10 servings.

ASPARAGUS WITH CREAMY TOMATO SAUCE

1 cup mayonnaise
1 tablespoon lemon juice
1 teaspoon lemon zest
1 teaspoon dried basil
Salt and pepper to taste
1 tomato, peeled, seeded, and finely chopped
2 bunches fresh asparagus, trimmed

Combine mayonnaise, lemon juice, lemon zest, basil, salt and pepper to taste, and tomato in a medium saucepan; warm gently over low heat. Cook asparagus in a small amount of boiling water until crisp and tender, about 4 or 5 minutes. Serve sauce over cooked asparagus. Makes 8 servings.

Sautéed Green Beans and Carrots with Bacon

½ **pound bacon, chopped**
2 **(10-ounce) packages green beans, thawed**
1 **pound carrots, peeled and thinly sliced**
2 **teaspoons garlic, minced**
Salt and pepper to taste

Cook bacon in large skillet over medium-low heat until crisp; drain and set aside. Drain off all but 2 tablespoons of bacon grease from skillet. Add green beans, carrots, garlic, and salt and pepper to taste. Cook and stir until vegetables are crisp and tender. Add cooked bacon to green beans and carrots. Makes 6 to 8 servings.

Better Green Bean Casserole

1 **tablespoon butter**
1 **tablespoon minced onion**
2 **tablespoons flour**
½ **cup sour cream**
Salt and pepper to taste
2 **(14-ounce) cans green beans, drained**
1 **cup Swiss cheese, shredded**
1 **cup cracker crumbs**

Melt butter in small saucepan over medium heat; add onion, and cook until tender. Add flour; cook and stir 2 minutes. Gradually add sour cream, stirring until thick and smooth. Add salt and pepper, green beans, and Swiss cheese. Pour into a greased 9-inch x 13-inch baking dish. Sprinkle with cracker crumbs. Bake at 350° for about 20 minutes. Makes 4 to 6 servings.

LIMA BEANS WITH WATER CHESTNUTS

3 (10-ounce) packages lima beans, cooked and drained
1 can sliced water chestnuts, drained
1 cup sour cream
1 (10¾-ounce) cream of mushroom soup
1 teaspoon soy sauce
Salt and pepper to taste

Combine all ingredients. Pour into a greased 9-inch x 13-inch baking dish. Bake at 350° for about 20 minutes. Makes 8 servings.

GREEN BEANS WITH CHEDDAR CHEESE

2 tablespoons butter
1 onion, chopped
2 tablespoons flour
2 tablespoons milk
2 tablespoons lemon juice
Salt and pepper to taste
2 (14-ounce) cans French-style green beans, cooked and drained
1 cup sour cream
½ cup shredded Cheddar cheese
½ cup breadcrumbs

Melt butter in medium saucepan over medium heat; add onion, and cook until tender. Add flour; cook and stir for 2 minutes. Add milk, lemon juice, and salt and pepper to taste; cook and stir until thickened. Add green beans and sour cream; pour into greased 9-inch x 13-inch baking dish. Sprinkle with cheese and breadcrumbs. Bake at 350° for about 20 minutes.

Simple Corn Pudding

2 (14-ounce) cans creamed corn
1 package Mexican-style cornbread mix
4 eggs, lightly beaten
1 cup shredded Cheddar cheese
⅔ cup vegetable oil
1 small onion, chopped

Combine all ingredients. Pour into greased 2-quart casserole. Bake at 350° for about 30 minutes or until set. Makes about 8 servings.

Honey-Glazed Carrots

½ cup brown sugar
1½ teaspoons cornstarch
Dash salt
1 cup water
1 (6-ounce) can crushed pineapple, drained, liquid reserved
2 tablespoons butter
1 tablespoon honey
1 pound baby carrots, cooked

Combine brown sugar, cornstarch, and salt in a small saucepan. Add water and reserved pineapple juice. Cook, stirring occasionally, until reduced to a thin syrup. Remove from heat and add butter and honey. Combine carrots, pineapple, and cooked syrup. Pour into a greased 9-inch x 13-inch baking dish. Bake at 350° for 30 minutes. Makes 4 to 6 servings.

MUSHROOMS AND CARROTS À LA GRECQUE

1 onion, chopped
⅓ cup olive oil
⅓ cup apple cider
¼ cup water
1 tablespoon lemon juice
1 teaspoon minced garlic
1 teaspoon sugar
Salt and pepper to taste
4 carrots, cut into chunks
1 pound whole mushrooms, cleaned and trimmed

Combine all ingredients except carrots and mushrooms in a large saucepan; bring to a boil. Add carrots, and cook for about 15 minutes. Add mushrooms. Cover, reduce heat, and simmer 5 minutes. Makes 6 to 8 servings.

HERBED CARROTS WITH GRAPES

½ cup butter
1 tablespoon lemon juice
1 teaspoon minced garlic
½ teaspoon dried thyme
¼ teaspoon celery salt
1½ pounds carrots, sliced
1 teaspoon dried basil
Salt and pepper to taste
1 cup red seedless grapes

Melt butter in a small saucepan; add lemon juice, garlic, thyme, and celery salt. Combine carrots, basil, and salt and pepper to taste in a large saucepan, adding water to cover. Bring to a boil, and cook 12 to 15 minutes or until crisp adn tender. Remove from heat and add grapes; cover and let stand for 2 minutes. Drain and toss with seasoned butter. Makes 6 to 8 servings.

SPINACH-CHEESE BAKE

2 (10-ounce) packages frozen spinach, thawed and drained
1 (16-ounce) container cottage cheese
2 cups Swiss cheese, shredded
3 eggs, beaten
¼ cup flour
¼ teaspoon nutmeg
Salt and pepper to taste

Combine all ingredients. Bake in a greased 2-quart casserole at 350°
for about 30 minutes. Makes 4 to 6 servings.

MAKE-AHEAD MASHED POTATOES

5 pounds potatoes, peeled and chopped
½ cup butter, melted
2 (3-ounce) packages cream cheese, softened
1 cup sour cream
1 cup shredded Cheddar cheese and softened
½ cup Parmesan cheese, grated
4 chopped green onions
Salt and pepper to taste

Cook potatoes in boiling water until tender; mash with electric mixer
or potato masher. Add remaining ingredients, and mix well. Pour into
a greased 3-quart casserole and chill up to 1 week. Bake uncovered at
350° for about 45 minutes. Makes 10 to 12 servings.

CREAMY GREEN NOODLES

2 tablespoons butter
3 tablespoons flour
Salt and pepper to taste
2 cups cream
Juice and zest of 1 lemon
1 (8-ounce) package dried green spinach noodles, cooked and
  drained
½ cup pimento-stuffed olives, sliced
½ cup grated Parmesan cheese

Melt butter in medium saucepan over medium heat; add flour and salt
and pepper to taste. Whisk for 3 minutes. Gradually add cream,
cooking and stirring until smooth and bubbly. Remove from heat, and
stir in lemon juice and zest. Toss with cooked noodles, olives, and
Parmesan cheese. Makes 4 servings.

BAKED ONION RICE

½ cup butter, melted
2 pounds onions, thinly sliced
½ cup rice
Salt and pepper to taste
¼ cup whipping cream
¼ Swiss cheese, shredded
2 tablespoons fresh parsley, chopped

Combine butter, onions, rice, and salt and pepper to taste in a shallow
baking dish. Cover tightly. Bake at 325° for about 1 hour, or until rice
and onions are tender. Stir in cream, Swiss cheese, and parsley.
Makes about 8 servings.

STOPLIGHT PEPPER RELISH

1 red bell pepper, chopped
1 green bell pepper, chopped
1 yellow bell pepper, chopped
1 onion, chopped
1 jalapeño pepper, seeded and finely chopped
2 cups water
¼ cup apple cider vinegar
¼ cup sugar
Salt to taste

Combine all ingredients; bring to a boil. Boil for 5 minutes, stirring occasionally. Drain and cool. Makes about 2 cups.

YELLOW RICE AND BLACK BEANS

1 (15-ounce) can black beans, undrained
1 (10-ounce) can diced tomatoes with chiles
Juice and zest of 1 lime
1 teaspoon cumin
½ teaspoon dried oregano
½ teaspoon minced garlic
½ cup sour cream
1 (5-ounce) package yellow rice mix, cooked

Combine black beans, tomatoes, lime zest and juice, cumin, oregano, and garlic. Simmer until heated through. Remove from heat, and stir in sour cream. Serve over yellow rice. Makes 4 servings.

ONION RELISH

2 cups sweet onions (such as Vidalia or Walla Walla), chopped
½ bell pepper, finely chopped
1 (4-ounce) jar diced pimento, drained
½ cup apple cider vinegar
¼ cup water
¼ cup sugar
½ teaspoon caraway seed
Salt and pepper to taste

Combine all ingredients in a medium saucepan; bring to a boil.
Reduce heat, and simmer about 5 minutes. Chill before serving. Serve
with grilled meats or burgers. Makes about 2½ cups.

CANDIED CRANBERRIES

2 cups fresh cranberries
1 cup sugar

Spread cranberries over the bottom of a large, shallow baking dish.
Sprinkle with sugar, and cover tightly. Bake at 350° for 1 hour,
stirring occasionally. Chill before serving. Makes 2 cups.

ZUCCHINI AND TOMATOES AU GRATIN

2 (14-ounce) cans zucchini with tomatoes, drained
½ teaspoon Italian seasoning
1 cup shredded mozzarella cheese

Pour tomatoes into a small greased baking dish. Toss Italian
seasoning with mozzarella, cheese and sprinkle over tomatoes. Bake
at 350° for about 20 minutes. Makes 4 servings.

MEXICAN RICE

¼ cup chopped onion
1 teaspoon minced garlic
1 cup rice, uncooked
3 tablespoons olive oil
½ teaspoon chili powder
Salt and pepper to taste
2½ cups water

Cook onion, garlic, and rice in oil over medium-high heat, about 3 minutes. Stir in remaining ingredients, and bring to a boil. Reduce heat, cover, and simmer about 20 minutes. Makes 8 servings.

GLAZED BUTTERNUT SQUASH

2 butternut squash, peeled, seeded, and chopped
¾ cup brown sugar
¼ cup sugar
2 tablespoons butter, melted
½ teaspoon cinnamon
¼ teaspoon ginger
Salt and pepper to taste

Cook squash in boiling water until tender; drain. Combine with remaining ingredients. Pour into a greased 9-inch x 13-inch baking dish. Bake at 350° for about 30 minutes. Makes 6 to 8 servings.

ZUCCHINI PARMESAN FRITTERS

½ cup all-purpose baking mix
½ cup grated Parmesan cheese
2 eggs, beaten
2 cups zucchini, grated
½ teaspoon Italian seasoning
Salt and pepper to taste
¼ cup butter

Combine baking mix, Parmesan cheese, eggs, zucchini, Italian seasoning, and salt and pepper to taste. Melt butter in large skillet over medium-high heat; drop zucchini mixture by tablespoonfuls into hot butter, and cook about 5 minutes, turning once. Makes about 6 servings.

SUCCOTASH

1 (15-ounce) can lima beans, drained
1 (15-ounce) can corn with red and green peppers, drained
1 (15-ounce) can diced tomatoes, undrained
½ cup chicken broth
Salt and pepper to taste

Combine all ingredients; simmer about 15 minutes. Makes about 6 servings.

RED RICE

2 tablespoons butter
4 chopped green onions
1 green bell pepper, chopped
2 teaspoons garlic, minced
1 cup quick-cooking rice
2 cups chicken broth
1 (14-ounce) can diced tomatoes with Italian seasoning
Salt and pepper to taste

Melt butter in large saucepan over medium-high heat; add green onions, green bell pepper, and garlic, stirring until tender. Add rice; cook and stir for about 2 minutes. Add chicken broth, undrained tomatoes, and salt and pepper to taste. Bring to a boil. Reduce heat, cover, and simmer for about 20 minutes. Makes 4 servings.

STEAMED BROCCOLI WITH LEMON BUTTER

1 bunch broccoli, trimmed
4 tablespoons butter, melted
Juice of 1 medium lemon

Steam broccoli until crisp-tender. Combine butter and lemon juice. Pour over steamed broccoli. Makes 6 to 8 servings.

ROASTED CARROTS WITH FRESH MINT

4 medium carrots, peeled and sliced
1 tablespoon olive oil
1 tablespoon fresh mint, chopped
Salt and pepper to taste

Combine all ingredients. Pour into a small greaed baking dish. Bake at 425° for about 20 minutes or until tender. Makes 4 servings.

CHEESY CORN WITH BACON

2 (15-ounce) cans corn, drained
1 cup shredded Cheddar cheese
3 slices bacon, cooked and crumbled
1 green onion, chopped
¼ cup milk
¼ teaspoon garlic salt
¼ teaspoon pepper

Combine all ingredients; pour into greased 2-quart baking dish. Bake at 400° for 10 to 15 minutes, stirring once. Makes 4 to 6 servings.

SAVORY HERBED RICE

2 cups chicken broth
1 teaspoon garlic salt
1 teaspoon dried oregano
1 teaspoon dried parsley
Pepper to taste
1 cup quick-cooking rice

Combine chicken broth, garlic salt, oregano, parsley, and pepper in a medium saucepan; bring to a boil. Stir in rice. Reduce heat to low; cover tightly and simmer 20 minutes. Makes 8 servings.

SAUTÉED FRESH SPINACH WITH GARLIC AND LEMON

1 teaspoon olive oil
1 teaspoon minced garlic
1 (9-ounce) bag fresh spinach
½ small lemon
Salt and pepper to taste

Heat oil and garlic in large skillet over medium heat. When garlic begins to sizzle and be fragrant, add spinach; skillet will be very full. Carefully turn spinach with tongs until wilted. Reduce heat to low. Cook until tender, stirring frequently, about 3 minutes. Squeeze lemon over spinach. Add salt and pepper to taste. Makes 2 to 3 servings.

BAKED SPINACH PASTA

1 (8-ounce) package dried pasta, cooked and drained
2 eggs, beaten
2 cups pasta sauce, divided
1 cup grated Parmesan cheese, divided
1 (10-ounce) package frozen chopped spinach, thawed and drained
1 (4-ounce) can sliced mushrooms, drained
1 cup cottage cheese
¼ teaspoon nutmeg

Combine cooked pasta, eggs, 1 cup pasta sauce, and ½ cup Parmesan cheese; pour into a greased 9-inch square pan. Combine spinach, mushrooms, cottage cheese, nutmeg, and remaining pasta sauce; spread over pasta. Top with remaining ½ cup Parmesan cheese. Bake at 350° for about 30 minutes. Makes 4 to 6 servings.

Mediterranean Pasta

1 (8-ounce) package orzo pasta, cooked and drained
1 (6-ounce) jar marinated artichoke hearts, drained and chopped
1 (4-ounce) can sliced black olives, drained
1 red bell pepper, chopped
½ cup red onion, chopped
1 cup Caesar salad dressing

Combine all ingredients, tossing well to coat. Serve warm or cold.
Makes 4 servings.

Southwestern Lentils and Corn

3 cups dried lentils
6 cups water
1 (14-ounce) can Mexican-style corn, drained
1 (10-ounce) can diced tomatoes with chiles
1 onion, chopped
1 (6-ounce) can tomato paste
½ cup bulgur wheat
2 tablespoons chili powder
1 tablespoon garlic, minced
2 teaspoons dried oregano
Salt and pepper to taste
1 tablespoon vinegar

Combine all ingredients except vinegar; bring to a boil. Reduce heat,
cover, and simmer for about 1½ hours. Stir in vinegar. Makes 10
servings.

BEEF AND PORK

ALL-PURPOSE GROUND MEAT MIX

5 pounds ground beef, turkey, or chicken
1 tablespoon salt
2 cups chopped onion
1 cup green bell pepper, diced

In a large pot or Dutch oven, brown the ground meat, stirring to break up any large pieces. Drain off excess grease. Stir in salt, celery, onion, and bell pepper. Cover; simmer until vegetables are crisp and tender, about 10 minutes. Remove from heat; set aside to cool.

Ladle meat mixture into 6 2-cup freezer containers with tight-fitting lids; leave ½ inch of space at the top of each. Draw a knife several times through the mixture in each container to prevent air pockets. Secure lids on the containers; label with date and contents. Store in the freezer. Use within 3 months. Makes 12 cups.

FAST AND EASY GOULASH

1 pound ground beef
1 large onion, chopped
1 (16-ounce) can tomatoes, chopped
1 (14-ounce) can corn or ½ pound frozen corn

Brown ground beef with onion in large pot or fry pan. Pour off grease. Add tomatoes with juice. Simmer for 15 to 20 minutes. Add corn and warm thoroughly, or cook frozen corn until done. Makes 4 servings.

Easy Moussaka

1 tablespoon olive oil
1 pound ground beef
1 onion, chopped
1 eggplant, peeled and chopped
1 (8-ounce) can tomato sauce
¼ cup ketchup
¼ teaspoon nutmeg
¼ teaspoon cinnamon
1 (10-ounce) container Alfredo sauce
2 cups cooked orzo pasta, drained

Heat olive oil in a large skillet; brown ground beef and onion until thoroughly cooked. Drain. Add eggplant, tomato sauce, ketchup, nutmeg, and cinnamon; cook until eggplant is tender. Stir in Alfredo sauce and heat through. Serve over hot cooked pasta. Makes 6 servings.

Cheesy Lumberjack Supper

1½ pounds ground beef
1 onion, chopped
2 (14-ounce) cans pork and beans
½ cup brown sugar
½ cup barbecue sauce
1 (10-count) can refrigerated biscuit dough
2 cups shredded Cheddar cheese

Brown ground beef and onion, cooking thoroughly; drain. Add pork and beans, brown sugar, and barbecue sauce; pour into a greased 3-quart baking dish. Lay biscuits over beef mixture and sprinkle with cheese. Bake at 350° for about 30 minutes. Makes 4 to 6 servings.

PICADILLO

1 tablespoon olive oil
1 pound ground beef
1 onion, chopped
1 teaspoon minced garlic
½ teaspoon cumin
½ teaspoon cinnamon
Dash ground cloves
Salt and pepper to taste
½ cup frozen black beans
1 (14-ounce) can diced tomatoes
¼ cup raisins
¼ cup green olives, sliced
3 cups rice, cooked and hot

Heat olive oil in a large skillet; brown ground beef and onion until thoroughly cooked. Drain. Add garlic, cumin, cinnamon, cloves, and salt and pepper to taste. Cook 2 to 3 minutes. Add peas, tomatoes, raisins, and green olives; cook until heated through. Serve over rice. Makes 4 servings.

GROUND BEEF CHOW MEIN

1 pound ground beef
1 onion, chopped
2 cups celery, chopped
1 (10¾-ounce) can cream of mushroom soup
1 cup milk
2 cups chow mein noodles

Brown ground beef with onion and celery; drain. Stir in remaining ingredients. Bake at 350° for about 30 minutes. Makes 4 servings.

Ranch Beef and Beans

1½ pounds ground beef, cooked and drained
1 (1½-ounce) package dry onion soup mix
2 (14-ounce) cans pork and beans
1 (14-ounce) can pinto beans, drained
1 cup ketchup
½ cup water
½ cup mustard
¼ cup brown sugar
1 tablespoon cider vinegar

Combine all ingredients. Bake at 400° for about 30 minutes. Makes 6 to 8 servings.

Bleu Burgers

1 pound ground beef
1 egg, beaten
1 (1½-ounce) package dry onion soup mix
1 (4-ounce) package bleu cheese crumbles

Combine all ingredients except cheese; form into 8 thin patties. Divide bleu cheese evenly over 4 patties; top with remaining 4 patties, and press edges to seal. Grill to desired doneness. Makes 4 servings.

Bacon-Wrapped Stuffed Hot Dogs

8 beef hot dogs
4 slices American cheese, torn into small pieces
8 slices bacon

Cut a lengthwise slit down each hot dog, cutting almost to the bottom. Stuff each hot dog with about ½ slice cheese. Wrap each stuffed hot dog with bacon. Bake or grill until bacon is thoroughly cooked. Makes 8 servings.

QUICK SPAGHETTI AND MEATBALLS

4¼ cups pasta sauce, any variety
1 pound frozen cooked meatballs
1 pound spaghetti
½ cup grated Parmesan cheese

Combine sauce and meatballs in a saucepan over medium-high heat. Bring to a boil. Reduce heat to low. Cover and cook 20 minutes, or until meatballs are heated through, stirring occasionally. Meanwhile, cook spaghetti in boiling water for 7 to 10 minutes or until al dente. Top with meatballs and sauce. Sprinkle with cheese. Makes 4 servings.

EASY AND FAST MEATLOAF

1½ pounds ground beef
4 crackers, crumbled
½ cup ketchup, plus more for topping
1 (1½-ounce) package dry onion soup mix
1 egg

Mix all ingredients. Bake at 350° for about 30 minutes. Pour small amount of ketchup on top before cooking, if desired. Makes 4 to 6 servings.

Easy Burgers

1 pound ground beef
½ cup onion, finely chopped
4 tablespoons soy sauce
¼ cup fresh mushrooms, sliced

Combine beef, onion, and 2 tablespoons soy sauce until well blended; shape into 4 patties. Heat frying pan until sizzling hot; add patties and cook over medium heat 5 minutes. Turn patties over; cook 5 minutes longer or to desired doneness. Remove patties; stir in remaining 2 tablespoons of soy sauce. Bring to rapid boil; add patties, remove pan from heat, and turn patties to coat both sides. Just before serving, sprinkle mushroom slices over patties. Makes 4 servings.

Grilled Nacho Cheeseburgers

4 frozen ground beef patties
½ teaspoon garlic-pepper seasoning blend
4 hamburger buns, split
⅓ cup spicy nacho cheese sauce

Sprinkle one side of each frozen patty with garlic pepper. Place on grill, cover, and cook patties, peppered sides up, 4 to 5 inches from medium coals for 12 to 15 minutes, turning once, until no longer pink in center. Place split hamburger buns, cut side down, on grill for about 1 to 2 minutes. Divide cheese sauce among patties. Cover and grill until cheese begins to melt, about 1 minute. Serve on toasted buns. Makes 4 servings.

BEEF POT PIE

4 cups beef, cooked and chopped
2 cups beef broth
4 hard-boiled eggs, chopped
1 (10¾-ounce) can cream of mushroom soup
1 (20-ounce) package frozen mixed vegetables, thawed
½ cup butter, melted
1 cup milk
1 cup self-rising flour

Combine beef, broth, eggs, soup, and vegetables; pour into a greased 9-inch x 13-inch baking dish. Combine butter, milk, and flour; pour over beef mixture. Bake at 350° for about 1 hour. Makes about 8 servings.

PESTO-STUFFED STEAKS

2 (1-pound) beef rib-eye steaks, about 1¼-inch thick
¼ cup pesto
3 tablespoons grated Parmesan cheese
1 tablespoon olive oil

Cut into side of each steak, forming a deep pocket. Be careful not to cut through to opposite side. Mix pesto and cheese and spread into pockets. Press closed and drizzle oil over beef. Place steaks carefully on grill, and cook 4 to 5 inches from medium coals for 12 to 15 minutes for medium doneness, turning once. Remove from grill, cover, and let stand for 5 to 10 minutes. Cut beef into thick strips to serve. Makes 4 to 6 servings.

BEEF STACKS

1 pound beef filet steak
Salt and pepper to taste
4 marinated artichoke hearts, plus some liquid, or 4 pickled
  onions
½ pound Cheddar or Swiss cheese, thinly sliced

Sprinkle beef with salt and pepper, and cook on grill or under broiler for about 14 to 16 minutes (medium), until desired doneness, turning once during cooking. Cover with foil, and let rest for 15 minutes; slice very thinly against the grain. Slice onions or artichoke hearts very thinly. Layer beef and cheese slices on each plate. Top with slices of artichoke heart or onion and drizzle with some of the pickling liquid. Season with salt and pepper, if desired. Makes 4 servings.

ALL-DAY ROAST

1 (3 to 4-pound) beef roast
1 (1½-ounce) package dry onion soup mix
Dash dried oregano
1 bay leaf
1 (10¾-ounce) can cream of mushroom soup

Place roast in covered dish. Sprinkle with onion soup mix. Add oregano and bay leaf. Pour cream of mushroom soup around roast. Soup will mix with juice from roast for gravy. Bake at 200° for 8 hours. Makes 6 to 8 servings.

MICROWAVE MEXICAN CUBE STEAKS

4 beef cube steaks
1 cup chunky salsa
1 cup pepper jack cheese, shredded
1 avocado, peeled and sliced

Arrange steaks in an 8-inch-square microwave-safe dish. Cover loosely with waxed paper, and cook on high for 6 to 8 minutes, turning beef over and rearranging after 3 minutes, until almost done. Drain. Top each steak with salsa.

Cover loosely with waxed paper and cook on high for 2 to 3 minutes or until salsa is hot. Sprinkle each with cheese and cover. Let stand 2 minutes until cheese is melted. Top with avocado slices. Makes 4 servings.

BAKED BEEF HASH

2 tablespoons onion, diced
2 tablespoons green bell pepper, diced
1 tablespoon margarine
2 cups beef, cooked and shredded
1 (10-ounce) can condensed beef soup with vegetables
1 cup potatoes, cooked and diced
1 egg

Sauté onions and green bell pepper in margarine until tender. Add beef, soup, and potatoes. Simmer for 5 minutes, stirring occasionally. Remove from stove top; add egg and mix thoroughly. Place in a greased 9-inch x 13-inch casserole. Bake at 400° for 45 minutes. Cut into squares for serving. Makes 6 servings.

EASY AND FAST LASAGNA

1 pound ground beef
Dash dried oregano
Dash garlic salt or powder
Tomato sauce
1 (8-ounce) package lasagna noodles, cooked
½ cup shredded Cheddar cheese
½ cup shredded mozzarella cheese

Brown ground beef and drain. Add oregano and garlic salt, to taste. Stir and let simmer. Put small amount of sauce in bottom of a 9-inch x 13-inch pan. Put a layer of noodles on top of the sauce. Pour half of sauce over noodles. Sprinkle with half of cheeses. Repeat with noodles, sauce, and cheeses. Cover with foil. Bake 10 minutes at 350°. Remove foil and cook 15 minutes. Let stand 10 minutes before serving. Makes 4 servings.

SALISBURY STEAK

1 pound ground beef
1 egg
1 (1½-ounce) package dry onion soup mix
2 tablespoons butter
1 onion, sliced
3 tablespoons flour
1½ to 2 cups beef broth
Salt and pepper to taste

Combine ground beef, egg, and onion soup mix. Form into 4 patties and cook in a large skillet until done. Remove and keep warm. Wipe skillet clean. Melt butter and cook onion, stirring until tender. Add flour and cook 3 minutes. Gradually add beef broth, cooking and stirring to desired consistency. Add salt and pepper to taste. Return cooked beef patties to pan, and cook covered until heated through. Makes 4 servings.

BEEFY BEAN CASSEROLE

1 pound ground beef
1 onion, chopped
2 (14-ounce) cans chili beans
1 (10-ounce) can diced tomatoes with chiles
1 cup shredded Cheddar cheese

Cook ground beef and onion in ovenproof skillet until thoroughly cooked; drain. Stir in beans and tomatoes, cooking until heated through. Top with shredded cheese, and run under broiler until cheese is melted and bubbly. Makes 4 to 6 servings.

BRAISED ROUND STEAK

2 pounds round steak, cut into pieces
1 teaspoon minced garlic
Salt and pepper to taste
2 (14-ounce) cans diced tomatoes

Season steak with garlic, salt, and pepper. Brown in large ovenproof skillet. Pour tomatoes over steak, and cover tightly. Bake at 325° for about 1 hour. Makes 4 to 6 servings.

BARBECUED CHUCK STEAK

½ cup mango chutney
⅓ cup ketchup
3 tablespoons lemon juice
Salt and pepper to taste
1 (1½-pound) beef chuck steak

Combine the first 4 ingredients. Rub half of chutney mixture over steak, and chill for 1 hour or more. Grill to desired doneness, and serve with remaining chutney mixture. Makes 4 to 6 servings.

BARBECUED BEEF

1 slice bacon, cut into 1-inch pieces
½ cup chopped onion
½ cup ketchup
½ cup apple juice
1 tablespoon white vinegar
1 teaspoon mustard
1 teaspoon Worcestershire sauce
⅛ teaspoon salt
⅛ teaspoon ground black pepper
2½ teaspoons sugar
12 ounces thinly sliced roast beef
4 Kaiser rolls (optional)

Cook bacon in medium saucepan over medium-high heat 3 to 4 minutes or until almost cooked. Add onion; cook 3 to 5 minutes, or until bacon is crisp and onion is tender, stirring occasionally.

Combine ketchup, apple juice, vinegar, mustard, Worcestershire sauce, salt, and pepper; add to bacon mixture. Reduce heat; cover and simmer until flavors are blended, 15 to 20 minutes. Stir in sugar and sliced beef. Serve warm on rolls, if desired. Makes 4 servings.

FAST BEEF AND RICE CASSEROLE

2 cans sliced beef
1 cup quick-cooking rice
1 (10-ounce) can beef broth
2 cups water

Mix beef, rice, broth, and water in a casserole dish. Cover. Bake at 350° until rice is done, about 1 hour. Makes 4 servings.

SWEET-AND-SOUR MEATBALLS

1¼ pound ground beef
¼ cup chopped onion
½ teaspoon salt
⅛ teaspoon pepper
1 (14-ounce) can pineapple in unsweetened juice
½ cup water
2 tablespoons light soy sauce
2 tablespoons vinegar
2 teaspoons cornstarch
½ green bell pepper, cut into bite-size chunks
¼ cup sugar

In a bowl, combine ground beef, onion, salt, and pepper; mix well.
Shape into 1-inch balls. Place on broiler rack. Broil about 4 inches
from heat for about 4 minutes or until cooked throughout.

Drain pineapple juice into saucepan, reserving pineapple. Add
water, soy sauce, and vinegar. Stir in cornstarch. Cook, stirring
constantly, until mixture boils and thickens. Stir in green bell pepper,
pineapple, and meatballs. Simmer for 5 minutes. Stir in sugar. Makes
4 servings.

BACON CHEESEBURGER PIZZA

1 (10¾-ounce) can cream of mushroom soup
1 (12-inch) baked pizza crust
1 pound ground beef, cooked and drained
½ pound bacon, cooked and crumbled
1 cup shredded Cheddar cheese

Spread soup over pizza crust. Sprinkle cooked beef and bacon over
soup, and top with cheese. Bake at 425° for about 15 minutes, or until
cheese is melted. Makes 4 to 6 servings.

Potato and Beef Casserole

1 pound ground round
½ onion, finely chopped
1½ cups mild shredded Cheddar cheese
Salt and pepper to taste
4 potatoes, thinly sliced
1 (10-ounce) can cream of mushroom soup
½ cup milk

Brown ground round and onion in skillet, stirring until ground meat is crumbly; drain. Spread beef mixture in a 9-inch x 13-inch baking dish; sprinkle with cheese, salt, and pepper. Layer potatoes over cheese. Spread mixture of soup and milk over top. Bake at 350° for 90 minutes. Makes 6 servings.

Stuffed Bell Peppers

3 large bell peppers
½ pound ground chuck
1 cup breadcrumbs
1 tablespoon onion, chopped
1 teaspoon salt
¼ teaspoon pepper
1 (8-ounce) can tomato sauce

Cut tops off peppers, and hollow out inside. Wash peppers thoroughly, and cook in salted boiling water. Mix remaining ingredients together, and stuff inside peppers. Stand them upright in a baking dish. Bake covered at 350° for 45 minutes. Remove the cover and cook for 15 more minutes. Makes 3 servings.

TACO PIE

1 pound ground beef
½ cup onion, chopped
2 (1-ounce) packages dry taco seasoning
¾ cup all-purpose baking mix
1¼ cup milk
3 eggs
1 cup shredded Cheddar cheese
¼ head lettuce, shredded
1 tomato, seeded and diced
¼ cup olives, sliced

Grease a 10-inch pie plate or 8-inch-square baking dish. Cook and stir the ground beef and onion in a 10-inch skillet until beef is brown; drain. Stir in seasoning mix; spoon into pie plate. Beat baking mix, milk, and eggs with wire whisk or hand beater, or until almost smooth, for about 1 minute. Pour into pie plate. Bake at 400° about 25 minutes or until knife inserted in center comes out clean. Sprinkle with cheese. Bake about 2 minutes longer, or until cheese is melted. Cool 5 minutes. Garnish with lettuce, tomato, and olives. Makes 4 to 6 servings.

SLOPPY JOES

1 pound ground beef
1 small onion, finely chopped
½ bell pepper, finely chopped
1 stalk celery, finely chopped
1 cup chili sauce
1 cup ketchup
Salt and pepper to taste
Burger buns

Brown ground beef with onion, bell pepper, and celery; drain fat. Add chili sauce, ketchup, and salt and pepper to taste. Simmer for about 20 minutes. Serve over burger buns. Makes 4 servings.

Ground Beef and Noodle Bake

2 tablespoons butter
2 pounds ground beef
2 (8-ounce) cans tomato sauce
1 teaspoon sugar
1 teaspoon salt
Pepper to taste
1 (8-ounce) package dried egg noodles, cooked and drained
1 (8-ounce) package cream cheese, cubed
1 cup sour cream
3 chopped green onions
½ cup mild shredded Cheddar cheese

Melt butter in skillet and add beef. Stir until crumbly; drain. Add tomato sauce, sugar, salt, and pepper; mix well. Simmer covered for 15 minutes. Layer noodles, cream cheese, sour cream, green onions, and ground beef mixture half at a time in a greased large baking dish. Top with cheese. Bake at 350° for 30 to 45 minutes or until heated through. Makes 8 servings.

Fast and Filling

2 (10¾-ounce) cans condensed tomato soup
1½ pounds ground beef, browned
1 (8-ounce) can green peas, drained
3 large potatoes, cooked and quartered

Heat soup. Drop in meat. Heat 10 more minutes. Add peas. Simmer for 10 minutes. Add potatoes and heat through. Makes 4 to 6 servings.

SHEPHERD'S PIE

2 cups meat, cooked and chopped
2 cups gravy
1 tablespoon finely chopped onion
2 cups mashed potatoes
1 teaspoon salt
⅛ teaspoon pepper
⅛ teaspoon paprika
1 or 2 tablespoons butter

Combine meat, gravy, and onion. Combine potatoes, salt, pepper, and parprika, and beat well. Line the bottom of a buttered 9-inch x 13-inch baking dish with potatoes. Dot with bits of butter. Bake at 400° until the potatoes are brown, or if cold potatoes have been used, until thoroughly heated and browned. Crumbs, macaroni, or rice may be substituted for potatoes. Makes 4 servings.

COUNTRY-FRIED STEAK

½ teaspoon salt
½ teaspoon pepper
1½ cups flour
1 cup vegetable oil
2 pounds boneless round steaks
1 onion, chopped
3 cups water

Combine salt, pepper, and 1 cup flour in a large bowl. Dredge steaks in flour mixture. Heat oil in a large skillet over medium-high heat. Brown steaks on both sides. Remove steaks from the skillet and reduce heat. Add onion and sauté until tender. Combine remaining flour and water; blend well. Pour flour mixture into the skillet, and stir slowly until it begins to thicken. Return steaks to skillet. Let simmer covered for 15 minutes or until steaks are cooked through. Makes 4 to 6 servings.

MEAT LOAF

2 eggs, beaten
⅓ cup milk
½ cup tomato sauce
1 teaspoon salt
Dash pepper
1½ cups breadcrumbs
2 pounds ground beef
1 cup onion, finely chopped
1 green bell pepper, chopped
1 cup tomatoes, seeded and diced
¼ tablespoon Worcestershire sauce

Combine eggs, milk, and tomato sauce in a large bowl. Add salt and pepper; stir to combine. Add breadcrumbs, ground beef, onion, green bell pepper, tomatoes, and Worcestershire sauce. Place mixture into a loaf pan. Bake at 375° for 45 minutes to 1 hour. Makes 6 to 8 servings.

MARINATED FLANK STEAK

¼ cup olive oil
2 tablespoons lemon juice
2 tablespoons soy sauce
2 tablespoons onion, minced
1 tablespoon meat tenderizer
1 tablespoon dried rosemary, crumbled
1 teaspoon minced garlic
1 teaspoon black pepper
4 pounds flank steaks

Combine all ingredients except steak. Add flank steaks to marinade, and refrigerate overnight. Grill about 10 minutes on each side. Slice thinly on the diagonal. Makes 8 servings.

BEEF FAJITAS

1 tablespoon olive oil
1 pound boneless steak, cut into strips
⅓ cup beef broth
2 tablespoons molasses
1 tablespoon lemon juice
1 tablespoon lime juice
1 teaspoon minced garlic
1 onion, sliced
1 red bell pepper, sliced
8 (10-inch) flour tortillas

Heat olive oil in large skillet; add steak and cook to desired degree of doneness; remove. Add beef broth, molasses, lemon juice, lime juice, and garlic to skillet; bring to a boil, scraping up browned bits of beef. Add onion and pepper; cook and stir until tender. Return meat to skillet and heat through. Serve with tortillas. Makes 4 servings.

VEAL SALTIMBOCCA

4 veal cutlets, pounded thin
½ teaspoon dried sage
Salt and pepper to taste
1 tablespoon olive oil
4 slices prosciutto
½ cup shredded mozzarella cheese

Season veal with sage, salt, and pepper. Cook in hot oil in ovenproof skillet until thoroughly cooked. Top each cooked veal cutlet with 1 slice prosciutto and 2 tablespoons shredded cheese; run under preheated broiler, until cheese is melted and golden brown. Makes 4 servings.

Steak Stroganoff

1 pound round steak cut into cubes
¼ cup flour
1 tablespoon oil
½ cup chopped onion
1 garlic clove, minced
1 (6-ounce) can mushrooms, undrained
1 cup sour cream
1 (10¾-ounce) can cream of mushroom soup
1 tablespoon Worcestershire sauce
½ teaspoon salt
⅛ teaspoon pepper
2 cups rice, cooked and hot
Parmesan cheese

Roll meat in flour; brown in hot oil in a large frying pan. Remove meat; add onion, garlic, and mushrooms. Cook gently until onions are golden. Add remaining ingredients except rice. Cook until thickened, and return meat and simmer, stirring occasionally, about 1 hour or until meat is tender. Serve over fluffy cooked rice. Sprinkle with Parmesan cheese if desired. Makes 4 servings.

Easy Veal Cordon Bleu

4 veal cutlets, pounded thin
½ teaspoon dried thyme
Salt and pepper to taste
1 tablespoon olive oil
4 slices ham
4 slices Swiss cheese

Season veal with thyme, salt, and pepper. Cook in hot oil in ovenproof skillet until done. Top each cooked veal cutlet with 1 slice ham and 1 slice Swiss cheese; run under preheated broiler, until cheese is melted and golden brown. Makes 4 servings.

SAVORY BEEF STROGANOFF

4 tablespoons butter
½ onion, finely chopped
2 tablespoons flour
1 pound lean ground beef
Salt and pepper to taste
¼ teaspoon paprika
1 (8-ounce) package sliced mushrooms
1 (10¾-ounce) can cream of mushroom soup
1 cup sour cream
1 (8-ounce) package dried egg noodles, cooked and drained

Melt butter in large skillet over medium-high heat; add onion and cook, stirring frequently, about 5 minutes. Add flour and cook and stir 2 minutes. Add ground beef, salt and pepper, and paprika. Cook until ground beef is fully done. Drain excess grease if necessary. Add mushrooms and soup; cook about 5 minutes. Reduce heat to low, and stir in sour cream; cook just until heated through. Serve over hot cooked noodles. Makes 4 servings.

EASY VEAL SARDOU

4 veal cutlets, pounded thin
½ teaspoon dried oregano
Salt and pepper to taste
1 tablespoon olive oil
1 (8-ounce) jar marinated artichoke hearts, drained and chopped
½ cup Parmesan cheese, grated

Season veal with oregano, salt, and pepper. Cook in hot oil in ovenproof skillet until thoroughly done. Top each cooked veal cutlet with chopped artichoke hearts and Parmesan cheese. Run under preheated broiler, until cheese is melted and golden brown. Makes 4 servings.

Pepper Steak

2 pounds round steak, cut into ½-inch strips, lightly salted
½ teaspoon salt
¼ teaspoon pepper
¼ cup flour
¼ cup oil
1 (16-ounce) can tomatoes
1¾ cups beef stock
½ cup chopped onion
1 garlic clove, minced
2 large green bell peppers, cut into strips
1½ teaspoons Worcestershire sauce

Mix salt, pepper, and flour. Dredge meat and brown in hot oil. Set aside remaining seasoned flour. Drain tomatoes, reserving liquid. Add tomato liquid, beef stock, onion, and garlic to the meat in the skillet. Cover and simmer for 1¼ hours. Add green bell pepper strips and Worcestershire sauce, and simmer for 5 minutes more. Blend in tomatoes and reserved flour, and simmer about 5 minutes. Makes 6 servings.

Breaded Veal Cutlets

4 veal cutlets, pounded thin
½ cup flour
2 eggs, beaten
½ cup Italian-seasoned breadcrumbs
2 tablespoons butter

Dredge each veal cutlet in flour; dip in egg, and coat with breadcrumbs. Cook breaded cutlets in hot butter until just done, for 1 or 2 minutes on each side. Makes 4 servings.

LEMONY VEAL SCALOPPINE WITH CAPERS

¼ cup flour
½ teaspoon garlic salt
½ teaspoon pepper
½ pound veal scallops
½ cup butter
1 (8-ounce) package sliced mushrooms
2 tablespoons lemon juice
½ cup chicken broth
1 lemon, thinly sliced
2 tablespoons capers, drained

Combine flour with garlic salt and pepper; dredge veal in flour mixture. Melt butter in large skillet over medium heat; add veal and brown 1 to 2 minutes on each side. Add mushrooms, lemon juice, and chicken broth; cover, reduce heat, and simmer about 5 minutes. Add lemon slices and capers, and cook just until heated. Makes 2 servings.

VEAL PARMESAN

4 veal cutlets, pounded thin
½ cup flour
2 eggs, beaten
½ cup Italian-seasoned breadcrumbs
2 tablespoons butter
1 cup pasta sauce, warm
1 cup shredded mozzarella cheese
½ cup grated Parmesan cheese

Dredge each veal cutlet in flour; dip in egg, and coat with breadcrumbs. Cook breaded cutlets in hot butter in an ovenproof skillet until just done, for 1 or 2 minutes on each side. Pour sauce over veal, and sprinkle with cheeses. Run under broiler for 2 minutes, or until cheese is melted. Makes 4 servings.

QUICK HAM-DILL CASSEROLE

1 (16-ounce) package frozen pasta and vegetables with cheese
1 cup ham, cooked and cubed
¼ cup milk
½ teaspoon dried dill

Prepare frozen pasta and vegetables according to package directions. Stir in remaining ingredients. Cook until thoroughly heated.

BARBECUE PORK AND COLESLAW

6 corn muffins
4 cups barbecued pork, shredded
1 cup creamy coleslaw

Place pork in an 8-inch-square microwave-safe dish, and cover with waxed paper. Microwave on high for 7 to 9 minutes or until hot, stirring once, or heat according to package directions. Split corn muffins and place two halves on each plate. Spoon barbecued pork over muffins, and top with coleslaw. Makes 6 servings.

PORK CHOP DINNER

4 to 6 pork chops
1 (10¾-ounce) can cream of celery soup
1 can baby carrots
Salt and pepper to taste
2 cups rice, cooked and hot

Place pork chops in a casserole dish. Pour in soup and carrots. Season with salt and pepper. Cover dish. Bake covered at 325° approximately 45 minutes. Serve with rice. Makes 4 to 6 servings.

PEACHY PORK CHOPS

6 pork chops, about 1-inch thick
2 (14-ounce) cans peach halves, drained, syrup reserved
1 envelope seasoned baking mix
¼ cup brown sugar
¼ cup ketchup
2 tablespoons apple cider vinegar

Dip pork chops in ¼ cup reserved peach syrup. Coat with baking mix and place in a large baking dish. Arrange peaches around pork chops. Combine remaining peach syrup, brown sugar, ketchup, and cider vinegar. Pour over pork chops and peaches. Cover tightly. Bake at 350° for about 1 hour. Makes 6 servings.

PORK AND BROCCOLI STIR-FRY

1 tablespoon olive oil
1 onion, chopped
4 boneless pork chops, cut into strips
1 teaspoon lemon pepper
1 (14-ounce) can chicken broth
1½ cups quick-cooking rice
1½ cups broccoli, chopped

Heat olive oil in large skillet; add onion and pork. Cook and stir for about 10 minutes, or until thoroughly done. Add lemon pepper, chicken broth, rice, and broccoli; bring to a boil. Reduce heat, cover, and simmer until rice and broccoli are cooked, about 20 minutes. Makes 4 servings.

SAUSAGE AND ZUCCHINI STIR-FRY

1 pound sausage
1 onion, chopped
1 (14-ounce) can chicken broth
2 cups quick rice
2 (14-ounce) cans zucchini and tomatoes
½ cup Parmesan cheese, grated

Brown sausage with onion in a large skillet, cooking until sausage is completely done; drain. Add chicken broth, rice, and zucchini; bring to a boil. Cover, reduce heat, and simmer until rice is cooked through, about 20 minutes. Sprinkle with Parmesan cheese. Makes 4 servings.

PORK CACCIATORE

1 pound boneless pork chops, cut into strips
1 onion, chopped
1 red bell pepper, chopped
1 teaspoon minced garlic
2 tablespoons olive oil
2 (14-ounce) cans diced tomatoes
1 (8-ounce) can tomato sauce
1 teaspoon Italian seasoning
Salt and pepper to taste
2 cups rice, cooked and hot

Brown pork, onion, bell pepper, and garlic in oil. Add tomatoes, tomato sauce, Italian seasoning, and salt and pepper to taste; bring to a boil. Reduce heat, cover, and simmer about 10 minutes, until pork is thoroughly cooked. Serve over hot cooked rice. Makes 4 servings.

Pork Chops and Wild Rice

1 (10¾-ounce) can cream of celery soup
1 (10¾-ounce) can cream of chicken soup
1 cup chicken broth
1 (1½-ounce) package dry onion soup mix
1 (6-ounce) package wild rice mix
6 boneless pork chops

Combine soups, broth, soup mix, and wild rice mix; pour into a greased 3-quart casserole. Lay pork chops over rice mixture. Cover tightly. Bake at 350° for about 1 hour. Makes 6 servings.

Teriyaki Pork Chops

6 boneless pork chops
1 onion, sliced
1 red bell pepper, chopped
1 (4-ounce) can sliced water chestnuts, drained
1 cup teriyaki sauce
1 (15-ounce) can pineapple chunks, drained

Combine all ingredients, coating pork chops well. Bake at 400° for 20 to 30 minutes. Makes 6 servings.

ASIAN PORK STIR-FRY

2 tablespoons olive oil
1 teaspoon sesame oil
3 boneless pork chops, cut into strips
1 onion, chopped
1 red bell pepper, chopped
1 carrot, chopped
2 cups fresh broccoli, chopped
2 tablespoons soy sauce
1 (8-ounce) can pineapple chunks, drained
1 tablespoon cornstarch
¼ cup water
2 cups rice, cooked and hot

Heat olive oil and sesame oil in large skillet; add pork and cook 2
minutes. Add onion, red bell pepper, carrot, broccoli, and soy sauce;
cook and stir several minutes. Add pineapple; cook about 10 minutes
more. Combine cornstarch and water. Add to pork mixture and cook
until thickened. Serve over hot cooked rice. Makes 4 to 6 servings.

CREAMY BAKED PORK CHOPS

6 boneless pork chops
1 (10¾-ounce) can cream of chicken soup
1 cup sour cream
½ cup Parmesan cheese, grated

Place pork chops in greased 9-inch x 13-inch baking dish. Combine
soup, sour cream, and cheese. Pour over pork chops, turning to coat.
Bake at 400° for about 30 minutes. Makes 6 servings.

CREAMY BAKED PORK CHOPS WITH MUSHROOMS

6 boneless pork chops
1 (8-ounce) package sliced mushrooms
1 (10¾-ounce) can cream of mushroom soup
1 cup sour cream
½ cup grated Parmesan cheese

Place pork chops and mushrooms in greased baking dish. Combine soup, sour cream, and cheese. Pour over pork chops, turning to coat. Bake at 400° for about 30 minutes. Makes 6 servings.

CREAMY BAKED PORK CHOPS AND ASPARAGUS

6 boneless pork chops
½ bunch asparagus, cut into 1-inch pieces
1 (10¾-ounce) can cream of asparagus soup
1 cup sour cream
½ cup grated Parmesan cheese

Place pork chops and asparagus in greased baking dish. Combine soup, sour cream, and cheese. Pour over pork chops, turning to coat. Bake at 400° for about 30 minutes. Makes 6 servings.

CREAMY BAKED PORK CHOPS AND BROCCOLI

6 boneless pork chops
1 (10-ounce) package frozen chopped broccoli, thawed
1 (10¾-ounce) can cream of broccoli soup
1 cup sour cream
½ cup shredded Cheddar cheese

Place pork chops and broccoli in greased baking dish. Combine soup, sour cream, and cheese. Pour over pork chops, turning to coat. Bake at 400° for about 30 minutes. Makes 6 servings.

HAM AND BROCCOLI WITH RICE

4 cups ham, cooked and chopped
1 (16-ounce) package frozen chopped broccoli, thawed
1½ cups quick-cooking rice
1 (10¾-ounce) can cream of mushroom soup
1 (10¾-ounce) can cream of celery soup
½ cup milk
1 (1½-ounce) package dry onion soup mix
1 cup shredded Cheddar cheese

Combine ham, broccoli, rice, soups, milk, and onion soup mix; pour into a greased 3-quart casserole. Top with shredded cheese. Bake at 350° for about 45 minutes. Makes 6 to 8 servings.

HAM AND NOODLES

½ cup butter
1 onion, chopped
1 bell pepper, chopped
2 stalks celery, chopped
1 (8-ounce) package processed cheese, cubed
1 (10¾-ounce) can cream of mushroom soup
1 (4-ounce) can sliced mushrooms, drained
4 cups ham, cooked and chopped
1 cup chicken broth
1 (16-ounce) bag dried egg noodles, cooked and drained
1 cup cheese crackers, crushed

Melt butter in large skillet. Add onion, bell pepper, and celery; cook until tender. Add cheese, soup, mushrooms, ham, and chicken broth, cooking and stirring until cheese is melted and mixture is smooth. Stir in cooked noodles. Pour into a greased 3-quart casserole and top with crushed cheese crackers. Bake at 350° for about 45 minutes. Makes 6 to 8 servings.

BAKED PORK CHOPS AND STUFFING

**1 (8-ounce) bag herb-seasoned stuffing mix, prepared according
to package directions**
6 boneless pork chops
1 (10¾-ounce) can cream of chicken soup
¾ cup milk

Sprinkle stuffing in bottom of greased baking dish; place pork chops
on top of dressing. Combine soup and milk and pour over pork chops.
Bake at 400° for about 30 minutes. Makes 6 servings.

POTATO CHIP PORK CHOPS

½ cup mayonnaise
2 tablespoons Dijon mustard
2 tablespoons milk
1 teaspoon Italian seasoning
1 teaspoon garlic salt
Pepper to taste
6 boneless pork chops
2 cups potato chips, crushed

Combine mayonnaise, Dijon mustard, milk, Italian seasoning, garlic
salt, and pepper to taste. Dip pork chops in mayonnaise mixture, then
roll in potato chip crumbs. Bake at 400° for about 30 minutes. Makes
6 servings.

DIJON PORK CHOPS

¼ cup Dijon mustard
2 tablespoons olive oil
1 tablespoon lemon juice
1 teaspoon garlic salt
1 teaspoon dried oregano
4 boneless pork chops

Combine Dijon mustard, olive oil, lemon juice, garlic salt, and oregano. Spread over pork chops. Bake at 400° for about 30 minutes. Makes 4 servings.

COLA PORK CHOPS

6 boneless pork chops
1 cup ketchup
1 cup cola beverage
2 tablespoons Worcestershire sauce
2 tablespoons grape jelly

Place pork chops in greased baking pan. Combine remaining ingredients and spread over pork chops. Bake at 400° for about 30 minutes. Makes 6 servings.

HONEY-GLAZED INDIAN PORK CHOPS

¼ cup butter, melted
¼ cup honey
¼ cup coarse grain mustard
1 tablespoon curry powder
1 teaspoon cinnamon
Dash cayenne pepper
6 boneless pork chops

Combine butter, honey, mustard, curry powder, cinnamon, and cayenne pepper. Spread over pork chops. Bake at 400° for about 30 minutes. Makes 6 servings.

PORK PEPPER SKILLET

1 tablespoon vegetable oil
4 boneless pork chops, cut into strips
2 garlic cloves, finely minced
3 bell peppers, cut into thin strips
2 medium onions, sliced
1 teaspoon cumin
1½ teaspoon dried oregano
2 teaspoons fresh jalapeño peppers, chopped
3 tablespoons fresh lemon juice
2 tablespoons fresh parsley, chopped
¼ teaspoon salt
Freshly ground black pepper to taste

In a large nonstick skillet, heat oil over medium-high heat. Add pork and stir-fry until done and lightly browned, about 3 to 4 minutes. Add garlic and cook 15 seconds, stirring constantly. Add bell pepper strips, sliced onion, cumin, oregano, and jalapeños. Stir-fry for 2 to 3 minutes or until crisp and tender. Add lemon juice, parsley, salt, and pepper; toss to combine well. Makes 4 servings.

TANGY LIME PORK CHOPS

6 boneless pork chops
1 cup Italian dressing
Juice and zest of 2 limes
Salt and pepper to taste

Place pork chops in greased baking dish. Combine dressing, lime juice, and lime zest. Season with salt and pepper. Pour over pork chops. Bake at 400° for about 30 minutes. Makes 6 servings.

ITALIAN BAKED PORK CHOPS

1 cup Italian breadcrumbs
½ cup grated Parmesan cheese
1 teaspoon garlic salt
½ cup butter
1 teaspoon minced garlic
6 boneless pork chops

Combine breadcrumbs, Parmesan cheese, and garlic salt. Melt butter in a small saucepan; add garlic and cook over low heat for 1 minute. Dip pork chops in garlic butter, and coat with breadcrumb mixture. Bake on greased baking sheet at 400° for about 20 minutes, or until thoroughly cooked. Makes 6 servings.

LEMON-ROSEMARY PORK CHOPS

Juice of 4 large lemons
1 onion, sliced
1 cup teriyaki sauce
1 cup chicken broth
¼ cup fresh rosemary, chopped
1 tablespoon Dijon mustard
2 teaspoons garlic, minced
8 boneless pork chops

Combine lemon juice, onion, teriyaki sauce, chicken broth, rosemary, Dijon mustard, and garlic. Lay pork chops in a single layer in a large baking dish or roasting pan. Pour lemon juice mixture over pork chops, turning to coat. Bake at 400° for about 20 minutes or until cooked through. Makes 8 servings.

BASIL PORK CHOPS

4 lean center-cut pork chops
1 teaspoon dried basil
½ teaspoon salt
1 cup tomato juice
1 teaspoon freshly ground black pepper

In a large frying pan, brown chops. Add remaining ingredients. Cover tightly. Simmer 40 minutes or until tender. Turn meat occasionally, and add a few tablespoons of water if necessary to prevent burning. Makes 4 servings.

Pork Chops with Ginger-Mustard Sauce

4 boneless pork chops
¼ teaspoon ground ginger
Salt and pepper to taste
1 tablespoon olive oil
¼ cup water
1½ teaspoons cornstarch
½ cup chicken broth
1 tablespoon Dijon mustard
2 teaspoons fresh ginger, peeled and chopped
3 tablespoons sour cream

Season pork chops with ground ginger and salt and pepper to taste;
sauté in olive oil until just cooked through. Remove from pan, and
cover to keep warm. Combine water and cornstarch, stirring until
cornstarch is dissolved. Add cornstarch mixture, chicken broth, Dijon
mustard, and fresh ginger to skillet. Cook, whisking constantly, until
mixture thickens; remove from heat. Pour any pork juices back into
skillet. Add sour cream; whisk until smooth. Pour over pork chops.
Makes 4 servings.

Sweet-and-Sour Pork Chops

6 boneless pork chops
1 (6-ounce) can frozen orange juice concentrate, thawed
¼ cup soy sauce
1 (1½-ounce) package dry onion soup mix
1 green bell pepper, chopped
1 (8-ounce) can pineapple chunks, drained

Place pork chops in greased baking dish. Combine orange juice
concentrate, soy sauce, and onion soup mix. Toss with bell pepper
and pineapple, and pour over chicken, turning chicken to coat. Bake
at 400° for 20 to 30 minutes. Makes 6 servings.

PORK CHOPS WITH NEW POTATOES

¼ cup butter
4 boneless pork chops
1 onion, sliced
1 garlic clove, minced
2 tablespoons flour
½ teaspoon salt
¼ teaspoon pepper
1 chicken bouillon cube
1 cup hot water
8 new potatoes, boiled

Melt butter in a large skillet, and sauté pork chops on both sides until brown. Add onion and garlic, and cook about 5 minutes. In a small bowl, combine flour, salt, and pepper. Add to skillet. Dissolve bouillon cube in hot water, and slowly pour over browned pork chops. Cover and cook on low heat for about 25 minutes or until pork chops are tender. Add hot new potatoes. Makes 4 to 6 servings.

ITALIAN PORK AND RICE

4 boneless pork chops, cut into strips
2 tablespoons olive oil
2 cups chicken broth
1 cup quick-cooking rice
2 teaspoons Italian seasoning
2 teaspoons garlic, minced
Salt and pepper to taste

Cook pork in oil in large skillet until done. Add chicken broth, rice, Italian seasoning, garlic, and salt and pepper to taste. Bring to a boil; reduce heat, cover, and simmer about 20 minutes. Makes 4 servings.

Italian Pork and Rice with Vegetables

4 boneless pork chops, cut into strips
1 onion, chopped
2 tablespoons olive oil
2 cups chicken broth
1 (14-ounce) can zucchini and tomatoes, drained
1 cup quick-cooking rice
2 teaspoons Italian seasoning
2 teaspoons garlic, minced
Salt and pepper to taste

Cook pork and onion in oil in large skillet until done. Add chicken broth, zucchini and tomatoes, rice, Italian seasoning, garlic, and salt and pepper to taste. Bring to a boil; reduce heat, cover, and simmer about 20 minutes. Makes 4 servings.

Creamy Pork Chops and Potatoes

6 pork chops
Salt and pepper to taste
2 tablespoons butter
6 medium potatoes, sliced
1 (10¾-ounce) can cream of mushroom soup
1 cup milk

Season pork chops with salt and pepper; brown in butter in a large skillet. Spread potatoes over pork chops. Combine soup and milk; pour over potatoes. Cover and cook over low heat for about 1 hour. Makes 6 servings.

CINNAMON APPLE PORK TENDERLOIN

1 (1-pound) pork tenderloin
2 apples, peeled, cored, and sliced
2 tablespoons cornstarch
2 tablespoons raisins
1 teaspoon cinnamon

Place the pork tenderloin in a roasting pan or casserole dish with a lid. Combine the remaining ingredients in a bowl and stir. Spoon the apple mixture around the pork tenderloin. Cover. Bake at 400° for 40 minutes. Remove the lid, and spoon the apple mixture over the tenderloin. Return to the oven, and bake 15 to 20 minutes longer until tenderloin is browned and cooked through. Makes 4 servings.

STIR-FRIED PORK WITH NAPA CABBAGE

4 tablespoons beef broth
½ teaspoon minced garlic
½ teaspoon fresh ginger, peeled and minced
8 chopped green onions
1 pound pork tenderloin, cut into thin strips
4 cups Napa cabbage, shredded
½ teaspoon salt
½ teaspoon cayenne pepper flakes

Heat broth in a large nonstick frying pan or in a wok. Stir-fry the garlic, ginger, and green onions for 1 minute. Add pork and stir-fry until pink color is nearly gone, about 1 minute. Mix in cabbage, cover, and continue cooking for 3 to 5 minutes or until cabbage is tender, stirring once. Season with salt and cayenne pepper flakes to taste. Makes 4 servings.

Marinated Grilled Pork Tenderloin

1 cup olive oil
⅔ cup fresh parsley, chopped
⅓ cup lemon juice
¼ cup garlic, minced
2 tablespoons soy sauce
1 tablespoon pepper
2 (1½-pound) pork tenderloins

Combine all ingredients except pork; pour over pork tenderloins and marinate overnight. Grill to desired doneness. Makes about 6 servings.

Pork Tenderloin with Dijon Cream Sauce

¼ cup apple juice
3 tablespoons olive oil
2 tablespoons fresh rosemary, chopped
Salt and pepper to taste
2 (1½-pound) pork tenderloins
1½ cups whipping cream
¼ coarse-grain Dijon mustard

Combine apple juice, olive oil, rosemary, salt, and pepper; pour over pork tenderloins and marinate overnight. Bake tenderloins at 375° for about 25 minutes, or to desired degree of doneness. While pork is cooking, combine cream, mustard, and salt and pepper to taste in small saucepan. Cook over medium heat (do not boil) until reduced to about 1 cup. Serve sauce over pork. Makes about 6 servings.

MACARONI AND CHEESE WITH SAUSAGE

1 pound Italian sausage
1 onion, chopped
2 tablespoons flour
Salt and pepper to taste
1 (14-ounce) can evaporated milk
1 (8-ounce) package dried elbow macaroni, cooked and drained
2 cups shredded Cheddar cheese, divided

Brown sausage and onion until sausage is thoroughly cooked; drain off grease. Add flour, salt, and pepper; cook and stir for 2 minutes. Gradually add milk, cooking until thickened. Stir in macaroni and 1 cup cheese. Pour into greased baking dish; top with remaining cheese. Bake at 400° for about 20 minutes. Makes 4 to 6 servings.

PORK TENDERLOIN WITH APPLES

2 (1½-pound) pork tenderloins
Salt and pepper to taste
¼ cup flour
2 teaspoons cumin
2 tablespoons olive oil
2 tart apples, peeled and quartered
½ onion, chopped
½ cup chicken broth
2 tablespoons apple cider vinegar
2 tablespoons honey
1 tablespoon tomato paste

Season pork with salt and pepper. Combine flour and cumin; dredge tenderloins with flour mixture. Heat oil in large skillet over medium-high heat; brown tenderloins on all sides. Add apples and onion; cook and stir about 5 minutes. Add all remaining ingredients, stirring until well combined. Cover, reduce heat, and simmer 20 minutes or until done. Makes about 6 servings.

STUFFED PORK CHOPS

6 double chops with pockets
2 tablespoons olive oil
¾ cup raisins
½ cup celery
½ cup green bell pepper, chopped
2 tablespoons onion, minced
1 cup apple, peeled, cored, and chopped
3 cups soft breadcrumbs
Salt and pepper to taste

Brown chops in oil. Stuff with the remaining ingredients, and put extra stuffing on top. Cover. Bake at 350° for 1½ hours.

PORK CHOPS WITH MILK GRAVY

3 tablespoons flour
1 teaspoon salt
4 pork chops
⅛ teaspoon pepper
½ tablespoon oil
1 cup water
½ cup evaporated milk

Combine the flour, salt, and pepper. Roll the pork chops in the flour mixture. Sprinkle over chops any flour that is left. Brown the chops on both sides in oil. Add water, cover, and cook slowly 30 minutes or until tender. Remove chops to warm platter. Stir evaporated milk into skillet, heat until steaming hot, but do not boil. Pour over chops. Makes 4 servings.

HAM POT PIE

4 cups ham, cooked and chopped
2 cups chicken broth
4 hard-boiled eggs, chopped
1 (10¾-ounce) can cream of celery soup
1 (20-ounce) package frozen mixed vegetables, thawed
½ cup butter, melted
1 cup milk
1 cup self-rising flour

Combine ham, broth, eggs, soup, and vegetables; pour into a greased baking dish. Combine butter, milk, and flour; pour over ham mixture. Bake at 350° for about 1 hour. Makes about 8 servings.

HAM CASSEROLE

1 (10¾-ounce) cream of mushroom soup
½ cup milk
1 teaspoon onion, minced
2 teaspoons mustard
1 cup sour cream
4 ounces dried egg noodles, cooked
2 cups ham, cooked and cut into 1-inch pieces
¼ cup dry breadcrumbs
1½ tablespoons butter, melted
1 tablespoon Parmesan cheese, grated

In a saucepan, combine soup and milk, stirring until smooth. Add onion, mustard, and sour cream, stirring to combine well. In prepared casserole, layer half of the noodles, ham, and sauce. Repeat. Toss breadcrumbs with butter; sprinkle over casserole. Top with cheese. Bake at 350° uncovered for 25 to 30 minutes or until golden brown. Makes 4 servings.

PORK CHOPS

8 center-cut or butterflied pork chops
Salt and pepper to taste
½ cup flour
2 tablespoons oil
1 cup sour cream
1 (10¾-ounce) can cream of mushroom soup
1 (1½-ounce) package dry onion soup mix
1 cup beef or pork broth

Rinse pork chops and pat dry. Sprinkle with salt and pepper; coat
with flour. Brown on both sides in oil in skillet; drain well. Arrange in
single layer in rectangular baking dish. Combine sour cream, soup,
soup mix, and broth in a bowl; mix well. Spoon over pork chops.
Bake at 325° for 45 minutes. Makes 8 servings.

RED RICE WITH HAM

2 tablespoons butter
4 chopped green onions
1 green bell pepper, chopped
2 teaspoons garlic, minced
1 cup quick-cooking rice
1 cup ham, cooked and chopped
2 cups chicken broth
1 (14-ounce) can diced tomatoes with Italian seasoning
Salt and pepper to taste

Melt butter in large saucepan over medium-high heat; add green
onions, green bell pepper, and garlic, stirring until tender. Add rice
and ham; cook and stir for about 2 minutes. Add remaining
ingredients, and bring to a boil. Reduce heat, cover, and simmer for
about 20 minutes. Makes 4 servings.

RED RICE WITH SMOKED SAUSAGE

2 tablespoons butter
4 chopped green onions
1 green bell pepper, chopped
2 teaspoons garlic, minced
1 cup quick-cooking rice
1 cup sliced smoked sausage
2 cups chicken broth
1 (14-ounce) can diced tomatoes with Italian seasoning
Salt and pepper to taste

Melt butter in large saucepan over medium-high heat; add green onions, green bell pepper, and garlic, stirring until tender. Add rice and smoked sausage; cook and stir for about 2 minutes. Add remaining ingredients, and bring to a boil. Reduce heat, cover, and simmer for about 20 minutes. Makes 4 servings.

POULTRY

ALMOND CHICKEN

¼ cup butter
¼ cup flour
2 cups chicken broth
2 eggs, beaten
1 cup mayonnaise
4 cups cooked and chopped chicken
1 cup chow mein noodles
½ cup slivered almonds

Melt butter in medium saucepan; add flour and cook for 4 minutes. Gradually add chicken broth, cooking and stirring until smooth and bubbly. Add remaining ingredients, and pour into a greased 2-quart casserole. Bake at 350° for about 45 minutes. Makes 4 servings.

EASY CHICKEN KIEV

½ cup butter, softened
1 teaspoon garlic salt
1 teaspoon dried parsley
4 boneless, skinless chicken breasts, pounded thin
½ cup flour
2 eggs, beaten
1 cup breadcrumbs
¼ cup vegetable oil

Combine butter, garlic salt, and parsley, mixing well. Divide into 4 equal pieces and freeze. Place 1 frozen butter piece in center of each piece of chicken; roll up and secure with toothpicks. Dredge each piece in flour, dip in egg, and roll in breadcrumbs. In an ovenproof skillet, brown in hot oil on all sides. Transfer to oven. Bake at 400° for about 20 minutes. Makes 4 servings.

CHICKEN CACCIATORE

1 pound boneless chicken breast strips
1 onion, chopped
1 red bell pepper, chopped
1 teaspoon minced garlic
2 tablespoons olive oil
2 (14-ounce) cans diced tomatoes
1 (8-ounce) can tomato sauce
1 teaspoon Italian seasoning
Salt and pepper to taste
2 cups rice, cooked and hot

Brown chicken, onion, bell pepper, and garlic in oil. Add tomatoes, tomato sauce, Italian seasoning, and salt and pepper to taste; bring to a boil. Reduce heat, cover, and simmer until chicken is thoroughly cooked. Serve over rice. Makes 4 servings.

CHICKEN AND WILD RICE

1 (10¾-ounce) can cream of celery soup
1 (10¾-ounce) can cream of chicken soup
1 cup chicken broth
1 (1½-ounce) package dry onion soup mix
1 (6-ounce) package wild rice mix
6 boneless, skinless chicken breasts

Combine soups, broth, soup mix, and wild rice mix; pour into a greased 3-quart casserole. Lay chicken breasts over rice mixture. Cover tightly. Bake at 350° for about 1 hour. Makes 6 servings.

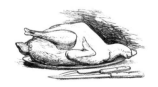

CHICKEN RATATOUILLE

3 tablespoons olive oil
3 boneless chicken breasts, cut into strips
1 zucchini, sliced
1 eggplant, cubed
1 onion, sliced
1 bell pepper, chopped
1 (8-ounce) package sliced mushrooms
2 teaspoons garlic, minced
2 teaspoons Italian seasoning
Salt and pepper to taste
1 (14-ounce) can diced tomatoes
2 cups rice, cooked and hot

Heat olive oil in large skillet; add chicken and cook several minutes.
Add zucchini, eggplant, onion, bell pepper, mushrooms, garlic, Italian
seasoning, and salt and pepper to taste. Cook until chicken is done
and vegetables are tender. Add tomatoes and cook until heated
through. Serve over rice. Makes 4 servings.

TERIYAKI CHICKEN

6 boneless, skinless chicken breasts
1 onion, sliced
1 red bell pepper, chopped
1 (4-ounce) can sliced water chestnuts, drained
1 cup teriyaki sauce
1 (15-ounce) can pineapple chunks, drained

Combine all ingredients, coating chicken well. Bake at 400° for 20 to
30 minutes. Makes 6 servings.

Asian Chicken Stir-Fry

2 tablespoons olive oil
1 teaspoon sesame oil
3 boneless chicken breasts, cut into strips
1 onion, chopped
1 red bell pepper, chopped
1 carrot, chopped
2 cups fresh broccoli, chopped
2 tablespoons soy sauce
1 (8-ounce) can pineapple chunks
1 tablespoon cornstarch
¼ cup water
2 cups rice, cooked and hot

Heat olive oil and sesame oil in large skillet; add chicken and cook 2 minutes. Add onion, red bell pepper, carrot, broccoli, and soy sauce; cook and stir several minutes. Add pineapple and cook about 10 minutes more. Combine cornstarch and water; add to chicken mixture and cook until thickened. Serve over rice. Makes 4 to 6 servings.

Forgotten Chicken

1 (3½-pound) whole fryer chicken, at room temperature
¼ cup butter, softened
Salt and pepper to taste

Rub chicken all over with butter; sprinkle with salt and pepper to taste. Bake at 300° for 3 hours. Makes 4 servings.

CHICKEN FAJITAS

1 tablespoon olive oil
1 pound boneless chicken breasts, cut into strips
⅓ cup beef broth
2 tablespoons molasses
1 tablespoon lemon juice
1 tablespoon lime juice
1 teaspoon minced garlic
1 onion, sliced
1 red bell pepper, sliced
Salt and pepper to taste
8 (10-inch) flour tortillas

Heat olive oil in large skillet; add chicken and cook thoroughly. Remove chicken from pan. Add beef broth, molasses, lemon juice, lime juice, and garlic to skillet; bring to a boil, scraping up browned bits of chicken. Add onion and salt and pepper; cook and stir until tender. Return chicken to skillet, and heat through. Serve with tortillas. Makes 4 servings.

SAVORY ITALIAN WINGS

1½ cups cracker crumbs
1 cup grated Parmesan cheese
1 (1-ounce) envelope Italian dressing mix
2 pounds chicken wings
½ cup butter, melted

Combine crumbs, cheese, and Italian dressing mix. Coat wings with melted butter, then crumb mixture. Bake on greased baking sheet at 350° for about 30 minutes. Makes about 6 servings.

Oven-Fried Chicken

6 to 8 pieces chicken
½ cup flour
1 teaspoon salt
¼ teaspoon pepper
½ teaspoon paprika
½ cup margarine, melted

Coat chicken with mixture of flour, salt, pepper, and paprika. Pour melted margarine in a baking pan. Dip chicken pieces in margarine; arrange on baking sheets. Bake at 400° for 30 minutes; turn. Bake for 25 minutes or until chicken is tender. Makes 8 servings.

Roasted Chicken

1 (3 to 4-pound) chicken
3 tablespoons butter
3 garlic cloves, minced
1 teaspoon salt
1 tablespoon pepper
3 sprigs rosemary
3 sprigs thyme
1 lemon, quartered

Rub the entire chicken with a mixture of butter, garlic, salt, and pepper. Place the rosemary and thyme sprigs along with the lemon inside the cavity. Tie legs together with butcher's string if necessary. Place on a lightly greased roasting pan. Bake at 450° for 30 minutes. Reduce heat to 350° and bake for 1 hour or until done.

BAKED CHICKEN BREASTS

1½ cups plain yogurt or sour cream
¼ cup lemon juice
½ teaspoon Worcestershire sauce
½ teaspoon celery seed
½ teaspoon Hungarian sweet paprika
1 garlic clove, minced
½ teaspoon salt (optional)
¼ teaspoon pepper
8 boneless, skinless chicken breast halves
2 cups fine dry breadcrumbs

In a large bowl, combine first 8 ingredients. Place chicken in mixture, and turn to coat. Cover and marinate overnight in the refrigerator.

Remove chicken from marinade; coat each piece with crumbs. Arrange on a lightly greased shallow baking pan. Bake uncovered at 350° for 45 minutes, or until juices run clear. Makes 8 servings.

CHICKEN CASSEROLE

1 (3-pound) chicken, cut up
Salt and pepper to taste
6 slices bacon
2 cups rice
1 (10¾-ounce) can cream of mushroom soup
2 cups milk

Rinse chicken and pat dry. Season with salt and pepper. Arrange bacon in baking dish. Sprinkle rice over bacon. Arrange chicken over rice. Pour mixture of soup and milk over top. Bake at 350° for 90 minutes. Makes 6 servings.

SAVORY RANCH WINGS

1½ cups cracker crumbs
1 cup grated Parmesan cheese
1 (1-ounce) envelope ranch dressing mix
2 pounds chicken wings
½ cup butter, melted

Combine crumbs, cheese, and Ranch dressing mix. Coat wings with melted butter, and then crumb mixture. Bake on a greaed baking sheet at 350° for about 30 minutes. Makes about 6 servings.

CREAMY BAKED CHICKEN

6 boneless, skinless chicken breast halves
1 (10¾-ounce) can cream of chicken soup
1 cup sour cream
½ cup grated Parmesan cheese

Place chicken breasts in greased baking dish. Combine soup, sour cream, and cheese. Pour over chicken, turning to coat. Bake at 400° for about 30 minutes. Makes 6 servings.

SAVORY SOUTHWESTERN WINGS

1½ cups cracker crumbs
1 cup grated Parmesan cheese
2 teaspoons chili powder
2 teaspoons cumin
2 teaspoons garlic salt
2 pounds chicken wings
½ cup butter, melted

Combine crumbs, cheese, chili powder, cumin, and garlic salt. Coat wings with melted butter, and then crumb mixture. Bake at 350° for about 30 minutes. Makes about 6 servings.

BARBECUE WINGS

1 (2-pound) package fresh mini-chicken legs
Barbecue sauce
Ranch salad dressing

Arrange the chicken legs on the rack of a roasting pan. Using a brush, coat both sides of each chicken leg with the barbecue sauce. Bake at 325° for 30 minutes or until tender. Serve with ranch dressing for dipping. Makes about 6 servings.

CREAMY BAKED CHICKEN WITH MUSHROOMS

6 boneless, skinless chicken breast halves
1 (8-ounce) package sliced mushrooms
1 (10¾-ounce) can cream of mushroom soup
1 cup sour cream
½ cup grated Parmesan cheese

Place chicken breasts and mushrooms in greased baking dish. Combine soup, sour cream, and cheese. Pour over chicken, turning to coat. Bake at 400° for about 30 minutes. Makes 6 servings.

CREAMY BAKED CHICKEN AND ASPARAGUS

6 boneless, skinless chicken breast halves
½ bunch asparagus, cut into 1-inch pieces
1 (10¾-ounce) can cream of asparagus soup
1 cup sour cream
½ cup grated Parmesan cheese

Place chicken breasts and asparagus in greased baking dish. Combine soup, sour cream, and cheese. Pour over chicken, turning to coat. Bake at 400° for about 30 minutes. Makes 6 servings.

CREAMY BAKED CHICKEN AND BROCCOLI

6 boneless, skinless chicken breast halves
1 (10-ounce) package frozen chopped broccoli, thawed
1 (10¾-ounce) can cream of broccoli soup
1 cup sour cream
½ cup shredded Cheddar cheese

Place chicken breasts and broccoli in greased baking dish. Combine soup, sour cream, and cheese. Pour over chicken, turning to coat. Bake at 400° for about 30 minutes. Makes 6 servings.

CHICKEN AND BROCCOLI WITH RICE

4 cups cooked and chopped chicken
1 (16-ounce) package frozen chopped broccoli, thawed
1½ cups quick-cooking rice
1 (10¾-ounce) can cream of mushroom soup
1 (10¾-ounce) can cream of celery soup
½ cup milk
1 (1½-ounce) package dry onion soup mix
1 cup shredded Cheddar cheese

Combine chicken, broccoli, rice, soups, milk, and onion soup mix; pour into a greased 3-quart casserole. Top with shredded cheese. Bake at 350° for about 45 minutes. Makes 6 to 8 servings.

CHICKEN AND NOODLES

½ cup butter
1 onion, chopped
1 bell pepper, chopped
2 celery stalks, chopped
1 (8-ounce) package processed cheese, cubed
1 (10¾-ounce) can cream of mushroom soup
1 (4-ounce) can sliced mushrooms, drained
4 cups cooked and chopped chicken
1 cup chicken broth
1 (16-ounce) package dried egg noodles, cooked and drained
1 cup cheese crackers, crushed

Melt butter in large skillet; add onion, bell pepper, and celery. Cook until tender. Add cheese, soup, mushrooms, chicken, and chicken broth, cooking and stirring until cheese is melted and mixture is smooth. Stir in cooked noodles. Pour into a greased 3-quart casserole, and top with crushed cheese crackers. Bake at 350° for about 45 minutes. Makes 4 servings.

BAKED CHICKEN AND STUFFING

1 (8-ounce) bag herb-seasoned stuffing mix, prepared according
  to package directions
6 boneless, skinless chicken breasts
1 (10¾-ounce) can cream of chicken soup
¾ cup milk

Sprinkle stuffing in bottom of greased 9-inch x 13-inch baking dish; place chicken breasts on top. Combine soup and milk, and pour over chicken. Bake at 400° for about 30 minutes. Makes 6 servings.

FRIED CHICKEN

1 (3 to 4-pound) chicken, cut into pieces
1 teaspoon salt
1 teaspoon pepper
2 cups buttermilk
2 cups flour
1 teaspoon garlic powder
1 teaspoon paprika
Vegetable oil

Season chicken with salt and pepper. In a large dish, pour buttermilk over chicken. Allow to soak in refrigerator for 2 hours. Combine flour, garlic powder, and paprika. Dredge chicken in flour mixture. Fry, a few pieces at a time, in preheated oil until golden brown, 8 to 10 minutes for white meat and 12 to 14 minutes for dark meat. Remove from oil and drain. Makes 4 servings.

PICNIC DRUMSTICKS

1 cup crushed saltine crackers
2 tablespoons dry onion soup mix
8 chicken legs
⅓ cup butter, melted

Stir together crackers and onion soup mix. Dip chicken legs into melted butter, and then coat with cracker mixture. Place remaining butter in a 9-inch x 13-inch baking pan, and then top with coated chicken legs. Sprinkle with any remaining crumb mixture.

Bake at 350° for 45 to 55 minutes, or until chicken is tender and thoroughly cooked. You can serve these with sour cream and salsa for dipping if desired. Makes 8 servings.

PINEAPPLE-TARRAGON CHICKEN

1 (6-ounce) can frozen pineapple juice concentrate, thawed
¼ cup honey
1 teaspoon dried tarragon leaves
Salt and pepper
6 chicken breasts, bone-in

Prepare and heat grill, placing coals to one side for indirect cooking. Make aluminum foil drip pan, and place opposite coals under grill rack. In small saucepan, combine juice concentrate, honey, tarragon, salt, and pepper. Cook over medium heat for 3 to 5 minutes until blended.

Place chicken breasts on grill over drip pan. Baste with sauce. Grill, turning and basting frequently with sauce, until chicken is thoroughly cooked, about 25 to 35 minutes. Cook any remaining sauce over medium heat until boiling. Boil for 2 minutes, stirring frequently. Serve with chicken. Makes 6 servings.

CATALINA CHICKEN

1 small jar apricot preserves or apricot/pineapple preserves
1 (1½-ounce) package dry onion soup mix
1 small bottle Catalina salad dressing
6 to 8 pieces of chicken

Combine the preserves, onion soup mix, and dressing. Spread over chicken. Bake on a greased baking sheet at 350° for 45 to 60 minutes. Makes 6 servings.

Barbecue Chicken

6 chicken thighs
½ cup barbecue sauce

Combine the chicken and barbecue sauce in a large bowl. Mix until the chicken is evenly coated. Place chicken in a small roasting pan, leaving a little space between each piece. Bake at 375° for 40 to 45 minutes, until done. Makes 6 servings.

Note: Cover the chicken with aluminum foil for the first 15 minutes, and then remove to brown.

Seasoned Coating for Chicken

½ cup flour
½ cup cracker crumbs or cornmeal
¼ cup grated Parmesan cheese
1 teaspoon paprika
1 teaspoon onion powder
1 teaspoon salt
½ teaspoon pepper
¼ teaspoon dried thyme
¼ teaspoon dried basil

Combine all ingredients and shake together in a jar. Store mix in a closed jar in the refrigerator. When ready to use, place chicken in a plastic bag with enough mix to coat. Shake until well coated. Bake chicken on a greased baking sheet at 375° for 35 to 45 minutes or until done. Makes about 1½ cups.

POTATO CHIP CHICKEN

½ cup mayonnaise
2 tablespoons Dijon mustard
2 tablespoons milk
1 teaspoon Italian seasoning
1 teaspoon garlic salt
Pepper to taste
6 boneless chicken breast halves
2 cups potato chips, crushed

Combine mayonnaise, Dijon mustard, milk, Italian seasoning, garlic salt, and pepper to taste. Dip chicken breasts in mayonnaise mixture, and then roll in potato chip crumbs. Bake on a greased baking sheet at 400° for about 30 minutes. Makes 6 servings.

DIJON CHICKEN

¼ cup Dijon mustard
2 tablespoons olive oil
1 tablespoon lemon juice
1 teaspoon garlic salt
1 teaspoon dried oregano
4 boneless, skinless chicken breasts

Combine Dijon mustard, olive oil, lemon juice, garlic salt, and oregano. Spread over chicken breasts. Bake on a greased baking sheet at 400° for about 30 minutes. Makes 4 servings.

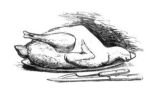

COLA CHICKEN

6 boneless, skinless chicken breasts
1 cup ketchup
1 cup cola beverage
2 tablespoons Worcestershire sauce
2 tablespoons grape jelly

Place chicken in greased baking pan. Combine remaining ingredients, and spread over chicken. Bake at 400° for about 30 minutes. Makes 6 servings.

HONEY-GLAZED INDIAN CHICKEN

¼ cup butter, melted
¼ cup honey
¼ cup coarse-grain mustard
1 tablespoon curry powder
1 teaspoon cinnamon
Dash cayenne pepper
6 boneless, skinless chicken breasts

Combine butter, honey, mustard, curry powder, cinnamon, and cayenne pepper. Spread over chicken breasts. Bake on a greased baking sheet at 400° for about 30 minutes. Makes 6 servings.

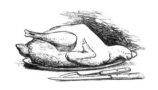

CHICKEN POT PIE

1 pound boneless chicken, cooked and cut into small pieces
1 (10¾-ounce) can cream of chicken soup
1 (14-ounce) can mixed vegetables, drained
2 deep-dish pie shells

Mix chicken, chicken soup, and vegetables. Heat in saucepan until warm. Prepare one pie crust according to package directions. Pour ingredients into prepared pie shell. Place second pie crust on top of mixture, crimp edges to seal, and crimp edges to seal. Bake in 350° oven until crust is done. Makes 4 servings.

CHICKEN POT PIE № 2

4 cups cooked and chopped chicken
2 cups chicken broth
4 hard-boiled eggs, peeled and chopped
1 (10¾-ounce) can cream of chicken soup
1 (20-ounce) package frozen mixed vegetables, thawed
½ cup butter, melted
1 cup milk
1 cup self-rising flour

Combine chicken, broth, eggs, soup, and vegetables; pour into a 3-quart greased baking dish. Combine butter, milk, and flour; pour over chicken mixture. Bake at 350° for about 1 hour. Makes about 4 servings.

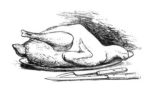

CHICKEN BISCUIT PIE

4 cups cooked and chopped chicken
2 cups chicken broth
4 hard-boiled eggs, peeled and chopped
1 (10¾-ounce) can cream of chicken soup
1 (20-ounce) package frozen mixed vegetables, thawed
1 (10-count) can refrigerated biscuit dough

Combine chicken, broth, eggs, soup, and vegetables; pour into a greased 3-quart baking dish. Top with biscuit dough. Bake at 350° for about 30 minutes. Makes about 4 servings.

CHICKEN AND DUMPLINGS

1 whole chicken, boiled and deboned
3 quarts plus ½ cup chicken broth
2 cups flour
1 egg

Place chicken in 3 quarts boiling broth. Mix together ½ cup broth, flour, and egg. Roll thin. Cut into strips and drop in boiling broth. Shake dumplings down as added. Do not stir. Cook about 30 minutes or until tender. Makes 4 to 6 servings.

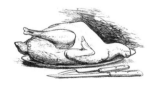

Easy Chicken Cordon Bleu

4 boneless, skinless chicken breast halves
½ teaspoon dried thyme
Salt and pepper to taste
1 tablespoon olive oil
4 slices ham
4 slices Swiss cheese

Season chicken with thyme, salt, and pepper. Cook in hot oil in ovenproof skillet until done. Top each breast with 1 slice ham and 1 slice Swiss cheese. Run under preheated broiler until cheese is melted and golden brown. Makes 4 servings.

Easy Chicken Saltimbocca

4 boneless, skinless chicken breast halves
½ teaspoon dried sage
Salt and pepper to taste
1 tablespoon olive oil
4 slices prosciutto
½ cup shredded mozzarella cheese

Season chicken with sage, salt, and pepper. Cook in hot oil in ovenproof skillet until done. Top each breast with 1 slice prosciutto and 2 tablespoons shredded cheese; run under preheated broiler until cheese is melted and golden brown. Makes 4 servings.

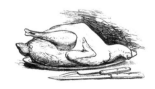

EASY CHICKEN SARDOU

4 boneless, skinless chicken breast halves
½ teaspoon oregano
Salt and pepper to taste
1 tablespoon olive oil
1 (8-ounce) jar marinated artichoke hearts, drained and chopped
½ cup Parmesan cheese, grated

Season chicken with oregano, salt, and pepper. Cook in hot oil in ovenproof skillet until thoroughly cooked. Top each cooked chicken breast with chopped artichoke hearts and Parmesan cheese; run under a preheated broiler until cheese is melted and golden brown. Makes 4 servings.

EASY CHICKEN BURRITOS

3 cups cooked and chopped chicken
1 (10¾-ounce) can cream of chicken soup
1 cup salsa
4 (10-inch) flour tortillas
1 cup shredded Monterey Jack cheese
2 chopped green onions

Combine chicken, soup, and salsa in a saucepan, and cook until heated through. Roll up in tortillas and place seam-side down in a greased baking dish. Sprinkle with cheese and green onions. Bake at 350°, just until cheese is melted. Makes 4 servings.

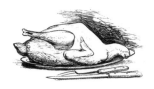

Easy Chicken Enchiladas

3 cups cooked and chopped chicken
1 (10¾-ounce) can cream of chicken soup
1 cup salsa
8 (6-inch) corn tortillas
1 can enchilada sauce
1 cup shredded Cheddar cheese

Combine chicken, soup, and salsa in a saucepan, and cook until heated through. Roll up in tortillas and place seam-side down in a greased 9-inch x 13-inch baking dish. Cover with enchilada sauce and Cheddar cheese. Bake at 350° for about 20 minutes. Makes 4 servings.

Easy Chicken Quesadillas

3 cups cooked and chopped chicken
1 (10¾-ounce) can cream of chicken soup
1 cup salsa
4 (8-inch) flour tortillas
1 cup shredded Cheddar cheese
1 cup shredded Monterey Jack cheese
2 tablespoons butter

Combine chicken, soup, and salsa in a saucepan, and cook until heated through. Place ¼ of chicken mixture on each tortilla; sprinkle evenly with cheeses. Fold over like an omelet. Melt butter in large skillet, and cook quesadillas one at a time, turning once, until cheese is melted and tortilla is crisp. Makes 4 servings.

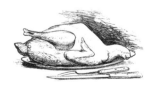

CHICKEN PEPPER SKILLET

1 tablespoon vegetable oil
4 skinless, boneless chicken breasts, cut into ½-inch strips
2 garlic cloves, finely minced
3 bell peppers (red, green, and yellow), cut into thin strips
2 medium onions, sliced
1 teaspoon ground cumin
1½ teaspoons dried oregano
2 teaspoons fresh jalapeño peppers, chopped
3 tablespoons fresh lemon juice
2 tablespoons chopped fresh parsley
¼ teaspoon salt
Freshly ground black pepper to taste

In a large nonstick skillet, heat oil over medium-high heat; add chicken and stir-fry until done and lightly browned, about 3 to 4 minutes. Add garlic and cook 15 seconds, stirring constantly. Add bell pepper strips, sliced onion, cumin, oregano, and jalapeños. Stir-fry for 2 to 3 minutes or until crisp and tender. Add lemon juice, parsley, salt, and pepper; toss to combine well and serve. Makes 4 servings.

QUICK ORIENTAL CHICKEN AND CASHEWS

1½ cups microwave spirals, uncooked
1 (14-ounce) can chicken chow mein
1 cup chicken broth
½ cup cashews

In a 2-quart microwave-safe casserole, stir together pasta, chow mein, and broth. Cover; microwave on high 8 to 10 minutes, stirring once, or until pasta is tender. Stir in cashews. Makes 2 servings.

FAST AND EASY CHICKEN AND DUMPLINGS

2 chicken breasts
2 (10-ounce) cans refrigerated biscuit dough
½ cup flour
Salt and pepper

Simmer chicken in water until done; remove from broth. Discard bone and skin from chicken. Cut each piece of biscuit dough into 3 pieces and drop into the chicken broth, stirring with a fork. Add more water if needed. Cover and simmer 12 to 15 minutes.

To thicken, stir 1 cup water into ½ cup flour. Gradually add to broth, mixing well. Return chicken to dumplings and salt and pepper to taste. Makes 2 servings.

QUICK AND TASTY CHICKEN

1 (10¾-ounce) can cream of chicken soup
1 (8-ounce) box Velveeta cheese
4 pieces baked chicken

In a small saucepan, heat soup. Add cheese. Keep on low heat until well blended. Spoon over baked chicken and serve.

FAST CHICKEN AND RICE CASSEROLE

1 whole chicken, cooked and deboned
3 cups chicken broth
1 cup dry onion soup mix
2 cups quick-cooking rice

Mix all ingredients together, and place in a 4-quart casserole. Bake covered for 1 hour at 350°. Makes 4 to 6 servings.

Fast and Easy Chicken Casserole

⅔ cup quick-cooking rice
1 (10¾-ounce) can cream of mushroom soup
2 chicken breasts

Wash off rice and drain. Place the uncooked rice in a casserole dish. Add cream of mushroom soup. Place chicken breasts on top. Bake uncovered at 350° for 1 to 1½ hours. Makes 2 servings.

Saucy Chicken

6 boneless, skinless chicken breasts
2 cups salsa
⅓ cup brown sugar
2 tablespoon honey Dijon mustard

Combine all ingredients and place in a 9-inch x 13-inch pan. Bake at 350° for 40 to 45, minutes until chicken is thoroughly cooked. Makes 6 servings.

Fast Chicken and Vegetable Stir-Fry

4 to 6 boneless chicken breasts
1 (1-pound) package mixed vegetables
1 (10¾-ounce) can Cheddar cheese soup
Cajun spice

Cut chicken into small pieces. Brown in electric skillet; season to taste. Add vegetables and stir-fry until tender to taste. Add Cheddar cheese soup and Cajun spice; mix thoroughly. Simmer until hot. Makes 4 to 6 servings.

ORZO PASTA WITH CHICKEN AND BROCCOLI

2¼ cups chicken broth
2 large boneless, skinless chicken breasts, cut into chunks
4 cups broccoli florets
6 ounces orzo pasta, cooked and drained
2 tablespoons olive oil
2 tablespoons vinegar
1 tablespoon Dijon mustard
1 teaspoon parsley flakes
½ teaspoon minced garlic
Salt and pepper to taste

Bring chicken broth to boil in a large saucepan. Add chicken and return to a boil. Reduce heat; cover and simmer for 5 minutes. Add broccoli and cook an additional 3 to 5 minutes, or until broccoli is crisp and tender and chicken is cooked through.

Drain chicken and broccoli. Toss with orzo and remaining ingredients. Makes 4 servings.

LEMON-PEPPER CHICKEN

1¼ pounds chicken breast fillets
1 cup breadcrumbs
2 tablespoons parsley, chopped
1 tablespoon lemon zest
1 teaspoon pepper
½ teaspoon salt
¼ cup plain yogurt

Rinse chicken fillets and pat dry. Combine breadcrumbs with parsley, grated lemon zest, pepper, and salt. Brush fillets with yogurt, and coat with breadcrumbs. Place on a nonstick baking sheet. Bake at 375° for 20 minutes or until tender. Makes 5 servings.

LEMON CHICKEN

6 boneless, skinless chicken breasts
1 (6-ounce) can frozen lemonade concentrate, thawed
¼ cup soy sauce
1 teaspoon minced garlic
1 teaspoon dried oregano
Pepper to taste

Combine all ingredients in a 9-inch x 13-inch baking dish, coating chicken well. Bake at 400° for 20 to 30 minutes. Makes 6 servings.

OVEN-FRIED PECAN CHICKEN

½ cup butter
1 cup flour
1 teaspoon baking powder
2 teaspoons garlic salt
2 teaspoons paprika
½ teaspoon pepper
½ cup pecans, chopped
1 tablespoon sesame seeds
1 egg, beaten
½ cup milk
6 boneless, skinless chicken breasts

Melt butter in large glass baking dish at 375°; set aside. Combine flour, baking powder, garlic salt, paprika, pepper, pecans, and sesame seeds in a large shallow dish. Combine egg and milk in a separate dish. Dip each chicken breast in egg mixture, then dredge in flour mixture. Place in melted butter, and bake about 25 minutes or until cooked through. Makes 6 servings.

CHICKEN PARMESAN

6 frozen fully-cooked breaded boneless chicken breasts, thawed
1 (28-ounce) jar pasta sauce
2 cups shredded mozzarella cheese
½ cup grated Parmesan cheese

Arrange chicken breasts in a greased 9-inch x 13-inch baking dish;
pour sauce evenly over chicken. Sprinkle cheeses over spaghetti
sauce. Bake at 350° for about 30 minutes, or until chicken is heated
through and cheese is melted and bubbly. Makes 6 servings.

ITALIAN BAKED CHICKEN BREASTS

1 cup Italian breadcrumbs
½ cup grated Parmesan cheese
1 teaspoon garlic salt
½ cup butter
1 teaspoon minced garlic
6 boneless, skinless chicken breasts

Combine breadcrumbs, Parmesan cheese, and garlic salt. Melt butter
in a small saucepan; add garlic and cook over low heat for 1 minute.
Dip chicken breasts in garlic butter, and coat with bread crumb
mixture. Bake on greased baking sheet at 400° for about 20 minutes
or until thoroughly cooked. Makes 6 servings.

LEMON-ROSEMARY CHICKEN

Juice of 4 large lemons
1 onion, sliced
1 cup teriyaki sauce
1 cup chicken broth
¼ cup fresh rosemary leaves, chopped
1 tablespoon Dijon mustard
2 teaspoons garlic, minced
8 boneless, skinless chicken breasts

Combine lemon juice, onion, teriyaki sauce, chicken broth, rosemary, Dijon mustard, and garlic. Lay chicken breasts in a single layer in a large baking dish or roasting pan. Pour lemon juice mixture over chicken, turning to coat. Bake at 400° for about 20 minutes or until cooked through. Makes 8 servings.

SWEET-AND-SOUR CHICKEN

6 boneless, skinless chicken breasts
1 (6-ounce) can frozen orange juice concentrate, thawed
¼ cup soy sauce
1 (1½-ounce) package onion soup mix
1 green bell pepper, chopped
1 (8-ounce) can pineapple chunks, drained

Place chicken in a large greased baking dish. Combine orange juice concentrate, soy sauce, and onion soup mix. Toss with bell pepper and pineapple, and pour over chicken, turning to coat. Bake at 400° for 20 to 30 minutes. Makes 6 servings.

CHICKEN CUTLETS WITH GINGER-MUSTARD SAUCE

1 pound chicken cutlets
¼ teaspoon ground ginger
Salt and pepper to taste
1 tablespoon olive oil
¼ cup water
1½ teaspoons cornstarch
½ cup chicken broth
1 tablespoon Dijon mustard
2 teaspoons fresh ginger, peeled and chopped
3 tablespoons sour cream

Season chicken with ginger and salt and pepper to taste; sauté in olive oil until just cooked through. Remove from pan, and cover to keep warm. Combine water and cornstarch, stirring until cornstarch is dissolved. Add cornstarch mixture, chicken broth, Dijon mustard, and fresh ginger to skillet. Cook, whisking constantly, until mixture thickens; remove from heat. Pour any chicken juices back into skillet, and add sour cream; whisk until smooth and pour over chicken cutlets. Makes 4 servings.

CHICKEN FOR CASSEROLES

3 pounds boneless, skinless chicken breasts

Place chicken breasts in large pot with water to cover. Bring just to a slow boil over high heat; reduce heat to low and cook covered for about 15 minutes or until cooked through. Cool and chop. Makes about 6 cups.

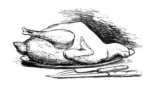

CHICKEN BREASTS WITH NEW POTATOES

¼ cup butter
4 to 6 large chicken breasts
1 onion, sliced
1 garlic clove, minced
2 tablespoons flour
½ teaspoon salt
¼ teaspoon pepper
1 chicken bouillon cube
1 cup hot water
8 new potatoes, boiled

Melt butter in a large skillet, and sauté chicken on both sides until brown. Add onion and garlic, and cook about 5 minutes. In a small bowl, combine flour, salt, and pepper. Dissolve bouillon cube in hot water, and slowly pour over browned chicken. Cover and cook on low heat for about 25 minutes, or until chicken is tender. Add new potatoes. Makes 4 to 6 servings.

CHIPPED BEEF CHICKEN

6 boneless, skinless chicken breasts
1 (5-ounce) jar chipped beef, chopped
1 (10¾-ounce) can cream of mushroom soup
1 cup sour cream
⅓ cup milk

Place chicken in larged greased baking dish. Combine chipped beef, soup, sour cream, and milk; pour over chicken. Bake at 400° for about 30 minutes. Makes 6 servings.

CHIPPED BEEF CHICKEN WITH BACON AND CHEESE

6 boneless, skinless chicken breasts
1 (5-ounce) jar chipped beef, chopped
6 slices bacon, cooked and crumbled
1 (10¾-ounce) can cream of mushroom soup
1 cup sour cream
⅓ cup milk
1 cup shredded Cheddar cheese

Place chicken in large greased baking dish. Combine chipped beef, bacon, soup, sour cream, and milk; pour over chicken. Sprinkle with shredded cheese. Bake at 400° for about 30 minutes. Makes 6 servings.

ITALIAN CHICKEN AND RICE

4 boneless, skinless chicken breasts, cut into strips
2 tablespoons olive oil
2 cups chicken broth
1 cup quick-cooking rice
2 teaspoons Italian seasoning
2 teaspoons garlic, minced
Salt and pepper to taste

Cook chicken in oil in large skillet until done; add chicken broth, rice, Italian seasoning, garlic, and salt and pepper to taste. Bring to a boil; reduce heat, cover, and simmer about 20 minutes. Makes 4 servings.

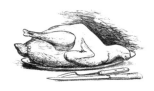

Italian Chicken and Rice with Vegetables

4 boneless, skinless chicken breasts, cut into strips
1 onion, chopped
2 tablespoons olive oil
2 cups chicken broth
1 (14-ounce) can zucchini and tomatoes
1 cup quick-cooking rice
2 teaspoons Italian seasoning
2 teaspoons garlic, minced
Salt and pepper to taste

Cook chicken and onion in oil in large skillet until done; add chicken broth, zucchini and tomatoes, rice, Italian seasoning, garlic, and salt and pepper to taste. Bring to a boil; reduce heat, cover, and simmer about 20 minutes. Makes 4 servings.

Tangy Lime Chicken

6 boneless, skinless chicken breasts
1 cup Italian dressing
Juice and zest of 2 limes
Salt and pepper to taste

Place chicken in large greased baking dish. Combine dressing, lime juice, and lime zest. Season with salt and pepper. Pour mixture over chicken. Bake at 400° for about 30 minutes. Makes 6 servings.

QUICK ARROZ CON POLLO

3 cups rice, cooked and hot
3 cups cooked and chopped chicken
1 (10¾-ounce) can nacho cheese soup
1 (10-ounce) can diced tomatoes with chiles, drained
2 cups shredded Monterey Jack cheese and divided

Combine rice, chicken, soup, tomatoes, and 1 cup cheese. Pour into large greased baking dish. Sprinkle remaining cup of cheese over top. Bake at 350° for about 40 minutes. Makes 6 servings.

CREAMY CURRIED CHICKEN OVER RICE

1 onion, chopped
2 tablespoons butter
3 tablespoons flour
1 to 2 teaspoons curry powder, or to taste
1 cup chicken broth
½ cup cream
1½ cups cooked and chopped chicken
Salt and pepper to taste
2 cups rice, cooked and hot
Chopped green onion, shredded coconut, chopped apples, raisins, chopped peanuts, mango chutney

Cook onion in butter in medium saucepan over medium heat about 5 minutes or until soft. Stir in flour and curry powder and cook, stirring constantly, for 3 minutes. Gradually add chicken broth and cream and cook until thick and bubbly, stirring constantly. Add chicken and salt and pepper to taste and cook until heated through. Serve over rice with desired accompaniments. Makes 4 servings.

FAST 'N' FANCY CORNISH HENS

1 box quick-cooking wild rice mix
2 (10¾-ounce) cans tomato soup
2 to 3 Cornish hens, cleaned and halved
1 (10¾-ounce) can golden mushroom soup

In a medium bowl, mix rice together with tomato soup and 1½ cans of water. Pour into 9-inch x 13-inch pan. Top with Cornish hens. Pour mushroom soup over hens. Cover with foil. Bake at 350° for 1 hour. Uncover and bake 15 minutes more or until browned.

CHICKEN POT PIE №3

2 (10½-ounce) cans cream of potato soup
1 (15-ounce) can mixed vegetables, drained
2 cups cooked and chopped chicken
½ cup milk
½ teaspoon dried thyme
½ teaspoon pepper
2 (9-inch) refrigerated pie crusts
1 egg, slightly beaten

Combine soup, mixed vegetables, chicken, milk, thyme, and pepper in a bowl; mix well. Spoon into pie crust; top with remaining pie crust; crimp edges to seal. Cut vents; brush with egg. Bake at 375° for 40 minutes. Makes 6 servings.

CHICKEN CROQUETTES

1½ cups chicken broth
2½ cups dry breadcrumbs, divided
1 medium onion, finely chopped
2 eggs, beaten
2 tablespoons Worcestershire sauce
1 tablespoon lemon juice
1 teaspoon sugar
Salt and pepper to taste
2 cups chicken, cooked and finely chopped

Combine chicken broth, 1½ cups breadcrumbs, onion, eggs, Worcestershire sauce, lemon juice, sugar, and salt and pepper to taste; mix well. Fold in chicken. Form into small cones, about 2 inches tall, and roll in remaining breadcrumbs. Bake at 375° for about 20 minutes or until golden. Makes 4 servings.

MARTIN'S CHICKEN HASH

1 medium onion, thinly sliced
2 tablespoons butter
4 ounces package sliced mushrooms
1 tablespoon chicken bouillon granules
1 teaspoon flour
½ cup water
2 cups cooked and chopped chicken
1 tablespoon lemon juice
½ teaspoon sugar
Salt and pepper to taste

Cook onions in butter over low heat until soft, being careful not to brown onions. Add mushrooms and cook 2 minutes more. Combine chicken bouillon granules with flour and water; stir into onion mixture. Add chicken and bring to a boil. Remove from heat and add lemon juice, sugar, and salt and pepper to taste. Makes 4 servings.

SESAME CHICKEN

1 (10¾-ounce) can golden mushroom soup
¾ cup milk
2 tablespoons butter, melted
2 cups cracker crumbs
¼ cup sesame seeds
6 boneless, skinless chicken breasts

Combine soup, milk, and butter. Combine cracker crumbs and sesame seeds. Dip chicken breasts in soup mixture, and coat with cracker crumb mixture. Place in large greased baking dish and pour remaining soup mixture over chicken. Bake at 400° for about 45 minutes. Makes 6 servings.

SOUTHWESTERN CHICKEN AND LENTIL BURRITOS

2 cups dried lentils
4 cups water
4 cups chicken, cooked and chopped
1 (14-ounce) can Mexican-style corn, drained
1 (10-ounce) can diced tomatoes with chiles
1 onion, chopped
1 (6-ounce) can tomato paste
½ cup bulgur wheat
2 tablespoons chili powder
1 tablespoon garlic, minced
2 teaspoons dried oregano
Salt and pepper to taste
1 tablespoon vinegar
12 (10-inch) flour tortillas
2 cups shredded Cheddar cheese

Combine all ingredients except vinegar, tortillas, and cheese; bring to a boil. Reduce heat, cover, and simmer for about 1½ hours. Stir in vinegar. Serve in flour tortillas with cheese. Makes 12 servings.

CHICKEN TETRAZZINI WITH BACON

3 slices bacon, chopped
½ onion, chopped
½ green bell pepper, chopped
1 (8-ounce) package elbow macaroni, cooked and drained
3 cups cooked and chopped chicken
2 cups shredded Cheddar cheese
1½ cups frozen green peas, thawed
¼ cup pimento, chopped
½ cup almonds, sliced

Cook bacon slices in skillet over medium heat until crisp; remove to paper towel-lined plate to drain. Discard all but 2 teaspoons bacon fat; add onion and pepper to skillet, and cook about 5 minutes or until tender. Combine cooked bacon and vegetables with macaroni, chicken, cheese, peas, and pimento. Pour into a greased 2-quart casserole and top with almonds. Bake at 350° for 20 to 30 minutes or until bubbly. Makes 6 to 8 servings.

TURKEY NACHOS

1 pound ground turkey
1 (1-ounce) package taco seasoning mix
½ cup water
1 (9-ounce) package tortilla chips
1 cup salsa
2 cups shredded Cheddar cheese

Brown ground turkey until thoroughly cooked; stir in taco seasoning and water. Layer half tortilla chips, half turkey mixture, half salsa, and half cheese in large baking dish. Repeat layers. Bake at 350° for about 10 minutes. Makes 4 to 6 servings.

Chicken à la King

1 medium onion, thinly sliced
½ green bell pepper, chopped
2 tablespoons butter
4 ounces sliced mushrooms
1 (4-ounce) jar pimento, drained
1 tablespoon chicken bouillon granules
1 teaspoon flour
½ cup water
2 cups cooked and chopped chicken
1 tablespoon lemon juice
½ teaspoon sugar
Salt and pepper to taste

Cook onions and pepper in butter over low heat until soft, being careful not to brown onions. Add mushrooms and pimento and cook 2 minutes more. Combine chicken bouillon granules with flour and water; stir into onion mixture. Add chicken and bring to a boil. Remove from heat, and add lemon juice, sugar, and salt and pepper to taste. Makes 4 servings.

Quick Italian Turkey

2 teaspoons olive oil
4 (4-ounce) turkey breast fillets
Salt and pepper
2 cups pasta sauce
2 cups mozzarella cheese, shredded

Heat oil in a heavy nonstick skillet over medium-high heat. Add turkey and season with salt and pepper to taste. Sauté 8 to 10 minutes, turning occasionally, until just cooked through. Pour sauce over turkey, and cook until hot. Serve turkey with sauce and cheese sprinkled over the top. Makes 4 servings.

TURKEY TACO SALAD

1 pound ground turkey
1 (1-ounce) envelope taco seasoning mix
½ cup water
1 (9-ounce) package tortilla chips
Salsa
Lettuce, shredded
Tomato, diced
Shredded Cheddar cheese
Sour cream

Brown ground turkey until thoroughly cooked; stir in taco seasoning and water. Top tortilla chips with turkey mixture, salsa, lettuce, tomato, cheese, and sour cream. Makes 4 to 6 servings.

TURKEY HASH AU GRATIN

½ pound ground turkey
1 cup chopped onion
2 cups potatoes, cooked and cubed
½ teaspoon salt
¼ teaspoon pepper
½ cup reduced-fat Cheddar cheese

In a medium skillet, over medium-high heat, combine turkey and onions. Cook 5 minutes, or until turkey is no longer pink. Add potato, breaking up larger pieces of potato with spoon if necessary; cook 2 to 3 minutes. Add salt and pepper. In a 1-quart casserole, lightly coated with vegetable cooking spray, bake turkey mixture at 375° for 10 to 15 minutes. Top casserole with cheese, and continue baking until cheese melts. Makes 2 servings.

(This recipe used by permission of the National Turkey Federation)

Southwest Turkey Casserole

1 pound ground turkey
1 small onion, chopped
1 garlic clove, minced
1 tablespoon vinegar
2 teaspoons chili powder
1½ teaspoons fresh oregano, crushed
½ teaspoon cumin
Cayenne pepper to taste
1 (16-ounce) can black beans, drained
¼ cup water
1 (16-ounce) jar mild salsa
6 (6-inch) corn tortillas, cut into strips
¾ cup shredded Cheddar cheese

Brown ground turkey with onion and garlic in a skillet, stirring until turkey is crumbly; drain. Stir in vinegar, chili powder, oregano, cumin, and cayenne pepper. Cook for 1 minute, stirring constantly. Add black beans and water; mix well. Remove from heat. Spread 2 tablespoons salsa in bottom of 2-quart baking dish. Layer half of tortilla strips, turkey mixture, and remaining salsa in baking dish; repeat with other half. Cover. Bake at 325° for 30 minutes. Remove cover; sprinkle with cheese. Bake for 5 to 10, minutes or until cheese melts. Makes 6 servings.

Fast-Bake Turkey

1 turkey
5 cups hot water
½ cup butter

Prepare turkey for baking as usual by thawing and cleaning. Place in pan. Add 5 cups hot water. Rub with butter, leaving remainder in pan. Cover with foil or lid. Seal well. Bake at 500° for 1 hour. Turn off oven. Do not open for 6 hours.

PECAN-CRUSTED TURKEY TENDERLOINS

1½ cups dried breadcrumbs
1½ cups pecans, very finely chopped
1 teaspoon fresh parsley, chopped
¼ teaspoon poultry seasoning
¼ teaspoon black pepper
2 eggs
1 cup water
1 to 1½ pounds turkey tenderloins, pounded to an even thickness

Mix first 5 ingredients together in a shallow dish. Mix eggs and water together in another shallow dish. Dip turkey tenderloins into egg wash and roll in dry mixture. Spray a baking pan with nonstick cooking spray. Place turkey in prepared pan. Bake at 350° until no longer pink in the center and the internal temperature reaches 170°, about 30 minutes. Makes 2 servings.

(This recipe used by permission of the National Turkey Federation)

FAST TURKEY CASSEROLE

2 cups cooked turkey, diced
1 (10¾-ounce) can cream of mushroom soup
2 cups stuffing

Place 2 cups diced cooked turkey in greased 2-quart casserole, spread with 1 can cream soup. Top with 2 cups stuffing. Bake at 325° for 25 minutes. Makes 2 servings.

CAROLINA MINCED TURKEY BARBECUE

2 cups grilled turkey
½ cup cider vinegar
½ cup water
2 tablespoons molasses
½ to ¾ teaspoon cayenne pepper flakes
½ teaspoon black pepper
½ teaspoon salt
1½ cups coleslaw
4 sandwich buns, split horizontally and toasted

Cut meat from bones and mince. In a saucepan, over high heat, combine vinegar, water, molasses, cayenne pepper flakes, black pepper, and salt with minced turkey. Bring mixture to boil, reduce heat, cover, and simmer 30 minutes. Uncover and simmer additional 30 to 35 minutes, or until liquid has evaporated. To serve, spoon barbecue mixture over buns and top with coleslaw.

(This recipe used by permission of the National Turkey Federation)

TURKEY SPAGHETTI

1 pound ground turkey breast
1 onion, chopped
1 tablespoon olive oil
1 (28-ounce) jar pasta sauce
1 (8-ounce) package spaghetti, cooked and drained
Grated Parmesan cheese

Brown turkey breast and onion in olive oil; add sauce and simmer until heated through. Serve over hot cooked spaghetti with Parmesan cheese. Makes 4 servings.

RICE PILAF WITH TURKEY

1 cup quick-cooking brown rice
½ teaspoon cumin seeds
¼ teaspoon ground ginger
¼ teaspoon cinnamon
4 cardamom seeds
4 whole cloves
1 tablespoon vegetable oil
2 cups turkey stock or water
¼ cup dark or golden raisins
2 cups cooked and chopped turkey
¼ cup pine nuts or cashews, lightly toasted

Sauté the rice, cumin seeds, ginger, cinnamon, cardamom seeds, and cloves in the oil in a saucepan until the rice is browned. Add the stock or water and bring the mixture to a boil. Lower the heat and simmer for 45 to 50 minutes or until the rice is cooked. Add the raisins, turkey, and nuts to the rice mixture. Serve hot or cold. Makes 4 servings.

SEAFOOD

Shrimp Fajitas

1 tablespoon olive oil
1 pound shrimp, peeled and deveined
⅓ cup beef broth
2 tablespoons molasses
1 tablespoon lemon juice
1 tablespoon lime juice
1 teaspoon minced garlic
1 onion, sliced
1 red bell pepper, sliced
Salt and pepper to taste
8 (10-inch) flour tortillas

Heat olive oil in large skillet; add shrimp and sauté until thoroughly cooked. Remove. Add beef broth, molasses, lemon juice, lime juice, and garlic to skillet; bring to a boil. Add onion and pepper; cook and stir until tender. Return shrimp to skillet, and heat through. Season with salt and pepper. Serve with tortillas. Makes 8 servings.

Zesty Baked Shrimp

3 pounds shrimp, unpeeled
1 cup butter, melted
1 cup Italian dressing
2 tablespoons pepper
Juice of 4 lemons

Combine all ingredients. Bake in a large baking pan at 450° for 15 minutes, until shrimp are cooked through. Makes 6 servings.

SHRIMP WITH TOMATO-CHILI SAUCE

¾ cup green bell pepper, chopped
2 tablespoons shallots, finely chopped
1 tablespoon jalapeño pepper, finely chopped
2 garlic cloves, minced
2 teaspoons olive or vegetable oil
1 teaspoon dried basil leaves
1 teaspoon dried mint leaves
1 tablespoon fresh parsley, minced
½ cup chicken broth
3 tablespoons ketchup
3 tablespoons rice wine or cider vinegar
3 tablespoons light soy sauce
3 tablespoons sugar
1 pound large shrimp, deveined, cooked, and peeled

Sauté first 4 ingredients in oil until tender in small saucepan. Stir in herbs; cook over medium heat 1 minute. Stir in broth, ketchup, vinegar, and soy sauce; heat to boiling. Reduce heat and simmer uncovered until sauce thickens. Remove from heat, and let stand 2 to 3 minutes; stir in sugar. Serve warm with shrimp. Makes 4 servings.

MARTIN'S SHRIMP ATHENIAN

5 tomatoes, seeded and chopped
1 onion, chopped
1 bell pepper, chopped
¼ cup fresh herbs (basil, oregano, thyme, parsley), chopped
¼ cup olive oil
3 pounds shrimp, peeled and deveined
1 (4-ounce) package feta cheese, crumbled

Cook tomatoes, onion, bell pepper, and herbs in olive oil until tender. Add shrimp and cook just until pink. Remove from heat, and toss with feta cheese. Makes 6 servings.

BROILED SHRIMP ON TOAST

½ cup olive oil
¼ cup soy sauce
3 tablespoons fresh parsley, chopped
1 tablespoon lemon juice
2 teaspoons garlic, minced
2 pounds shrimp, peeled and deveined
8 slices toasted French bread

Combine olive oil, soy sauce, parsley, lemon juice, and garlic. Pour over shrimp and marinate for 2 hours in refrigerator. Place under preheated broiler and cook about 7 minutes, depending on size of shrimp. Serve over toasted French bread. Makes 4 generous servings.

SHRIMP AND BROCCOLI CASSEROLE

2 heads broccoli, chopped into florets
1 (10¾-ounce) can cream of shrimp soup
1 (10¾-ounce) can cream of broccoli soup
1 (8-ounce) carton sour cream
1½ cups shredded mozzarella cheese
1½ pounds shrimp, peeled and deveined
½ cup cracker crumbs

Arrange broccoli in bottom of greased 9-inch x 13-inch baking dish. Combine soups, sour cream, and cheese; spread over broccoli. Arrange shrimp over soup mixture. Bake at 350° for 30 minutes. Sprinkle cracker crumbs over and bake 10 minutes more. Makes about 6 servings.

CREAMY SHRIMP WITH MUSHROOMS

1 (8-ounce) package sliced mushrooms
1 medium onion, chopped
1 red bell pepper, chopped
¼ cup butter, melted
1 to 2 cups chicken broth
Salt and pepper to taste
Dash cayenne pepper
2 pounds shrimp, peeled and deveined
1 (16-ounce) carton sour cream
2 tablespoons flour
3 cups rice, cooked and hot

Sauté mushrooms, onion, and bell pepper in butter in large skillet over medium-high heat until tender. Add chicken broth, salt and pepper, and cayenne pepper. Stir in shrimp, and cook until pink. Combine sour cream and flour, whisking until smooth. Stir into shrimp mixture, and cook until bubbly. Serve over rice. Makes 6 servings.

CAROLINA SHRIMP SAUCE

1 onion, chopped
1 green bell pepper, chopped
¼ cup butter
¼ cup flour
Salt and pepper to taste
2 (14-ounce) cans diced tomatoes
½ cup ketchup
Dash hot sauce
1 pound shrimp, peeled, deveined, cooked, and chopped
Hot cornbread

Sauté onion and bell pepper in butter until tender; add flour, salt, and pepper, and cook and stir for 4 minutes. Add tomatoes, ketchup, and hot sauce; cook and stir until thickened. Stir in shrimp and cook just until heated through. Serve over hot cornbread. Makes 4 servings.

SHRIMP WITH LEMON BUTTER

1 cup butter, melted
¼ cup lemon juice
1 teaspoon minced garlic
1 teaspoon dried parsley
1 teaspoon Worcestershire sauce
1 teaspoon soy sauce
¼ teaspoon garlic powder
Salt and pepper to taste
2 pounds shrimp, peeled and deveined
2 cups rice, cooked and hot

Combine butter, lemon juice, garlic, parsley, Worcestershire sauce, soy sauce, garlic powder, salt, and pepper in large skillet over medium heat; bring to a boil. Add shrimp; cook and stir about 5 minutes, or until shrimp are pink. Serve over hot cooked rice. Makes 4 to 6 servings.

GRILLED SHRIMP PACKETS

1½ pounds shrimp, peeled and deveined
4-ounces sliced mushrooms
6 tablespoons butter, melted
⅓ cup parsley, chopped
3 chopped green onions
½ teaspoon garlic salt
Dash Worcestershire sauce
Dash hot sauce
Pepper to taste

Divide shrimp evenly among 4 large square pieces of aluminum foil; top evenly with mushrooms. Combine the remaining ingredients and pour evenly over shrimp and mushrooms. Fold packets tightly to seal and grill 5 to 10 minutes. Makes 4 servings.

SHRIMP PASTA AU GRATIN

2 tablespoons butter
1 onion, chopped
1 pound shrimp, peeled
1 (8-ounce) package sliced mushrooms
¼ cup flour
2 cups milk
¼ cup mayonnaise
1 (8-ounce) package dried pasta, cooked and drained
½ cup grated Parmesan cheese

Melt butter over medium heat; add onion, cooking until tender. Add shrimp and mushrooms, and cook for about 5 minutes, just until shrimp are pink. Remove from skillet. Add flour to skillet; cook and stir for 4 minutes. Gradually add milk; cook and stir until bubbly. Whisk in mayonnaise. Toss cream sauce with shrimp mixture and cooked pasta. Top with Parmesan cheese. Bake at 350° for about 30 minutes. Makes 4 to 6 servings.

Steamed Shrimp with Dijon Dill Sauce

¼ cup Dijon mustard
¼ cup plain yogurt
¼ cup vinegar
¼ cup fresh dill, chopped
Salt and pepper to taste
1½ pounds shrimp, peeled, deveined, steamed, and chilled

Combine Dijon mustard, yogurt, vinegar, dill, and salt and pepper to taste. Serve with chilled shrimp. Makes 4 to 6 servings.

Shrimp Fettuccine

2 cups whipping cream
½ cup chicken broth
3 tablespoons garlic, minced
2 tablespoons olive oil
Salt and pepper to taste
1½ pounds shrimp, peeled and deveined
4 chopped green onions
1 pound dried fettuccine, cooked and hot
Grated Parmesan cheese

Combine cream, chicken broth, garlic, olive oil, and salt and pepper to taste in a large saucepan; bring to a boil. Add shrimp and green onions. Reduce heat, and simmer several minutes, or until shrimp is cooked through. Serve over fettuccine with Parmesan cheese. Makes about 8 servings.

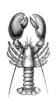

SHRIMP CASSEROLE

1 onion, chopped
1 green bell pepper, chopped
¼ cup margarine
2 pounds shrimp, peeled and deveined
1 (10¾-ounce) can French onion soup
1 (10¾-ounce) can cream of mushroom soup
2 cups quick-cooking rice
1 (10-ounce) can chopped tomatoes

Sauté onion and green bell pepper in margarine in a skillet until tender. Add shrimp, soups, rice, and tomatoes; mix well. Spoon into a greased baking dish. Bake at 325° for 1 hour. Makes 6 servings.

BAKED SHRIMP

3 pounds shrimp, peeled and deveined
1 cup butter or margarine
1 (8-ounce) bottle Italian dressing
½ teaspoon black pepper
Loaf of fresh bread

Place shrimp in a casserole dish, spread evenly. On top of stove in boiler, melt butter, then add Italian dressing and black pepper. Pour over shrimp. Bake at 450° for 15 minutes. Shrimp should be bright orange when done. Serve with loaf of fresh bread to dip in sauce. Makes 6 servings.

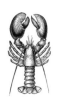

BAKED SHRIMP WITH FLORENTINE NOODLES

4 tablespoons butter
2 pounds shrimp, peeled and deveined
1 teaspoon garlic salt
1 (10¾-ounce) can cream of mushroom soup
1 cup sour cream
1 cup mayonnaise
1 tablespoon Dijon mustard
1 (8-ounce) package dried spinach pasta, cooked and drained
1 cup mozzarella cheese, shredded

Melt butter in large skillet over medium-high heat; add shrimp and garlic salt, cooking and stirring until shrimp are pink. Remove from heat and add soup, sour cream, mayonnaise, and Dijon mustard, stirring well. Layer half of cooked spinach noodles in a greased 9-inch x 13-inch inch baking dish; top with half of shrimp mixture, and repeat layers. Bake at 375° for 20 minutes. Top with mozzarella cheese, and bake 15 minutes more. Makes about 8 servings.

SHRIMP KABOBS

1 pound medium shrimp, peeled and deveined
2 red bell peppers, cut into chunks
1 (8-ounce) package button mushrooms, cleaned and trimmed
¼ cup Italian salad dressing, divided

On each of 8 metal kabobs, thread shrimp, pepper chunks, and whole mushrooms, allowing a bit of space in between each ingredient. Brush kabobs with salad dressing. Grill or broil 4 to 6 inches from heat for 4 to 6 minutes until shrimp are cooked, turning once and brushing once with salad dressing. Makes 8 servings.

BAKED SHRIMP AND TORTELLINI

4 tablespoons butter
3 tablespoons lemon juice
2 teaspoons garlic, minced
1 pound shrimp, peeled and deveined
¾ cup sour cream
½ cup plain yogurt
¼ cup chicken broth
1 teaspoon oregano
Salt and pepper to taste
3 cups cooked cheese tortellini
6 chopped green onions
½ cup Parmesan cheese, grated

Melt butter in large skillet over medium-high heat; add lemon juice and garlic and cook for 2 minutes. Add shrimp and cook 3 to 5 minutes more. Remove from heat. Combine sour cream, yogurt, chicken broth, oregano, and salt and pepper to taste; combine with cooked shrimp and cooked tortellini. Pour into a greased 2-quart baking dish. Top with green onions and Parmesan cheese. Bake at 350° for about 20 minutes. Makes about 6 servings.

SHRIMP AND WILD RICE

1 (10¾-ounce) can cream of celery soup
1 (10¾-ounce) can cream of chicken soup
1 cup chicken broth
1 (1½-ounce) package dry onion soup mix
1 (6-ounce) package quick-cooking wild rice mix
2 pounds peeled, raw shrimp

Combine all ingredients; cover tightly. Bake at 350° for about 30 minutes. Makes 6 to 8 servings.

SHRIMP AND GRITS

6 cups chicken broth
2 cups quick-cooking grits
4 tablespoons butter
1 cup shredded Cheddar cheese
2 tablespoons extra virgin olive oil
1 small onion, finely chopped
1 pound shrimp, peeled and deveined
Salt and pepper, to taste

In a medium saucepan, bring the chicken broth to a boil. Stir in the grits, cover, and reduce heat to low. Simmer, stirring occasionally, until done, about 5 minutes. Stir in the butter and cheese; continue stirring until melted. Cover. In a skillet, heat olive oil over medium heat. Add onion and cook until translucent, about 5 minutes. Season shrimp with salt and pepper and add to skillet. Cook until shrimp turn pink, about 4 to 5 minutes. Stir shrimp and onions into grits. Cook for another 10 minutes. Makes 4 servings.

SHRIMP CREOLE

1 onion, minced
2 garlic cloves, minced
1 tablespoon oil
1 pound shrimp, peeled and deveined
1 bay leaf
½ small bell pepper, chopped
1 (8-ounce) can tomato paste
⅔ cup water
2 cups rice, cooked and hot

Sauté onions and garlic in cooking oil until they turn yellow. Add shrimp, and cook a few minutes longer, turning and stirring often. Add remaining ingredients, and simmer for 1 hour. Serve over rice. Makes 4 servings.

SHRIMP AND RED RICE

2 tablespoons butter
4 chopped green onions
1 green bell pepper, chopped
2 teaspoons garlic, minced
1 cup quick-cooking rice
1 pound shrimp, peeled and deveined
2 cups chicken broth
1 (14-ounce) can diced tomatoes with Italian seasoning
Salt and pepper to taste

Melt butter in large saucepan over medium-high heat; add green onions, green bell pepper, and garlic, stirring until tender. Add rice and shrimp; cook and stir for about 2 minutes. Add chicken broth, undrained tomatoes, and salt and pepper to taste. Bring to a boil. Reduce heat, cover, and simmer for about 20 minutes. Makes 4 servings.

TERIYAKI SHRIMP

2 pounds shrimp, peeled and deveined
1 onion, sliced
1 red bell pepper, chopped
1 (4-ounce) can sliced water chestnuts, drained
1 cup teriyaki sauce
1 (15-ounce) can pineapple chunks, drained

Combine all ingredients, tossing well to mix. Bake in a large casserole dish at 400° for 20 to 30 minutes. Makes 6 servings.

ASIAN SHRIMP STIR-FRY

2 tablespoons olive oil
1 teaspoon sesame oil
2 pounds shrimp, peeled and deveined
1 onion, chopped
1 red bell pepper, chopped
1 carrot, chopped
2 cups fresh broccoli, chopped
2 tablespoons soy sauce
1 (8-ounce) can pineapple chunks, drained
1 tablespoon cornstarch
¼ cup water
2 cups rice, cooked and hot

Heat olive oil and sesame oil in large skillet; add shrimp and cook 2 minutes. Remove shrimp from skillet and keep warm. Add onion, red bell pepper, carrot, broccoli, and soy sauce; cook and stir several minutes. Add pineapple and cook about 10 minutes more. Return shrimp to skillet. Combine cornstarch and water; add and cook until thickened. Serve over rice. Makes 4 to 6 servings.

TUNA TORTELLINI

1 pound refrigerated or frozen cheese tortellini
2 cups frozen green peas
1 (12-ounce) can tuna in olive oil
Parmesan cheese, grated

Cook the tortellini in boiling salted water until tender, adding the peas for the last minute of cooking. Drain. Return to pot, and add the tuna in its oil, along with salt and pepper to taste. Heat through, stirring gently. Sprinkle with Parmesan cheese. Makes 4 servings.

TUNA ARTICHOKE SKEWERS

3 (10-ounce) tuna steaks
Salt and pepper to taste
2 lemons
24 oil-marinated artichoke hearts from bottle, drained
  and liquid reserved

Cut the tuna into 36 1-inch cubes and sprinkle with salt and pepper. Cut lemons into 6 wedges each. Thread tuna cubes, artichoke hearts, and lemon wedges onto six 12-inch metal skewers or bamboo skewers that have been soaked in water. Pierce the tuna against the grain (perpendicular to the stripes of flesh) so it doesn't fall off when cooked. Brush with some of the oil from the artichoke hearts. Cook in a nonstick skillet for 3 to 6 minutes on each side to desired doneness, or grill 4 to 5 inches from medium hot coals for 3 to 6 minutes on each side. Makes 6 servings.

FAST AND EASY TUNA CASSEROLE

2 (7-ounce) cans tuna
2 (8-ounce) boxes macaroni and cheese

Prepare macaroni and cheese according to instructions on package. In a large bowl, mix drained tuna with macaroni and cheese. Makes 4 servings.

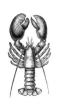

TUNA-NOODLE CASSEROLE

1 (10¾-ounce) can cream of celery soup
1 cup sour cream
¼ cup milk
1 (8-ounce) package dried egg noodles, cooked and drained
2 (6-ounce) cans tuna, drained
1 cup frozen green peas
2 cups potato chips, crushed

Combine soup, sour cream, and milk, stirring until smooth. Add noodles, tuna, and peas, tossing until well coated. Pour into a greased 2-quart baking dish. Top with potato chips. Bake at 350° for about 30 minutes. Makes 6 servings.

TUNA FISH LOAF

1 (7-ounce) can tuna
½ cup dry breadcrumbs
2 tablespoons green bell pepper, finely chopped
½ cup celery, diced
1 tablespoon onion, diced
3 eggs, beaten
1 (10¾-ounce) can vegetarian vegetable soup
3 green bell pepper rings
1 hard-boiled egg, peeled and sliced

Combine first 7 ingredients. Grease a loaf pan and arrange bell pepper rings in bottom. Place a slice of hard-boiled egg in center of each ring. Pack loaf mixture in pan. Bake at 350° for 45 to 60 minutes or until firm. Invert onto plate to serve. Makes 4 servings.

SEAFOOD CASSEROLE

1 cup shrimp, cooked
1 cup crabmeat, picked over to remove bits of shell
1 cup green peas, cooked
½ teaspoon salt
⅛ teaspoon pepper
2 tablespoons onion, chopped
1 green bell pepper, chopped
1 cup celery, diced
1½ cups brown rice, cooked
1 teaspoon Worcestershire sauce
1⅛ cups mayonnaise
¾ cup whole wheat breadcrumbs

Combine all ingredients in a 2-quart casserole dish, reserving some breadcrumbs for topping. Bake at 350° for about 30 minutes. Makes about 4 servings.

FRESH TUNA WITH PENNE PASTA

1 pint grape tomatoes, halved
2 tablespoons capers, drained and chopped
1 tablespoon dried dill
2 teaspoons garlic, minced
Juice and zest of 1 lemon
2 teaspoons olive oil
Salt and pepper to taste
1 (8-ounce) package dried penne pasta
2 (10-ounce) bags fresh spinach, chopped
8 ounces fresh tuna, cubed
1 tablespoon olive oil
½ (4-ounce) package crumbled feta cheese

Combine tomatoes, capers, dill, garlic, lemon juice and zest, olive oil, and salt and pepper to taste. Cook penne pasta according to package directions, stirring spinach in during last minute of cooking time. Drain. Add pasta and spinach to tomato mixture, tossing well. Cook tuna in oil until just cooked through, and add to pasta mixture. Top with feta cheese and serve. Makes 4 servings.

SALMON CROQUETTES

4 eggs
¼ teaspoon baking soda
½ cup buttermilk
2 cups cracker crumbs
1 (12-ounce) can salmon, drained and flaked
Oil for frying

Beat eggs and add soda to buttermilk. Combine all ingredients and form into patties. Fry in hot oil until brown. Makes about 12 croquettes.

SALMON CROQUETTES №2

1 (12-ounce) can salmon, drained and flaked
½ cup flour or more
1 egg, beaten
Salt and pepper to taste
Oil for frying

Combine all ingredients. Fry in a skillet, browning on both sides.
Makes about 12 croquettes.

OVEN-FRIED OYSTERS

1 dozen large oysters, shucked
1 cup flour
1 teaspoon salt
¼ teaspoon pepper
1 egg, slightly beaten
Breadcrumbs
Salad oil
Tartar sauce
Lemon slices

Roll oysters in flour seasoned with salt and pepper. Dip in the egg,
and roll in breadcrumbs. Dip in salad oil and place in a shallow pan.
Bake at 400° for 30 minutes or until brown. Serve with tartar sauce
and slices of lemon.

OYSTERS BAKED IN CREAMED CORN

1½ cups small oysters, shucked
2 eggs, beaten
1 cup saltine cracker crumbs
½ cup half-and-half
1 (16-ounce) can creamed corn
⅓ cup butter, melted
¼ teaspoon salt

Combine oysters, eggs, cracker crumbs, half-and-half, corn, butter, and salt in a bowl; mix well. Spoon into a greased 2-quart baking dish. Bake at 350° for 25 minutes; do not overbake. Makes 4 servings.

SCALLOPED OYSTERS

1 cup butter, melted
2½ cups cracker crumbs
1 tablespoon onion, finely chopped
1 tablespoon lemon juice
2 teaspoons salt
¼ teaspoon Worcestershire sauce
Dash cayenne pepper
2 quarts small oysters, drained
⅔ cup whipping cream

Combine melted butter, cracker crumbs, onion, lemon juice, salt, Worcestershire sauce, and cayenne pepper, tossing until well combined. Layer ⅓ of crumb mixture in a greased 2-quart casserole; top with half of oysters and half of heavy cream. Repeat layers, ending with final ⅓ of crumb mixture. Bake at 450° for about 30 minutes. Makes 12 servings.

Sautéed Scallops with Zucchini

1 tablespoon olive oil
1 pound scallops
1 zucchini, sliced
½ teaspoon basil
Salt and pepper to taste
1 (4-ounce) jar pimentos, drained
2 cups rice, cooked and hot

Heat olive oil in large skillet over medium-high heat. Add scallops, zucchini, basil, and salt and pepper to taste. Cook until scallops are just cooked through; add pimentos and cook and stir for 30 seconds. Serve over rice. Makes 4 servings.

Orange Roughy and Peppers

2 tablespoons olive oil
2 red bell peppers, seeded and sliced
8 orange roughy fillets
1 teaspoon dried thyme

Heat olive oil in a heavy skillet. Add bell peppers, and cook over medium-high heat for 2 to 3 minutes. Place fillets over peppers, and sprinkle with thyme and salt. Lower heat to medium-low, cover skillet, and cook 15 to 20 minutes, shaking pan occasionally, until fish flakes easily with fork. Makes 8 servings.

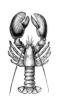

FAST GRILLED FISH

1 pound fish (whole trout, sole, cod, etc.)
2 tablespoons butter
½ cup plain Italian dressing
Garlic salt and pepper

Make a boat out of tin foil to hold the fish and make sure there is enough foil to seal the boat. Place fish in boat with all other ingredients. Broil over grill until fish flakes easily with a fork, about 15 minutes. Makes 2 servings.

SLOW-BAKED SALMON WITH LIME-MUSTARD COATING

1 teaspoon lime zest
2 tablespoons olive oil
1 tablespoon dry breadcrumbs
1 tablespoon finely chopped flat-leaf parsley
2 teaspoons mustard seeds
Juice of large 1 lime
1 teaspoon Dijon mustard
⅛ teaspoon sugar
4 (5-ounce) skinless salmon fillets
Freshly ground pepper

In a small bowl combine the lime zest, olive oil, breadcrumbs, parsley, mustard seeds, lime juice, Dijon mustard, and sugar. Place the salmon fillets in a baking dish, and sprinkle with pepper. Place some of the lime coating on each fillet. Bake at 250° for 25 to 30 minutes until done. Serve hot or at room temperature. Makes 4 servings.

TROUT AMANDINE

¼ cup butter, melted
Juice and zest of 2 lemons
6 trout fillets
Salt and pepper to taste
½ cup slivered almonds

Combine butter, lemon juice, and zest in a large baking dish. Season trout with salt and pepper, and lay in lemon-butter, turning to coat. Bake at 375° for about 20 minutes, or until fish begins to flake easily. Sprinkle almonds over fish, and bake 5 more minutes. Makes 6 servings.

FISH DISH FOR TWO

2 fish fillets
Lemon juice
2 to 3 tablespoons mayonnaise
Grated Parmesan cheese

Place fish fillets in a foil-lined broiler-safe dish. Sprinkle with lemon juice, and coat with a layer of mayonnaise. Broil 5 minutes (7 if frozen); turn the fillets, coat the other side with mayonnaise, sprinkle on some Parmesan cheese. Broil another 5 minutes. Serve immediately. Makes 2 servings.

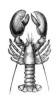

FISH BAKED IN MILK

2 tablespoons butter
1½ pounds fish fillets
1 teaspoon salt
⅔ cup water
⅔ cup evaporated milk

Melt butter in a large baking pan. Place fish on top of melted butter, and sprinkle with salt. Add water and milk. Bake at 350° until fish is tender, about 45 minutes. Makes 6 servings.

LEMON-BATTERED FISH

1 cup flour
⅔ cup water
⅔ cup lemon juice, divided
1 egg, beaten
1 teaspoon baking powder
½ teaspoon sugar
¾ teaspoon salt
1 pound fresh or frozen fish fillets
½ cup flour
Oil for frying

Combine 1 cup flour, water, ⅓ cup lemon juice, egg, baking powder, sugar, and salt in a bowl; mix well. Dip fish in ⅓ cup lemon juice; coat with ½ cup flour. Dip into batter, coating well. Deep-fry in hot oil until golden brown. Makes 3 servings.

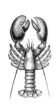

FRIED CATFISH

4 (6-ounce) catfish fillets
Seasoning salt and pepper to taste
¼ cup flour
¾ cup yellow cornmeal
½ teaspoon salt
Oil for frying

Sprinkle seasoning salt and pepper over each fillet. In a large bowl, combine the flour, cornmeal, and salt. Dredge the catfish in the flour mixture, and fry in hot oil until golden brown, about 7 minutes. Makes 4 servings.

PAN-FRIED FISH

½ cup flour
½ cup cornmeal
1 tablespoon salt
1 teaspoon cayenne pepper
¼ teaspoon dry mustard
½ teaspoon celery seed
1 teaspoon onion powder
1 teaspoon garlic powder
4 white fish fillets
1 cup milk
Oil for frying

In a shallow dish, combine the flour, cornmeal, salt, cayenne pepper, dry mustard, celery seed, onion powder, and garlic powder. Soak each fillet in the milk, then dredge in flour mixture. Fill a large cast-iron skillet with about ½-inch of oil, and heat to frying temperature. Fry fillets two at a time, until crispy. Makes 4 servings.

SAUTÉED FISH FILLETS À LA PROVENÇAL

1 pound mild fish fillets, such as tilapia
Salt and pepper to taste
2 tablespoons olive oil
1 large tomato, seeded and chopped
½ cup kalamata olives, pitted and chopped
2 tablespoons fresh basil, chopped
2 tablespoons fresh parsley, chopped
1½ teaspoons garlic, minced

Season fish to taste with salt and pepper. Sauté in olive oil over medium-high heat until cooked through, about 3 minutes per side. Remove fish from pan. Add tomato, olives, basil, parsley, and garlic to pan. Cook and stir until heated through, about 3 minutes. Serve over fish. Makes 4 servings.

OVEN-FRIED FISH

1 pound white fish fillets
Salt and pepper to taste
¼ cup breadcrumbs
¼ cup grated Parmesan cheese
1 teaspoon dried Italian seasoning
¼ cup flour
2 eggs, beaten

Season fish with salt and pepper. Combine breadcrumbs, Parmesan cheese, and Italian seasoning in a shallow dish. Roll each fish piece in flour, then dip in beaten eggs, then roll in breadcrumb mixture. Bake on greased baking sheet at 450° for about 8 minutes or until cooked through. Makes 4 servings.

LIME BROILED CATFISH

1 tablespoon margarine
2 tablespoons lime juice
¼ teaspoon pepper
¼ teaspoon garlic powder
2 catfish fillets

Melt margarine in a saucepan. Stir in lime juice, pepper, and garlic powder; mix well. Remove from the heat and set aside. Place fillets in a shallow baking dish. Brush each generously with lime sauce. Broil for 5 to 8 minutes, or until fish flakes easily with a fork. Transfer to a warm serving dish; spoon pan juices over each fillet. Makes 2 servings.

CRAB CAKES

3 tablespoons butter
1 small onion, chopped
¼ cup red bell pepper, finely chopped
1 garlic clove, minced
2 cups breadcrumbs
¼ cup mayonnaise
2 eggs, beaten
1 teaspoon salt
½ teaspoon pepper
½ teaspoon cayenne pepper
1 pound lump crabmeat, picked over to remove bits of shell
2 tablespoons vegetable oil

In a saucepan, melt butter over medium heat. Add the onion, bell pepper, and garlic; sauté for 2 minutes. Remove from heat. Pour into a mixing bowl. Add breadcrumbs, mayonnaise, eggs, and seasonings. Stir to combine. Gently fold in crabmeat. Form into cakes about ½ inch thick and refrigerate until firm, about 2 hours. In a heavy cast-iron skillet, heat vegetable oil over medium heat. Fry crab cakes until browned, about 3 minutes per side. Makes 4 servings.

WEST INDIES SALAD

1 pound lump crabmeat, picked over to remove bits of shell
1 onion, finely chopped
1 cup olive oil
¾ cup vinegar
Juice of 1 lemon
Salt and pepper to taste

Layer crabmeat and onion in a glass bowl. Combine olive oil, vinegar, lemon juice, and salt and pepper, and pour over top. Cover surface with plastic wrap and than a layer of ice cubes. Chill overnight. Drain before serving. Makes 6 servings.

RICH CRAB FETTUCINE

1 bunch chopped green onions
1 teaspoon minced garlic
1 cup butter, melted
1 pound fresh lump crabmeat, picked over to remove bits of shell
⅓ cup whipping cream
1 cup grated Parmesan cheese
8 ounces fettuccine, cooked and hot

Cook green onions and garlic in butter until tender; add crab and cream, tossing gently and heating just until heated through. Add Parmesan cheese and toss lightly. Serve over hot cooked fettuccine. Makes 4 servings.

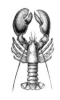

CRAB NORFOLK

2 pounds fresh lump crabmeat, picked over to remove bits of shell
3 tablespoons vinegar
Salt and pepper to taste
½ cup butter, cut up

Combine crab, vinegar, and salt and pepper, tossing very lightly to combine. Transfer to a greased 1-quart baking dish; dot with butter. Bake at 350° for 20 to 30 minutes. Makes 6 servings.

SPICY SEAFOOD WONTONS

4 ounces Neufchatel cheese
1 cup crabmeat, picked over to remove bits of shell
5 chopped green onions
½ teaspoon hot sauce
1 garlic clove, minced
25 wonton wrappers
1 tablespoon vegetable oil
¼ cup water

Combine first five ingredients in food processor or blender until smooth. Add 2 teaspoons of this filling to the middle of a wonton wrapper, fold in half over the mixture, and seal edges. Heat oil in a large skillet over medium heat. Place wontons in skillet, and cook just until lightly browned on both sides. Gradually pour water into skillet; cover immediately. Allow to steam 1 minute. Drain wontons with slotted spoon. Serve immediately. Makes 12 servings.

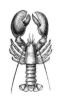

GRILLED LOBSTER TAILS WITH GARLIC BUTTER

4 lobster tails
½ cup butter, softened
2 garlic cloves, minced
1 lemon, cut into wedges

With a sharp knife, cut each lobster tail down the back of the shell. Place on a medium-high grill, cut-side down. Grill for 5 minutes; then flip the tails over and grill for another 2 to 3 minutes, or until done.

Meanwhile, in a medium saucepan, melt the butter. Add the garlic and sauté until fragrant, about 1 minute. Remove from heat. Drizzle garlic butter over each lobster tail, and serve with lemon wedges. Makes 4 servings.

BAKED OLD BAY CRAB

2 pounds lump crabmeat, picked over to remove bits of shell
1 cup mayonnaise
2 tablespoons vinegar
1 tablespoon white Worcestershire sauce
2 teaspoons sugar
2 teaspoons salt
½ teaspoon Old Bay seasoning
Juice and zest of 1 lemon
½ cup grated Parmesan cheese
Paprika

Combine crab, mayonnaise, vinegar, white Worcestershire sauce, sugar, salt, Old Bay seasoning, and lemon juice and zest; toss very lightly to combine. Transfer to a greased 1-quart baking dish; sprinkle with Parmesan cheese and paprika. Bake at 375° for 20 to 30 minutes. Makes 6 servings.

SLOW COOKER

CHILI CON QUESO

1 pound Mexican or plain processed cheese spread
1⅓ cups chunky salsa
1 (4-ounce) can chopped green chiles, drained
¼ teaspoon pepper

Combine all ingredients in a 3 to 4-quart slow cooker. Cover and cook on low for 2 to 2½ hours, or until cheese is melted, stirring twice during cooking. Remove the lid from the slow cooker, and cook on high for 1 hour longer, until mixture is hot. Makes about 6 to 8 servings.

SAUSAGE CHEESE DIP

1 pound sausage
1 pound ground beef
½ onion, chopped
1 (16-ounce) package processed cheese spread, cubed
1 (10-ounce) can diced tomatoes with chiles
1 (10¾-ounce) can cream of mushroom soup

Brown sausage and ground beef with onion until thoroughly cooked. Drain and add to slow cooker with remaining ingredients. Cook on low 4 hours or until thoroughly melted, stirring occasionally. Makes about 8 servings.

BOILED PEANUTS

2 pounds fresh peanuts, uncooked and in shells
½ cup salt

Fill a slow cooker with peanuts. Cover with water and add salt; stir. Cover and cook on low for 12 to 18 hours, or until peanuts are soft. Drain and serve. Makes 8 servings.

CHILI CON CARNE

3 pounds ground beef
2 (15-ounce) cans diced tomatoes
2 (15-ounce) cans kidney beans, drained
1½ cups water
½ onion, chopped
½ green or red bell pepper, chopped
3 tablespoons chili powder
1 tablespoon minced garlic
Cayenne pepper to taste

Brown ground beef until thoroughly cooked. Drain off all fat. Add ground beef and all other ingredients to slow cooker. Cook on low for 8 hours. Makes about 10 servings.

BEEF AND BROCCOLI SLOW COOKER

¾ pound thin beef strips
2 cups fresh broccoli flowerets
1 (1-ounce) package brown gravy mix
1 cup water

Place beef and broccoli in the bottom of slow cooker. Mix together gravy mix and water. Pour over the top. Cover and cook on low for 6 to 8 hours. Makes 4 servings.

VIENNESE POT ROAST

1 onion, chopped
2 carrots, chopped
2 turnips, chopped
8 new potatoes
4 dried figs, chopped
1½ cup beef stock
1 (4-pound) rump roast
4 gingersnap cookies, crushed

Place vegetables in the bottom of a slow cooker. Add the figs and the beef stock. Add the roast on top. Cover and cook on low for 8 to 10 hours. Set to high heat and add gingersnap cookies; cook until thickened. Makes 8 servings.

TERIYAKI STEAK

2 tablespoons vegetable oil
1 teaspoon ground ginger
½ cup soy sauce
1 tablespoon sugar
1 garlic clove, crushed
2½ pounds boneless chuck steak, cut into thin slices
2 cups rice, cooked and hot

Combine all ingredients except steak in a bowl. Place meat in a slow cooker. Pour sauce on top of steak. Cook on low for 6 to 8 hours. Serve over hot rice. Makes 4 to 6 servings.

CHILI BEEF SANDWICHES

3 pounds boneless beef chuck roast
1 (1-ounce) package taco seasoning mix
½ cup barbecue sauce
8 Kaiser rolls, split and toasted

Trim excess fat from beef, and brown on all sides in heavy skillet over medium-high heat; transfer to a 4-quart slow cooker. Sprinkle with seasoning mix and pour sauce over. Cover and cook on low for 8 to 10 hours. Remove beef from slow cooker and shred; return to slow cooker. Make sandwiches with Kaiser rolls. Makes 8 servings.

SPICED BEEF BRISKET

1 (4 to 5-pound) fresh beef brisket
2 cups water
1 (1-ounce) package dry onion soup mix
¼ cup ketchup
2 tablespoons Worcestershire sauce
½ teaspoon minced garlic
¼ cup water
4 tablespoons flour

Place brisket in a slow cooker. Combine water with soup mix, ketchup, Worcestershire sauce, and garlic. Pour over brisket. Cover and cook on low heat for 8 to 10 hours.

To make gravy, combine ¼ cup cold water and 4 tablespoons flour in a small saucepan. Stir until flour dissolves. Add ¾ cup cooking liquid. Cook and stir until bubbly. Continue cooking for an additional minute. Makes 8 to 12 servings.

HUNGRY MAN

1 pound ground beef
1 (16-ounce) can baked beans
¾ cup barbecue sauce
⅔ cup shredded Cheddar cheese

Brown ground beef and drain. Mix ground beef, baked beans, and barbecue sauce together in slow cooker. Cover and cook on low for 6 to 8 hours. Sprinkle with cheese last 15 minutes of cooking. Makes 4 servings.

MEXICAN RIBS

4 pounds beef short ribs
1¼ cups beef stock
2½ tablespoons taco seasoning mix

Place ribs in the bottom of a slow cooker. Thoroughly mix beef stock and taco seasoning mix and pour over the ribs. Cover and cook on low for 6 to 8 hours. Makes 4 servings.

ONION MEATBALLS

3 pounds frozen cooked meatballs
1 (1½-ounce) package dry onion soup mix
3 garlic cloves, minced
1 (10-ounce) jar beef gravy
3 tablespoons water
⅛ teaspoon pepper

Combine all ingredients in a 4 to 6-quart slow cooker and stir. Cover and cook on low for 4 to 5 hours until thoroughly heated. Makes 6 to 8 servings.

Sweet-and-Sour Meatballs

2 pounds frozen meatballs
1 cup grape jelly
2 cups cocktail sauce

Heat meatballs in oven as directed on package. Place in 3 to 4-quart slow cooker. Mix jelly and cocktail sauce thoroughly, pour over meatballs and stir well. Cover and cook on high 1 to 2 hours until sauce is hot. Turn heat to low until ready to serve, stirring occasionally. Makes 4 servings.

Tender Shredded Beef

1 (2-pound) fresh beef brisket
1 tablespoon olive oil
1 (10-ounce) can condensed beef broth
2 garlic cloves, minced
1 onion, chopped, if desired
½ teaspoon salt
¼ teaspoon pepper

Trim excess fat from beef. Heat oil in 10-inch skillet over medium heat. Cook beef for 10 minutes, turning frequently, to brown all sides. Place beef in a 3½ to 6-quart slow cooker. Pour remaining ingredients over beef. Cover and cook on low for 8 to 10 hours, until beef is tender. Remove beef from slow cooker and shred, using two forks. Skim fat from juices in slow cooker, and add beef. Keep on low setting until ready to serve. Makes 4 servings.

BEEF AND BLACK-EYED PEAS

1 (16-ounce) package dried black-eyed peas
1 (10-ounce) can bean and bacon soup
3 cups water
4 carrots, peeled and chopped
3 pounds beef chuck roast, cut into 2-inch cubes
¼ teaspoon pepper

Sort through the black-eyed peas to remove any stones or shriveled peas; rinse and drain. Combine all ingredients in a 4 to 5-quart slow cooker. Cover and cook on low for 9 to 10 hours, or until peas are tender and beef is done. Makes 6 to 8 servings.

SAUCY BEEF

2 pounds beef stew meat
2 (10-ounce) cans tomato soup
1 (10-ounce) can Cheddar cheese soup
2 cups rice or egg noodles, cooked and hot

Place meat in a 3 to 4-quart slow cooker, pour the soups over the meat, and mix well to combine. Cover and cook 8 to 10 hours, until meat is tender. Stir well and serve over rice or noodles. Makes 4 to 6 servings.

Savory Short Ribs

4 pounds beef short ribs
½ teaspoon pepper
1 (12-ounce) jar beef gravy
1 pound frozen bell peppers and onions, thawed and drained

In a 3 to 4-quart slow cooker, place ribs and sprinkle with pepper. Pour gravy over top. Cover and cook on low for 9 to 11 hours until beef is tender. Skim fat from surface of liquid and remove ribs. Cover with foil to keep warm. Add bell peppers and onions to slow cooker, cover, and cook on high 15 to 20 minutes. Serve vegetables and sauce over ribs. Makes about 4 servings.

Beef and Potatoes

3 to 4 potatoes, sliced thin
1 teaspoon salt
½ teaspoon pepper
2 tablespoons butter, melted
1 pound ground beef
1 medium onion, chopped
1 (10½-ounce) can tomato sauce

Put potatoes in the bottom of a slow cooker. Sprinkle with salt and pepper. Add remaining ingredients. Cover and cook on low for 8 to 10 hours. Makes 4 to 6 servings.

ALL-DAY-LONG BEEF

3 carrots, diced
2 celery stalks, diced
1 green bell pepper, chopped
1 yellow onion, sliced
1½ pounds beef roast, cut into serving-sized pieces
½ teaspoon black pepper
2 garlic cloves, minced
1 (1½–ounce) package dry onion soup mix
1 teaspoon steak sauce
2 teaspoons Worcestershire sauce
½ cup water
½ cup tomato juice

Place the vegetables in the bottom of a slow cooker. Sprinkle the beef pieces with black pepper, garlic, and onion soup mix. Place on top of the vegetables. Mix the steak sauce and Worcestershire sauce in a small bowl with ½ cup water and ½ cup tomato juice. Pour over the meat. Cover and cook on low for 7 to 9 hours. Makes 4 servings.

MEATBALL SOUP

1 (16-ounce) bag frozen cooked meatballs
2 (14-ounce) cans condensed beef broth
1 cup water
2 (14-ounce) cans diced tomatoes with herbs, undrained
1 (16-ounce) bag frozen mixed vegetables

Combine frozen meatballs, broth, water, and tomatoes in a 3 to 4-quart slow cooker. Cover and cook on low for 9 to 10 hours, or until meatballs are tender when pierced with a fork. Stir in the frozen vegetables and mix well. Cover and cook on high for 1 hour. Makes 6 to 8 servings.

SPANISH CHICKEN WITH MUSHROOMS

1 teaspoon paprika
1 teaspoon garlic powder
Salt and pepper to taste
3 pounds chicken breasts
1 (6-ounce) can tomato paste
1 cup water
1 (8-ounce) can mushrooms, sliced
3 cups rice, cooked and hot

Combine paprika, garlic powder, salt, and pepper. Sprinkle spice mixture on each piece of chicken. Place chicken in a slow cooker. Mix tomato paste and water together. Pour over the chicken. Add sliced mushrooms. Cover and cook on low for 7 to 9 hours. Serve over rice. Makes 6 to 8 servings.

TANGY RUMP ROAST

1 (3 to 5-pound) rump roast, trimmed
1 (1½-ounce) package dry onion soup mix
1 can cranberry sauce, jellied
2 tablespoons butter, softened
2 tablespoons flour

Rinse rump roast and pat dry. Sprinkle onion soup mix in bottom of a slow cooker. Place rump roast in next; spoon cranberry sauce around and over roast. Cover and cook on low 10 to 12 hours. Remove roast from slow cooker, and allow to rest while you thicken gravy. Turn slow cooker up on high. Blend softened butter and flour into a paste. Whisk it into the gravy. Cover and cook on high for about 10 minutes, until thick. Slice roast into ¼-inch thick slices, and serve with gravy. Makes 6 to 10 servings.

SMOKY BARBECUE BRISKET

1 teaspoon chili powder
½ teaspoon garlic powder
¼ teaspoon celery seed
⅛ teaspoon pepper
1 (2 to 3-pound) beef brisket
½ cup ketchup
½ cup chili sauce
¼ cup packed brown sugar
2 tablespoons vinegar
2 tablespoons Worcestershire sauce
1½ teaspoons liquid smoke
½ teaspoon dry mustard

Combine chili powder, garlic powder, celery seed, and pepper; rub
evenly over meat, and place in slow cooker. Combine remaining
ingredients. Pour over brisket. Cover and cook on low for 8 to
12 hours or on high for 4 to 5 hours. Makes 6 to 8 servings.

ROULADE STEAK

3 pounds round steaks, cut thin
1 teaspoon salt
1 teaspoon pepper
¾ cup chopped onion
¾ cup bacon, chopped
¼ cup water

Season steaks with salt and pepper. Mix onion and bacon, spread over
each steak. Roll steaks (as you would for a jelly roll) and tie tightly in
several places with a string. Put steaks into a slow cooker. Add water.
Cover and cook on low for 8 hours. For gravy, remove meat when
done, and thicken liquid with a mixture of flour and water; cook at
high for 15 minutes. Makes 4 to 6 servings.

MUSHROOM-SMOTHERED BEEF

½ pound fresh white mushrooms, sliced
1 medium onion, sliced
1 (10¾-ounce) can cream of mushroom soup
½ cup beef stock
2 tablespoons Worcestershire sauce, divided
1 (4-ounce) can diced green chilies
2½ pound boneless beef chuck or cross rib-roast, sliced
  into 1½ to 2-inch cubes
3 tablespoons flour

Combine mushrooms and onion in bottom of a slow cooker. Whisk together undiluted soup with the stock, 1 tablespoon of the Worcestershire sauce, and chilies. Pour half of soup mixture over the mushrooms and onion. Place beef on top of the mushroom mixture. Pour the remaining soup mixture on top. Do not mix. Cover and cook on low for 8 hours. Increase the heat setting to high. Mix remaining Worcestershire sauce with flour and several spoonfuls of the liquid from the slow cooker until smooth. Stir the flour mixture into the sauce in the slow cooker. Cover and cook on high for 30 minutes. Makes 5 to 6 servings.

FRENCH DIP SANDWICH

1 (1-pound) fresh beef brisket
1 (1½-ounce) package dry onion soup mix
1 (10-ounce) can condensed beef broth

Combine all ingredients in a 3 to 4-quart slow cooker. Cover and cook on low for 8 to 10 hours, until beef is tender. Skim any fat from liquid in slow cooker. Remove beef and cut across grain into thin slices. Serve on crusty baguette rolls, with the hot broth for dipping. Makes 4 to 6 servings.

HUNGARIAN GOULASH

1½ pounds stewing beef, cut into ¾-inch pieces
½ cup water
1 (8-ounce) can tomato sauce
2 onions chopped
1 garlic clove, chopped
1 tablespoon paprika
2 teaspoons salt
2 teaspoons beef bouillon
¼ teaspoon freshly ground black pepper
1 cup sour cream
8 ounces dried egg noodles, cooked and hot

Place all ingredients except sour cream in the bottom of a slow cooker. Cover and cook for 8 to 18 hours on low. Add sour cream to slow cooker 10 minutes before serving. Serve over noodles. Makes 4 servings.

BARBECUE SANDWICH

1½ pounds boneless beef round steak
½ teaspoon salt
¼ teaspoon pepper
2 cups coleslaw
½ cup barbecue sauce
Sandwich buns

Trim beef and cut into 1-inch pieces; sprinkle with salt and pepper. In medium bowl, combine coleslaw and barbecue sauce and mix thoroughly. Layer beef and coleslaw mixture in slow cooker. Cover and cook on low for 8 to 9 hours, until beef is tender. Stir well with fork so beef falls apart. Serve on crusty sandwich buns. Makes 4 to 6 servings.

TAMALE PIE

¾ cup yellow cornmeal
1 cup beef broth
1 pound extra-lean ground beef
1 teaspoon chili powder
½ teaspoon ground cumin (optional)
1 (14 to 16-ounce) jar thick and chunky salsa
1 (16-ounce) can whole-kernel corn, drained
¼ cup sliced ripe olives
½ cup shredded Cheddar cheese

In a large bowl, mix cornmeal and broth; let stand 5 minutes. Stir in beef, chili powder, cumin, salsa, corn, and olives. Pour into a slow cooker. Cover and cook on low 4 to 8 hours or until set. Sprinkle cheese over top; cover and cook another 5 minutes, or until cheese melts. Makes 6 to 8 servings.

CHILI BEEF SANDWICHES

1 (3-pound) boneless beef chuck roast
1 (1-ounce) package taco seasoning mix
½ cup barbecue sauce
8 Kaiser rolls, split and toasted

Trim excess fat from beef, and brown on all sides in heavy skillet over medium-high heat; transfer to 4-quart slow cooker. Sprinkle with seasoning mix, and pour sauce over. Cover and cook on low for 8 to 10 hours. Remove beef from slow cooker and shred; return to slow cooker. Make sandwiches with Kaiser rolls. Makes 8 servings.

CAJUN BEEF AND POTATOES

1½ pounds round steak
3 tablespoons Caribbean jerk marinade
4 potatoes, cut into chunks
⅓ cup flour
1 (14-ounce) can diced tomatoes

Trim excess fat from round steak, and cut into 1-inch pieces.
Combine marinade and beef in a large glass dish, and stir to coat. Let
stand for 15 to 30 minutes. Place potatoes in slow cooker. Add flour
to marinade/beef mixture, mix to coat, and place on top of potatoes.
Add undrained tomatoes. Cover and cook on low for 8 to 9 hours,
until beef and potatoes are tender. Makes 6 servings.

CHUCK ROAST AU GRATIN

6 potatoes, peeled and cut into quarters
3½ pounds boned chuck roast
1 tablespoon dried chives
2 cans cream of mushroom soup
½ cup Cheddar cheese, grated
Paprika

Place potatoes in the bottom of a slow cooker. Place roast over the top
of the potatoes. Combine the chives with the soup, and pour over top
of roast. Cover and cook on low for 8 hours. Sprinkle with cheese and
paprika. Cover and cook until cheese melts. Makes 8 servings.

OLD-FASHIONED POT ROAST

6 small potatoes, peeled and diced
6 small onions, chopped
6 medium carrots, chopped
1 (3-pound) boneless beef chuck roast
Salt and pepper to taste
1 cup water

Place all ingredients in a slow cooker in the order listed. Cover and cook on low for 8 hours. Makes 8 servings.

CORNED BEEF AND CABBAGE

4 cups hot water
2 tablespoons cider vinegar
2 tablespoons sugar
½ teaspoon black pepper
1 onion, cooked and cut into wedges
2¼ pounds whole corned beef brisket
8 small potatoes, scrubbed and quartered
1 head green cabbage, cored and cut into wedges

Combine first 5 ingredients in a slow cooker on high heat. Mix thoroughly. Add meat and potatoes. Cover and cook 4 hours. Remove lid, and add cabbage wedges. Cover and cook another 3 to 4 hours, or until meat is tender. Carve beef into slices, and serve with cabbage, potatoes, and sauce. Makes 6 to 8 servings.

FRENCH ONION BEEF

1¼ pounds boneless beef round steak, cut into 1-inch cubes
1 cup fresh mushrooms, sliced
1 large onion, sliced
1 (10¾-ounce) can French onion soup
6 (¼-ounce) packages 15-minute stuffing mix
¼ cup margarine or butter, melted
½ cup mozzarella cheese, shredded

Place beef, mushrooms, and onion in bottom of a slow cooker. Pour soup on top. Cover and cook on low for 8 to 10 hours. Mix stuffing mix and contents of seasoning packet with melted margarine and ½ cup liquid from pot. Place stuffing in slow cooker. Cover. Increase heat to high setting, and cook for 10 minutes or until stuffing is fluffy. Sprinkle with cheese. Cover and cook until cheese is melted. Makes 4 servings.

CRANBERRY POT ROAST

4 potatoes, peeled and cut into 1-inch chunks
1 (3-pound) boneless center-cut pork loin roast, rolled and tied
1(16-ounce) can whole-berry cranberry sauce
1 (5-ounce) can apricot nectar
1 cup pearl onions
½ cup dried apricots, coarsely chopped
½ cup sugar
1 teaspoon dry mustard
¼ teaspoon crushed cayenne pepper

Place the potatoes in the bottom of a slow cooker; place the roast over the potatoes. In a large bowl, combine the remaining ingredients; mix well and pour over roast. Cover and cook on low for 5 to 6 hours. Remove the roast to a cutting board and thinly slice. Serve with the potatoes and sauce. Makes 6 to 8 servings.

Pork Loin with Fruit

2 pounds boneless pork loin roast
1½ cups mixed dried fruit
½ cup apple juice
½ teaspoon salt
¼ teaspoon pepper

Place pork in a 3 to 4-quart slow cooker, and top with fruit. Pour apple juice over pork and sprinkle with salt and pepper. Cover and cook on low for 7 to 9 hours until pork is tender. Makes 4 to 6 servings.

Mexican Pork

1 pound boneless pork loin roast, cut into 1-inch pieces
1 (20-ounce) jar chunky salsa
1 (15-ounce) can pinto beans, rinsed and drained

Mix pork and salsa in a 3 to 4-quart slow cooker. Cover and cook on low for 6 to 8 hours until pork is tender. Add beans, Cover and cook 10 to 15 minutes until hot. Makes 4 servings.

Sweet Barbecue Ribs

3½ pounds pork loin back ribs
½ teaspoon salt
¼ teaspoon pepper
½ cup cola beverage
⅔ cup barbecue sauce

Place ribs in slow cooker, sprinkle with salt and pepper, and pour cola over. Cover and cook on low for 8 to 9 hours until the ribs are tender. Drain liquid and discard. Pour barbecue sauce into slow cooker and mix so ribs are coated. Cover and cook on low for 1 hour, until ribs are glazed. Makes 4 servings.

BABY BACK RIBS

¼ cup spicy chili rub (below)
¼ cup dark brown sugar
4 (1-pound) racks baby back ribs
¼ cup barbecue sauce

Mix spicy blend and brown sugar; rub on ribs. Curl racks, meaty side out; stand upright on thick ends in 5 to 6-quart slow cooker. Cover and cook on low for 7 to 8 hours, or on high for 3 to 3½ hours, until meat is very tender. Remove ribs to cutting board. Let rest for 5 minutes, and brush with barbecue or sweet-and-sour sauce. Serve. Makes 4 to 6 servings.

SPICY CHILI RUB

1 tablespoon black pepper
2 tablespoons cayenne pepper
2 tablespoons chili powder
2 tablespoons cumin
1 tablespoon ground oregano
4 tablespoons paprika
2 tablespoons salt
1 tablespoon pepper

Combine all ingredients. Makes about 1 cup.

PORK IN A BUN

1 (3 to 4-pound) pork butt roast, well trimmed
Salt and pepper
2 onions, chopped
1 (16-ounce) bottle barbecue sauce

Season pork with salt and pepper. Place the onions in a 4 to 5-quart slow cooker; place the meat on top. Pour ½ cup barbecue sauce over the meat. Cover and cook on low for 9 to 10 hours. Remove the cooked meat from the slow cooker. Drain the juices from the pot, reserving the onions. Coarsely shred the meat into chunks, using two forks. Put the shredded meat and onions back in the slow cooker; mix in the remaining barbecue sauce. Cover and cook on low for about 1 hour. Serve. Makes 6 to 8 servings.

HONEY BARBECUE PORK AND CARROTS

3 pounds boneless pork roast
1 (16-ounce) bag baby carrots
½ cup barbecue sauce
¼ cup honey
½ teaspoon salt
¼ teaspoon pepper

Place pork and carrots in a 3 to 4-quart slow cooker. Combine barbecue sauce, honey, salt, and pepper in a small bowl, and pour over ingredients in slow cooker. Cover and cook on low for 8 to 10 hours, or until pork is thoroughly cooked. Makes 6 to 8 servings.

POLISH KRAUT AND APPLES

1 pound fresh or canned sauerkraut
1 pound lean smoked Polish sausage
3 tart cooking apples, cored and thickly sliced
½ cup packed brown sugar
¾ teaspoon salt
⅛ teaspoon pepper
½ teaspoon caraway seeds (optional)
¾ cup apple juice or cider

Rinse sauerkraut and squeeze dry. Place half of the sauerkraut in a slow cooker. Cut sausage into 2-inch lengths. Place in slow cooker. Continue to layer in slow cooker, in order, apples, brown sugar, salt, pepper, and, if desired, caraway seeds. Top with remaining sauerkraut. Add apple juice. Do not stir. Cover and cook on high for 3 to 3½ hours or on low for 6 to 7 hours, or until apples are tender. Stir before serving. Makes 4 to 6 servings.

CARIBBEAN RIBS

3 pounds pork loin back ribs, cut into 4-inch pieces
1 teaspoon pepper
½ teaspoon allspice
1 teaspoon dry mustard
1 teaspoon salt
½ cup water
1½ cups barbecue sauce

Combine all spices in a small bowl. Rub ribs with spice mixture. Place in a 3 to 4-quart slow cooker, and pour water over. Cover and cook on low for 8 to 9 hours, or until ribs are tender when pierced with a fork. Remove ribs from slow cooker, and discard cooking liquid. Put ribs back in slow cooker, and add barbecue sauce. Cover and cook on low for 1 hour. Makes 3 to 4 servings.

EASIEST PORK CHOPS

4 pork chops, well trimmed
1 (1½-ounce) package dry onion soup mix
1 (10-ounce) can chicken broth

Brown the pork chops, if desired, in a nonstick skillet, 3 to
4 minutes on each side. Place pork chops in a 3½ to 4-quart slow
cooker. In a medium bowl, combine soup mix and chicken broth and
stir until blended. Pour this mixture over the pork chops. Cover and
cook on low heat for 6 to 8 hours. Makes 4 servings.

PIZZA FONDUE

¼ pound Italian sausage
1 onion, chopped
1 garlic clove, minced
8 cups tomato sauce
1 cup fresh mushrooms, sliced and cooked
1½ cups pepperoni, chopped
1 teaspoon fresh oregano, crushed
Italian bread

Sauté sausage, onion, and garlic in a skillet over medium-high heat
until meat is browned. Drain and discard fat. Combine tomato sauce,
mushrooms, pepperoni, and oregano in a 4-quart slow cooker. Stir in
meat mixture. Cover and cook on low 3 hours. Makes 4 servings.

CANTONESE PORK

1½ pounds pork steak, cubed
1 green onion, sliced
1 (4-ounce) can mushrooms, drained
1 onion, sliced
2 teaspoons Worcestershire sauce
1 (8-ounce) can tomato sauce
2 tablespoons brown sugar
1½ tablespoons vinegar
2 cups rice, cooked and hot

Put all of the ingredients except rice into a slow cooker. Cover and cook on low for 8 to 10 hours or on high for 4 to 6 hours. Serve over rice. Makes 4 servings.

HAM AND SCALLOPED POTATOES

2 pounds ham, chopped into bite-size chunks
6 medium potatoes, peeled and thinly sliced
2 medium onions, chopped
1 (10¾-ounce) can cream of mushroom soup
2 cups Colby cheese, shredded

Combine ham with potatoes and onions, and place in the bottom of a slow cooker. Pour cream of mushroom soup over the top. Cover and cook on low for 6 to 8 hours. About an hour before serving, stir in cheese. Makes 6 to 8 servings.

Pork Chops and Applesauce

6 boneless pork chops, browned
Salt and pepper
¼ cup brown sugar
½ teaspoon cinnamon
1 (8-ounce) can tomato sauce
¼ cup applesauce
¼ cup vinegar

Season pork chops with salt and pepper, and then place in a slow cooker. Combine sugar, cinnamon, tomato sauce, and vinegar. Place applesauce on top of the chops, and pour tomato mixture over. Cover and cook on low for 4 to 6 hours. Makes 6 servings.

Chutney Ham

3 pounds boneless ham, cooked
¼ teaspoon pepper
2 (6-ounce) jars mango chutney
1 onion, chopped
1 tablespoon balsamic vinegar

Place ham in a slow cooker. Mix remaining ingredients in a medium bowl, and pour over the ham. Cover and cook on low for 6 to 8 hours, until thoroughly heated. Makes 8 servings.

HONEY BARBECUE RIBS

1 (3-pound) boneless pork roast
1 (16-ounce) bag baby carrots
½ cup barbecue sauce
¼ cup honey
½ teaspoon salt
¼ teaspoon pepper

Place pork and carrots in a 3 to 4-quart slow cooker. Combine barbecue sauce, honey, salt, and pepper in a small bowl, and pour over ingredients in slow cooker. Cover and cook on low for 8 to 10 hours, or until pork is thoroughly cooked. Makes 6 servings.

APPLEY KIELBASA

2 pounds kielbasa sausage, cut into 1-inch pieces
¾ cup brown sugar
1 cup chunky applesauce
2 garlic cloves, minced

Combine sausage with brown sugar and applesauce in a 3-quart slow cooker. Cover and cook on low for 6 to 8 hours until thoroughly heated. Makes 12 servings.

SWEET AND SPICY KIELBASA

1 cup brown sugar
1 tablespoon spicy mustard
2 pounds kielbasa sausage, cut into 1-inch pieces

Combine brown sugar and mustard in slow cooker; add kielbasa and stir evenly to coat. Cover and cook on low 2½ to 3 hours, stirring occasionally, until kielbasa is thoroughly heated. Makes 12 servings.

TENDER PORK ROAST

1 (3 to 4-pound) pork roast
½ cup apple juice
1 teaspoon dry mustard
1 teaspoon dried basil
½ teaspoon onion powder
½ cup soy sauce

Place roast in a slow cooker. Combine remaining ingredients, and pour over roast. Cover and cook on low for 8 hours. Makes 6 to 8 servings.

CHEESY TORTELLINI

1 pound Italian sausage
1 (26-ounce) jar pasta sauce
1 (14-ounce) can diced tomatoes with Italian seasonings, undrained
1 (9-ounce) package refrigerated cheese tortellini
1 cup mozzarella or Parmesan cheese, shredded

Cook sausage in heavy skillet over medium heat until browned, about 10 minutes. Stir sausage frequently to break up as it cooks. Drain well and place in a 4 to 5-quart slow cooker. Add pasta sauce and tomatoes, and stir well. Cover and cook on low 7 to 8 hours. Then stir in tortellini, cover again and cook on low for 30 to 40 minutes, until pasta is tender and heated. Sprinkle with cheese, and let stand 5 minutes before serving. Makes 4 servings.

ITALIAN PORK CHOPS

6 (1-inch thick) boneless pork loin chops
Salt and pepper to taste
1 tablespoon olive oil
1 onion, chopped
2 cups chunky pasta sauce
1 cup shredded mozzarella cheese

Trim any excess fat from pork chops and sprinkle with salt and pepper. Cook chops in olive oil in a heavy skillet over medium heat until browned, about 5 minutes, turning once during cooking. Place in a 3 to 4-quart slow cooker. Top with onion and pasta sauce. Cover and cook on low for 4 to 6 hours, until pork is tender and thoroughly cooked. Top with cheese just before serving. Makes 6 servings.

BACON ONION DIP

6 slices bacon, finely chopped
1 (8-ounce) package light cream cheese, softened
1 cup light sour cream
½ cup shredded Cheddar cheese
2 green onions, finely chopped
Potato chips or crackers

In a nonstick skillet over medium-high heat, cook bacon 7 to 8 minutes or until crisp. Transfer to a paper towel-lined plate to drain. Place all ingredients, except bacon, in a slow cooker. Crumble the bacon and sprinkle on top. Cover and cook on high for 1 hour, or until cheese is melted (do not stir). Reduce heat to low. Serve with potato chips or crackers. Makes about 8 servings.

Honey Mustard Pork Roast

1 onion, chopped
2 apples, peeled, cored, and cut into 1-inch pieces
3 tablespoons honey mustard
¼ teaspoon salt
¼ teaspoon pepper
1 (2-pound) boneless pork roast
1 tablespoon cornstarch
2 tablespoons water

Peel apples and cut into 1-inch pieces. In a 4 to 6-quart slow cooker, mix onion and apples. Spread honey mustard over pork roast and sprinkle with salt and pepper. Place coated roast on top of onions and apples. Cover and cook on low for 7 to 8 hours.

Remove roast and cover with foil to keep warm. Combine cornstarch and water in a medium saucepan, and blend with wire whisk. Add juices, apples, and onions from slow cooker to saucepan, and cook over medium heat until mixture boils and thickens, stirring frequently. Serve roast with sauce. Makes 6 servings.

Smoked Sausage

1 (10½-ounce) can beef broth
1 cup water
⅛ teaspoon pepper
2 medium onions, quartered
6 carrots, julienned
1½ cups celery, diced
2 potatoes, pared and diced
1 pound smoked sausage

Combine broth, water, and all vegetables except potatoes in a slow cooker. Cover and cook for 1 hour on low. Add potatoes. Cover and cook for 6 hours on low. Add sausage and cook for an additional hour. Makes 4 servings.

RED BEANS AND RICE

1 pound dried red kidney beans, soaked overnight and drained
1 cup ham, cut into pieces
1 onion, chopped
1 tablespoon Worcestershire sauce
1 teaspoon hot sauce
2 bay leaves
2 garlic cloves, minced
4 tablespoon parsley
4 cups water
3 cups rice, cooked and hot

Combine all ingredients in a slow cooker. Cover and cook on low for 8 hours, or until beans are tender. Serve over rice. Makes 6 servings.

CHICKEN STROGANOFF

1 cup light sour cream
1 tablespoon flour
1 (1-ounce) package chicken gravy mix
1 cup water
1 pound boneless, skinless chicken breasts
1 (16-ounce) bag frozen mixed vegetables, thawed

In a 3 to 4-quart slow cooker, mix sour cream, flour, gravy mix, and water; stir with wire whisk until well blended. Cut chicken breasts into 1-inch pieces, and add to slow cooker. Stir in vegetables and cover. Cook on low for 4 hours, until chicken is tender. Turn heat to high and cook for 1 hour longer, until sauce is thickened and chicken is thoroughly cooked. Makes 4 servings.

SOUTH OF THE BORDER CHICKEN

4 boneless chicken breast halves
1 (10-ounce) can broccoli cheese soup
⅓ cup evaporated milk
4 cups rice, cooked and hot
Salsa
Sour cream
1 small avocado, sliced (optional)

Place chicken in bottom of a slow cooker and cover with soup and milk. Cover and cook on low for 7 to 8 hours. Serve with rice. Top with salsa, sour cream, and avocado. Makes 4 servings.

WILD RICE-STUFFED TURKEY

1½ cups wild rice
1 onion, finely chopped
½ cup dried cranberries
2 apples, chopped
3 cups water
1 (4 to 5-pound) boneless whole turkey breast, thawed if frozen

Combine rice, onion, dried cranberries, and apples; place in bottom of a 4 to 5-quart slow cooker. Pour water over, making sure all wild rice is submerged. Place turkey on top of rice mixture.

Cover and cook on low for 8 to 9 hours, or until turkey is thoroughly cooked and reaches 180° on a meat thermometer, and wild rice is tender. Makes 10 servings.

Lemon Pepper Chicken №2

4 boneless, skinless chicken breasts
1 teaspoon black pepper
Juice of half of a lemon

Place chicken in a slow cooker. Squeeze lemon juice over the chicken. Sprinkle with pepper. Cover and cook on low for 6 to 8 hours. Add more lemon juice if needed. Makes 4 servings.

Brown Sugar Chicken

2 pounds boneless chicken breasts
1 cup packed brown sugar
⅔ cup vinegar
¼ cup lemon-lime soda
2 tablespoons garlic, minced
2 tablespoons soy sauce
1 teaspoon black pepper

Place chicken pieces in a slow cooker. Combine remaining ingredients, and pour over the top of chicken. Cover and cook on low for 6 to 8 hours. Serve with rice. Makes 4 servings.

GARLIC-PEPPER CHICKEN

4 chicken leg quarters
2 tablespoons garlic, minced
2 teaspoons pepper
1 can zucchini with tomato sauce
½ cup shredded mozzarella cheese

Place chicken in a slow cooker. Sprinkle with garlic and pepper. Pour zucchini with tomato sauce over chicken. Cook for 6 hours on high. Sprinkle with cheese, and cook until cheese melts, about 30 minutes. Makes 4 servings.

CURRIED CHICKEN

3 to 4 chicken breasts
½ cup honey
½ cup Dijon-style mustard
2 tablespoons soy sauce
¼ teaspoon curry powder

Place all ingredients in a slow cooker. Cover and cook on low for 8 hours. Makes 3 to 4 servings.

SUNSHINE CHICKEN

8 skinless, boneless chicken breasts
1 cup barbecue sauce
1 cup orange juice

Place chicken breasts in a slow cooker. Combine barbecue sauce with orange juice. Pour over the chicken breasts. Cover and cook on low for 8 hours. Makes 8 servings.

SMOTHERED CHICKEN AND VEGETABLES

3 carrots, sliced
3 celery stalks, sliced
1 large onion, cut into thin wedges
3 cups chicken, cooked and cubed
1 (10¾-ounce) can cream of celery soup
¾ cup chicken broth

Place vegetables in the bottom of a slow cooker. Top with chicken. Add soup and broth. Cover and cook for 4 to 6 hours on low. Makes 3 to 4 servings.

APRICOT CHICKEN

4 boneless, skinless chicken breasts
1 tablespoon freshly grated ginger root
½ cup apricot preserves
⅓ cup Italian salad dressing

Combine all ingredients in a large zip-lock bag. Shake bag to mix; refrigerate at least 2 hours, up to 24 hours. When ready to cook, place chicken in a baking dish; reserve marinade. Cover and cook on low for 6 to 8 hours, until chicken is thoroughly cooked, basting occasionally with marinade. Discard remaining marinade. Makes 4 servings.

CHICKEN TACOS

1 fryer chicken, skinned if desired
1 (18-ounce) jar salsa
2 tablespoons taco seasoning mix
Taco shells

Place chicken in a 3 to 4-quart slow cooker. In a medium bowl, combine salsa and taco seasoning, and mix to blend. Pour over top of chicken, Cover and cook on low for 6 to 8 hours until chicken is tender and thoroughly cooked.

Remove skin and bones from chicken. Shred meat, and stir back into liquid in slow cooker. Cook 20 to 30 minutes longer until thoroughly heated. Serve in taco shells. Makes 4 to 6 servings.

TURKEY TERIYAKI SANDWICH

1½ pounds boneless, skinless turkey thighs
½ cup teriyaki sauce
3 tablespoons orange marmalade
¼ teaspoon pepper
Hoagie buns

Combine all ingredients in a 3 to 4-quart slow cooker. Cover and cook on low for 9 to 10 hours. Remove turkey from slow cooker, shred turkey using two forks, and return to slow cooker. Cook on high for 10 to 15 minutes, until sauce is thickened. Serve on hoagie buns. Makes 4 to 6 servings.

Southwest Turkey Loaf

⅔ **cup salsa**
1 egg, beaten
¼ **teaspoon pepper**
¼ **teaspoon salt**
1¼ **pounds ground turkey**

In a medium bowl, combine salsa, egg, pepper, and salt, and mix well. Add ground turkey and combine. Form into a 6-inch-round loaf, and place loaf on a rack or balled-up foil in a 3-quart slow cooker. Cover and cook on low for 4 to 5 hours, until turkey is thoroughly cooked. Makes 4 to 6 servings.

Turkey Dijon

1 fresh bone-in turkey breast
3 tablespoons Dijon mustard
1 teaspoon salt
⅛ **teaspoon pepper**
⅔ **cup 100% fruit juice**

Put turkey breast, skin side up, in a 3 to 4-quart slow cooker. Spread with Dijon mustard and season with salt and pepper to taste. Pour juice over the turkey. Cover and cook on low 8 to 9 hours, until turkey is tender and thoroughly cooked. Makes 4 to 6 servings.

FAKE CHICKEN CORDON BLEU

6 boneless, skinless chicken breasts
6 pieces Swiss cheese
1 (10¾-ounce) can cream of mushroom soup with roasted garlic
3 tablespoons water
¼ teaspoon pepper

Flatten each chicken breast with wooden mallet or rolling pin. Place a piece of cheese in the center of each. Fold up and secure with toothpicks. Place in a slow cooker. Combine remaining ingredients, and pour over chicken bundles, making sure pieces are fully covered. Cover and cook on low 6 to 7 hours, until chicken is thoroughly cooked. Makes 6 servings.

CHEESY CHICKEN

6 boneless, skinless chicken breasts
1 (10¾-ounce) can cream of chicken soup
1 (10¾-ounce) can fiesta cheese soup
3 cups rice or noodles, cooked and hot

Place chicken breasts in a 3½ to 4-quart slow cooker. Pour the undiluted soups over the chicken, and stir to combine. Cover and cook on low 6 to 8 hours, until chicken is tender and thoroughly cooked. Serve over rice or noodles. Makes 6 servings.

THREE-INGREDIENT TURKEY

1 frozen turkey breast, unthawed
1 (16-ounce) can cranberry sauce
1 (1½-ounce) package dry onion soup mix

Put all ingredients into a 5 to 6-quart slow cooker, cover, and cook for 2 hours on high. Then reduce heat to low, and continue cooking for 4 to 5 hours, until turkey registers 180° on an instant meat thermometer. Slice turkey breast, and serve with sauce. Makes 8 servings.

PEANUT CHICKEN

3½ pounds boneless, skinless chicken breasts
⅓ cup peanut butter
2 tablespoons low-sodium soy sauce
3 tablespoons orange juice
⅛ teaspoon pepper
4 cups rice or noodles, cooked and hot

Combine all ingredients in a slow cooker; mix well. Cover and cook on low for 6 to 8 hours or until chicken is tender and thoroughly cooked. Serve with rice or noodles. Makes 8 servings.

CHICKEN COLA

1 whole chicken
1 cup ketchup
1 cup cola beverage

Place whole chicken in a slow cooker on low heat. Pour ketchup and cola over chicken. Cook 9 hours. Makes 4 to 6 servings.

SWEET-AND-SOUR CHICKEN №2

2 pounds boneless, skinless chicken thighs
1 (26-ounce) jar sweet-and-sour simmer sauce
1 (16-ounce) package frozen broccoli, carrots, and peppers,
thawed and drained

Cut chicken thighs into 1½-inch pieces. Mix with simmer sauce in slow cooker. Cover and cook on low for 8 to 10 hours, or until chicken is tender and no longer pink. Ten minutes before serving, stir in vegetables. Cover, increase heat to high, and cook for 10 to 15 minutes, or until vegetables are crisp and tender. Makes 4 to 6 servings.

CHICKEN WINGS

5 pounds chicken wings, each wing cut into 3 pieces
2 cups brown sugar
½ cup mustard
½ cup ketchup
4 tablespoons Worcestershire sauce

Put chicken in a slow cooker. Combine remaining ingredients, and pour over chicken. Cook on low for 6 to 8 hours. Makes 10 servings.

ITALIAN CHICKEN

1½ pounds boneless, skinless chicken breasts
½ cup zesty Italian salad dressing
⅛ teaspoon pepper
4 garlic cloves, minced
4 potatoes, cubed

Combine all ingredients in a 3 to 4-quart slow cooker. Cover and cook on low for 6 to 8 hours, until chicken is thoroughly cooked and potatoes are tender. Makes 4 servings.

Chicken à la Marengo

1 whole chicken, cut up
2 (1-ounce) packages spaghetti sauce mix
1 cup chicken stock
2 fresh tomatoes, quartered
4 ounces fresh mushrooms, sliced

Place chicken parts in bottom of a slow cooker. Combine dry spaghetti sauce packets with stock; pour over chicken. Cover and cook on low 6 to 7 hours. Turn control to high. Add tomatoes and mushrooms. Cover and cook on high for 30 to 40 minutes or until tomatoes are done. Makes 4 to 5 servings.

Enchilada Dip

2 pounds boneless, skinless chicken thighs
1 (10-ounce) can enchilada sauce
2 (8-ounce) packages cream cheese, cut into cubed and softened
4 cups pepper jack cheese, shredded

Combine chicken and enchilada sauce in a 3 to 4-quart slow cooker. Cover and cook on low for 8 to 10 hours, or until chicken is thoroughly cooked. Using two forks, shred chicken in the sauce. Stir cheeses into the slow cooker; mix well. Cover and cook on low for 30 minutes, stirring twice, until mixture is blended and cheese is melted. Makes 6 to 8 servings.

ORANGE-GLAZED CHICKEN

½ cup orange marmalade
⅓ cup Russian dressing
½ package dry onion soup mix
6 frozen chicken breasts, unthawed

Mix the first 3 ingredients together. Place chicken in slow cooker, and cover with marmalade mixture. Cover and cook on low 6 to 8 hours. Makes 6 servings.

ALOHA CHICKEN

⅓ cup steak sauce
2 tablespoons honey
1 (8-ounce) can pineapple chunks, drained, reserving
  2 tablespoons juice
1 medium green bell pepper, chopped
4 skinless, boneless chicken breasts

Mix steak sauce with honey and reserved pineapple juice. Place bell peppers in bottom of a slow cooker. Add chicken breasts on top. Pour honey mixture over top of chicken breasts. Cover and cook on low for 4 to 6 hours. Add pineapple chunks, and cook an additional 30 to 60 minutes. Makes 4 servings.

SOUR CREAM AND BACON CHICKEN

8 bacon slices
8 boneless, skinless chicken breasts
2 (10¾-ounce) cans cream of mushroom soup with roasted garlic
1 cup sour cream
½ cup flour

Wrap one slice of bacon around each boneless chicken breast and place in a 3 to 4-quart slow cooker. In medium bowl, combine condensed soups, sour cream, and flour, and mix with wire whisk to blend. Pour over chicken. Cover and cook on low for 6 to 8 hours until chicken and bacon are thoroughly cooked. Makes 8 servings.

CREAMY ITALIAN CHICKEN

2 pounds boneless, skinless chicken breasts
¼ cup butter, melted
1 (8-ounce) container cream cheese with chives, softened
1 (10¾-ounce) can condensed golden cream of mushroom soup
1 (7-ounce) package Italian dressing mix
½ cup water
2 cups rice or noodles, cooked and hot

Cut chicken breasts into strips, and place into a 3 to 4-quart slow cooker. In a medium bowl, combine melted butter, softened cream cheese, soup, Italian dressing mix, and water, and stir until blended. Pour over chicken. Cover and cook on low for 6 to 8 hours. Stir well, and serve over pasta or rice. Makes 4 to 6 servings.

CHICKEN TORTILLAS

1 whole chicken, cooked and removed from bone
1 (10¾-ounce) can cream of chicken soup
½ cup green chili salsa
2 tablespoons quick-cooking tapioca
12 corn tortillas
1 medium onion, chopped
1½ cups Monterey Jack cheese, grated
Black olives

Tear chicken into bite-size pieces, and mix with soup, chili, salsa, and tapioca. Line bottom of a slow cooker with 3 corn tortillas, torn into bite-size pieces. Add ⅓ of the chicken mixture. Sprinkle with ⅓ of the onion and ⅓ of the grated cheese. Repeat layers of tortillas topped with chicken mixture, onions, and cheese. Cover and cook on low 6 to 8 hours. Garnish with sliced black olives. Makes 12 servings.

CHICKEN AND DUMPLINGS №2

4 boneless, skinless chicken breasts, cut into small chunks
2 (10¾-ounce) cans cream of chicken soup
¼ cup onion, finely diced
2 cups water
1 chicken bouillon cube
2 (10-ounce) packages refrigerated biscuits

Combine all ingredients, except biscuits, in slow cooker. Cover and cook on low for 5 to 6 hours. Thirty minutes before serving, tear biscuit dough into 1-inch pieces. Add to slow cooker, stirring gently. Cover and cook on high for an additional 30 minutes, or until biscuits are cooked through. Makes 4 to 6 servings.

CHICKEN DIVAN

1 (10-ounce) package frozen broccoli spears
2 to 3 boneless, skinless chicken breasts
1 (10¾-ounce) can cream of chicken soup
1¼ cups mayonnaise
1 teaspoon lemon juice

Place broccoli in the bottom of a slow cooker. Put chicken on top of broccoli. Mix together soup, mayonnaise, and lemon juice. Pour over chicken, mixing slightly. Cover and cook on low for 8 hours. Makes 2 to 3 servings.

CHICKEN CASSEROLE №2

1½ pounds boneless, skinless chicken breasts
6 carrots, sliced
1 (8-ounce) can green beans
2 (10¾-ounce) cans cream of mushroom soup
2 tablespoons mayonnaise
½ cup shredded Cheddar cheese

Place chicken in bottom of a slow cooker. Mix carrots, green beans, mushroom soup, and mayonnaise. Pour over chicken. Cover and cook for 8 to 10 hours on low. Sprinkle with Cheddar cheese before serving. Makes 6 to 8 servings.

CREAMY CHICKEN

6 to 8 chicken pieces
1 cup evaporated milk
1 (10¾-ounce) can cream of mushroom soup
Salt and pepper to taste
Paprika

Place chicken in a slow cooker. Mix together evaporated milk and soup. Pour over chicken. Sprinkle with salt, pepper, and paprika. Cover and cook on low for 8 hours. Makes 6 to 8 servings.

MAPLE-GLAZED TURKEY BREAST

1 (6-ounce) package long-grain and wild rice mix
1¼ cups water
2 pounds boneless turkey breast, thawed if frozen
1 onion, chopped
¼ cup maple syrup
¼ teaspoon cinnamon
½ teaspoon salt
⅛ teaspoon white pepper

Combine rice and its seasoning mix packet with water in a 3 to 4-quart slow cooker. Place turkey breast on top, sprinkle with onions, and drizzle with maple syrup. Sprinkle with cinnamon, salt, and pepper. Cover and cook on low for 5 to 6 hours, until turkey is thoroughly cooked and registers 180° on a meat thermometer. Makes 4 servings.

TURKEY CASSOULET

1½ cups dried Great Northern beans, soaked overnight and drained
1 pound turkey breast tenderloin
2 onions, chopped
1 (14-ounce) can chicken broth
1½ cups water
1 (14-ounce) can diced tomatoes, undrained
⅛ teaspoon white pepper
¼ teaspoon salt
½ teaspoon dried thyme

Place beans in a 3 to 4-quart slow cooker. Cut turkey into 1-inch pieces, and place in slow cooker along with onions, chicken broth, and water. Cover and cook on low for 8 to 10 hours. Then stir in tomatoes, pepper, salt, and thyme. Cover again and cook on low for 30 minutes until hot. Makes 6 servings.

CARAMELIZED ONIONS

6 large onions
2 tablespoons olive oil

Peel the onions, and cut them into ¼-inch slices. Place the onions in the slow cooker and sprinkle with oil. Cover and cook 8 to 10 hours, until the onions caramelize. Makes 3 cups.

CHILI DIP

1 bottle picante sauce
2 (16-ounce) cans refried beans
1 pint sour cream
½ teaspoon chili powder
1 pound ground beef, browned
1 medium onion, chopped
Salt and pepper to taste
1 cup shredded Cheddar cheese
1 jalapeño pepper, seeded and chopped
Raw vegetables or chips

Combine all ingredients in a slow cooker. Cover and cook 4 to 6 hours on low. Serve with raw vegetables or chips. Makes 12 servings.

APPLE CIDER

1 gallon apple cider
12 whole cloves
3 (3-inch) cinnamon sticks
2 whole nutmegs
2 chunks crystallized ginger

Place all of the ingredients into a slow cooker. Heat on high for 2 hours. Reduce to low to keep warm until ready to serve. Makes 20 servings.

GRANOLA

5 cups rolled oats (not instant or quick)
½ cup honey
¼ cup vegetable oil
Raisins, coconut, nuts, seeds (optional)

Place oats, honey, and oil in a slow cooker. Mix well. Cook on low, stirring every 30 minutes or so until dry and golden, about 3 hours, adding optional ingredients during the last hour of cooking. Keep lid propped open while cooking. Cool and store in airtight container. Makes about 5 to 6 cups.

MULLED CRANBERRY CIDER

Juice and zest of 1 orange
4¼ cups cranberry juice
¼ cup brown sugar
1 cinnamon stick
3 star anise
1 teaspoon whole cloves

Combine orange juice, cranberry juice, and brown sugar in a slow cooker. Combine orange zest, cinnamon, star anise, and cloves in the center of a double-thick piece of cheesecloth; bring corners together and tie with clean kitchen string. Add this bag to slow cooker. Cover and cook on low 5 to 6 hours or on high about 3 hours. Remove spice bag before serving. Makes about 5 cups.

Vegetarian Enchilada Casserole

3⅓ cups canned crushed tomatoes, in tomato purée
1⅔ cups chunky salsa
1 (6-ounce) can tomato paste
2 (16-ounce) cans black beans, rinsed and drained
1 pound corn kernels, thawed if frozen
1 (4-ounce) can diced mild green chilies, drained
1½ tablespoons ground cumin
½ teaspoon garlic powder
5 corn tortillas
¼ cup olive, sliced and drained

Combine first 8 ingredients in a bowl. Mix thoroughly. Pour about 1 cup of mixture into the bottom of a slow cooker on low heat. Spread evenly and top with 1½ tortillas, cutting to fit pot. Spread ⅓ of remaining tomato mixture over top. Repeat layering process, ending with tomato mixture. Spread top evenly. Sprinkle with olives. Cover and cook about 5 hours. Serve hot. Makes 8 servings.

Dinner Party Stew

1 pound lean beef chuck, cut into 1½ to 2-inch cubes
3 medium onions, sliced
½ cup tomato juice
1¾ cups beef broth
1 tablespoon sugar
1 small can mushrooms
½ cup sour cream

Place all ingredients except sour cream in a slow cooker. Cover and cook on low for 8 to 10 hours. Thirty minutes before serving, stir in sour cream. Makes 4 servings.

HAMBURGER STEW

1 (10-ounce) package frozen mixed vegetables
1 pound lean ground beef or turkey
½ cup chopped onion
1 (1-ounce) package beef stew seasoning mix
2 tablespoons all-purpose flour
¾ cup water
¼ cup beef broth or apple juice
1 (15-ounce) can small whole potatoes, drained and halved

Place all ingredients in a slow cooker. Cover and cook on high for 4 to 6 hours or on low 6 to 8 hours. Makes 4 servings.

CHICKEN MUSHROOM STEW

6 boneless, skinless chicken breasts
2 tablespoons cooking oil
1 cup fresh mushrooms, sliced
1 medium onion, sliced
3 cups zucchini, diced
1 cup green bell pepper, diced
4 garlic cloves, minced
3 medium tomatoes, diced
1 (6-ounce) can tomato paste
¾ cup water
2 teaspoons salt
1 teaspoon each dried thyme, oregano, marjoram, and basil

Place ingredients in a slow cooker in the order listed. Cover and cook on low for 6 to 8 hours. Makes 6 servings.

Prospector's Stew

2 to 3 large potatoes, peeled and cut into bite-size pieces
1 pound kielbasa, sliced
2 (15-ounce) cans green beans, drained
1 small onion, quartered
1 garlic clove, minced
2 cans cream of mushroom soup
1 cup shredded Cheddar cheese

Place all ingredients except cheese in a slow cooker. Cover and cook on low for 6 to 10 hours. Sprinkle with cheddar cheese before serving. Makes 4 to 6 servings.

Best Bean Chili

1 pound lean ground beef
1½ cups onions, chopped
1 cup green bell pepper, chopped
1 teaspoon minced garlic
2½ tablespoons chili powder
1½ teaspoons ground cumin
1 (16-ounce) can red kidney beans
1 (16-ounce) can pinto beans
2¼ pounds tomatoes, diced
2 tablespoons brown sugar
1 tablespoon unsweetened cocoa

Combine all ingredients in a slow cooker. Cover and cook on low 5 to 6 hours. Makes 6 servings.

BLACK BEAN CHILI

1 (1-pound) pork tenderloin, cubed
2 cups chunky salsa
1 (45-ounce) can black beans, rinsed and drained
½ cup chicken broth
1 red bell pepper, chopped
1 onion, chopped
1 teaspoon cumin
2 teaspoons chili powder
1 teaspoon dried oregano
¼ cup sour cream

Place tenderloin in a slow cooker. Add remaining ingredients except sour cream. Cover and cook on low for 8 hours. Serve with sour cream. Makes 4 servings.

BEEF STEW WITH MUSHROOMS

1½ pounds beef stew meat
1 (10¾-ounce) can cream of mushroom soup
1 (4-ounce) can sliced mushrooms, drained
½ cup beef broth
1 (1½-ounce) package dry onion soup mix

Combine all the ingredients in a slow cooker. Cover and cook for 8 to 10 hours on low or 4 to 6 hours on high. Makes 4 servings.

SOUTHWESTERN BEEF SOUP

1 pound boneless beef round, cut into thin strips
1 tablespoon vegetable oil
1 onion, chopped
2 garlic cloves, finely chopped
1 (14-ounce) can diced tomatoes
1 cup whole kernel corn, frozen
1 (4-ounce) can diced green chiles
2 tablespoons fresh cilantro, chopped
1 cup beef broth
½ teaspoon ground cumin
2 corn tortillas, in strips
2 tablespoons green onion, chopped

Stir-fry beef in hot oil, 2 to 3 minutes. Place all ingredients except tortilla strips and green onion into a slow cooker. Cover and cook for 6 to 8 hours on low. Place tortilla strips in soup bowls, cover with soup. Sprinkle with green onion. Makes 4 servings.

HAM AND LENTIL STEW

3 cups ham, cooked and chopped
3 cups carrots, chopped
2 cups dried lentils, sorted and rinsed
2 onions, chopped
2 (10-ounce) cans chicken broth
4 cups water

Combine all ingredients in a 3 to 4-quart slow cooker, and mix to combine. Cover and cook on low for 7 to 9 hours. Makes 4 to 6 servings.

FRENCH ONION SOUP №2

3 large onions, sliced
2 tablespoons butter or margarine
4 cups water
6 beef bouillon cubes
1 teaspoon Worcestershire sauce
½ teaspoon paprika
Dash of pepper
French bread
Parmesan cheese, grated

In a large frying pan, cook onions in butter until golden. Place the onion mixture in a slow cooker. Add water, bouillon cubes, Worcestershire sauce, paprika, and pepper. Cover and cook on low for 4 to 6 hours or on high for 1½ to 2 hours. Serve with a slice of toasted French bread sprinkled with cheese. Makes 4 to 6 servings.

DOUBLE CORN STEW

3 cups frozen corn
1 (14-ounce) can creamed corn
1 onion, chopped
1 (14-ounce) can chicken broth
⅛ teaspoon pepper

Combine all ingredients in a 3 to 4-quart slow cooker, and stir gently to mix. Cover and cook on low for 5 to 6 hours, or until corn is tender. Makes 4 servings.

IRISH STEW

1 cup chicken broth
1 teaspoon dried marjoram
1 teaspoon dried parsley
¾ teaspoon salt
½ teaspoon garlic powder
¼ teaspoon pepper
1¼ pounds white potatoes, peeled and cut into 1-inch pieces
1 pound lean lamb stew meat, cubed
1 (8-ounce) package frozen cut green beans
2 small leeks, cut into slices
1½ cups carrots, coarsely chopped

Mix together broth, marjoram, parsley, salt, garlic powder, and pepper in a slow cooker. Add potatoes, lamb, green beans, leeks, and carrots. Cover and cook on low for 7 to 9 hours. Makes 4 to 6 servings.

CHICKEN CHILI

2 pounds boneless, skinless chicken thighs
3 (14-ounce) cans diced tomatoes with chiles and garlic
1 (1-ounce) package taco seasoning mix
2 (15-ounce) cans white beans, drained and rinsed

Combine all ingredients in a 4 to 5-quart slow cooker. Cover and cook on low for 7 to 9 hours, or until chicken is tender. Stir well so that the chicken breaks into small pieces. Makes 6 servings.

FIREHOUSE CHILI

3 pounds lean beef, cut into ¼-inch pieces
2 tablespoons onion powder
1 teaspoon garlic powder
2 (8-ounce) cans tomato sauce
4 tablespoons chili powder
2 tablespoons cumin
1 tablespoon paprika
¼ teaspoon ground oregano
½ teaspoon cayenne pepper
½ teaspoon white pepper
½ teaspoon onion powder
1 tablespoon garlic powder
½ teaspoon salt

Place first six ingredients in a slow cooker. Cover and cook on high 1 hour. Pour spices over top of beef. Cover and cook on low for 4 to 6 hours. Makes 6 to 8 servings.

SUPER BOWL MEATBALLS

1 (16-ounce) jar cheese sauce (may use mild nacho cheese sauce)
1 (1-ounce) package taco seasoning mix
1 (14-ounce) can diced tomatoes
1 (1-pound) package frozen cooked meatballs (plain, not Italian)

Mix cheese, taco seasoning, and tomatoes in a large bowl. Put meatballs in slow cooker, and cover with cheese mixture. Cover and cook on high for 1½ to 2 hours. Makes 4 servings.

Vegetarian Chili

2 large onions, diced
2 tablespoons olive oil
3 garlic cloves, minced
2 teaspoons cumin
2 teaspoons cayenne pepper
1 red bell pepper, chopped
1 green bell pepper, chopped
3 (14-ounce) cans diced tomatoes, undrained
1 tablespoon chili powder
½ teaspoon crushed cayenne pepper flakes
1 (10-ounce) package frozen corn
2 (15-ounce) cans black beans, drained and rinsed
1 cup picante sauce

In a heavy skillet, sauté onions in the olive oil until tender, stirring frequently. Add garlic and cook 2 minutes longer. Add cumin and cayenne pepper. Cook for 2 minutes longer. Mix all ingredients into a 4 to 5 quart slow cooker. Cover and cook on low about 10 hours. Makes 8 to 10 servings.

DESSERTS

Double Chocolate Cake

1 cup butter, softened
2 cups sugar
1 large can chocolate syrup
6 chocolate bars without nuts, chopped
4 eggs
2½ cups flour
½ teaspoon baking soda
½ teaspoon salt
1 cup buttermilk

Cream butter and sugar until light and fluffy; beat in chocolate syrup and stir in chopped candy bars. Add eggs, beating well. Whisk together flour, baking soda, and salt; add to chocolate mixture alternately with buttermilk. Pour into a greased tube pan. Bake at 350° for about 1 hour. Makes about 16 servings.

Pound Cake

1½ cups butter, softened
1 (16-ounce) box powdered sugar
6 eggs
3 cups flour
1 teaspoon vanilla extract
½ teaspoon lemon extract
½ teaspoon almond extract

Cream butter and powdered sugar until light and fluffy. Alternately add eggs, one at a time, and flour, ½ cup at a time. Stir extracts into batter, and pour into a greased tube pan. Bake at 325° for about 1 hour. Makes about 16 servings.

Sour Cream Pound Cake

1 cup butter, softened
3 cups sugar
6 eggs
1 cup sour cream
3 cups flour
¼ teaspoon baking soda
1 teaspoon vanilla extract

Cream butter and sugar until light and fluffy. Add eggs, beating well. Stir in sour cream. Combine flour and baking soda; gradually add to butter mixture. Stir in vanilla extract. Pour into a greased tube pan. Bake at 325° for about 1 hour. Makes 16 servings.

Easy Coconut Cake

1 (18-ounce) package yellow cake mix
1 cup hot milk
1 container whipped cream topping
1 package flaked sweetened coconut

Prepare cake mix according to package directions for sheet cake; punch holes in top of baked cake with a fork. Pour hot milk over cake and let cool. Cover completely with whipped cream topping, and sprinkle with coconut. Makes about 12 servings.

MOCHA ANGEL FOOD TORTE

1 cup whipping cream
1 cup milk
2 teaspoons instant coffee
1 (3-ounce) package chocolate pudding mix
1 angel food cake, cut horizontally into 3 layers

Combine cream, milk, instant coffee, and pudding mix, beating until thick. Spread between layers of angel food cake and on top. Makes about 14 servings.

DUMP CAKE

1 (20-ounce) can crushed pineapple
1 cup coconut, grated
1 (18-ounce) box yellow cake mix
1 cup nuts, chopped
1 cup butter, cubed

Layer ingredients in order listed in a shallow 3-quart baking dish. Bake at 350° for about 45 minutes. Makes 8 servings.

CARAMEL CAKE

1 (16-ounce) package German chocolate cake mix
1 (7-ounce) can sweetened condensed milk
½ jar caramel ice cream sauce
Whipped cream topping
6 to 8 Skor or Heath candy bars, crushed

Prepare cake according to instructions on package. When done and still hot, poke pencil size holes in cake. Pour condensed milk over cake. Next, pour caramel sauce over cake. Frost with whipped cream topping. Top with crushed candy bars. Makes 12 servings.

CREAM CHEESE PECAN CAKE

1 (18-ounce) box pound cake mix
½ cup butter, softened
4 eggs
1 (8-ounce) package cream cheese, softened
1 box powdered sugar
1 cup pecans, chopped

Combine pound cake mix, butter, and 2 eggs, mixing well. Spread in greased 3-quart baking dish. Combine remaining 2 eggs, cream cheese, and powdered sugar, and spread over batter. Sprinkle with pecans. Bake at 350° for about 40 minutes. Makes about 20 servings.

CINNAMON CAKE

¾ cup sugar
¼ cup shortening
1 egg
½ cup milk
1 teaspoon vanilla extract
1 cup flour
1½ teaspoons baking powder
¼ teaspoon salt
1 tablespoon butter, melted
3 tablespoons powdered sugar
1 teaspoon cinnamon

Cream sugar and shortening until light and fluffy; beat in egg, milk, and vanilla extract. Add flour, baking powder, and salt, beating until smooth. Pour into a greased 8-inch-square pan. Bake at 375° for about 25 minutes. Brush with melted butter. Combine powdered sugar and cinnamon, and sprinkle over top. Makes about 6 servings.

LEMON-LIME CAKE

1 cup shortening
½ cup butter, softened
2 cups sugar
5 eggs
2 teaspoons coconut extract
1 teaspoon lemon extract
1 teaspoon vanilla extract
3 cups flour
1 cup lemon-lime soda

Cream shortening and butter with sugar until light and fluffy. Add eggs and extracts, beating well. Alternately add flour and soda, mixing well. Pour into greased tube pan. Bake at 325° for about 1 hour. Makes about 16 servings.

BITTERSWEET CHOCOLATE CUPCAKES

4 squares bittersweet chocolate
1 cup butter
1½ cups pecans, chopped
4 eggs, beaten
1¾ cups sugar
1 cup flour
2 tablespoons vegetable oil
2 teaspoons vanilla

Melt chocolate and butter over low heat, stirring until smooth; add pecans and stir to coat. Combine eggs, sugar, flour, oil, and vanilla, whisking until just combined. Fold in chocolate and pecans. Spoon batter into lined muffin cups. Bake at 325° for about 20 minutes. Makes about 18 cupcakes.

FASTEST CHEESECAKE

1 (8-ounce) package cream cheese, softened
1 (14-ounce) can sweetened condensed milk
1 (9-inch) graham cracker crust

In a medium bowl, beat cream cheese until smooth and fluffy. Add sweetened condensed milk, and mix until very well combined. Pour into graham cracker crust and chill. Makes 8 servings.

CHERRY CHEESECAKE

1 Fastest Cheesecake (above)
1 (15-ounce) can cherry pie filling

Top cheesecake with cherry pie filling before serving. Makes 8 servings.

BLUEBERRY CHEESECAKE

1 Fastest Cheesecake (above)
1 (15-ounce) can blueberry pie filling

Top cheesecake with blueberry pie filling before serving. Makes 8 servings.

TURTLE CHEESECAKE

1 Fastest Cheesecake (p. 387)
1 jar caramel ice cream topping
1 cup chocolate chips
1 cup roasted pecans, chopped

Top cheesecake with caramel topping, chocolate chips, and pecans before serving. Makes 8 servings.

QUICK TOFFEE CHOCOLATE CAKE

¾ cup semisweet chocolate chips
⅔ cup sour cream
1 (11-ounce) ready-to-serve pound cake
2 English toffee bars, chopped

In a small saucepan over low heat, melt chocolate, stirring often. Remove from heat; stir in sour cream until smooth. Cut pound cake horizontally in half. Place 1 cake layer on serving plate; spread with ⅓ frosting; sprinkle ⅓ chopped candy. Top with second layer; frost cake with remaining frosting; sprinkle top with remaining candy. Makes 8 servings.

CHESS CAKE

1 (18-ounce) box yellow cake mix
½ cup butter
4 eggs
1 (8-ounce) package cream cheese, softened
1 (16-ounce) box powdered sugar

Mix cake mix, butter, and 1 egg, and press in the bottom of oblong pan. Mix cream cheese, 3 eggs, and powdered sugar and pour over the first mixture. Bake at 350° for 30 to 35 minutes or until lightly brown on top. Makes 12 servings.

COCONUT CAKE

1 (18-ounce) box yellow or white cake mix
1 (8-ounce) can sweetened condensed milk
1 can cream of coconut, shredded
Whipped cream topping
2 cups coconut, shredded

Bake cake according to directions on the box. While still warm, prick with fork. Mix milk and cream of coconut and spread over cake. When cool, cover with whipped cream topping and sprinkle with coconut. Makes 12 servings.

TWO-INGREDIENT CAKE

1 (18-ounce) box angel food cake mix
1 (20-ounce) can crushed pineapple

Combine cake mix and pineapple, mixing well. Pour into an ungreased pan, and bake according to package instructions. Makes 12 servings.

PINEAPPLE UPSIDE-DOWN CAKE

½ cup butter
1 cup brown sugar
1 (21-ounce) can sliced pineapple
12 maraschino cherries, halved
1 cup pecans, chopped
1 (16-ounce) package yellow cake mix

Melt butter and sugar in a cake pan; remove and spread evenly. Arrange pineapple, cherries, and nuts. Mix cake according to directions and spread in pan. Bake according to directions. Makes 16 servings.

MISSISSIPPI MUD CAKE

2 cups sugar
1 cup butter
4 eggs
½ cup cocoa
1½ cups pecans, chopped
1½ cups plain flour
Dash salt
1 teaspoon vanilla
Miniature marshmallows
Icing

Cream sugar and butter together. Add eggs and blend well. Add cocoa, pecans, flour, salt, and vanilla; mix well. Pour into a greased and floured pan. Bake at 350° for 35 minutes. When cake is done, immediately cover the top with miniature marshmallows. Do not remove cake from pan. Pour icing over marshmallows after the cake cools.

BLACK FOREST CAKE

1 (18-ounce) package devil's food cake mix
1 (20-ounce) can cherry pie filling
3 cups whipped cream topping
1 cup miniature chocolate chips

Prepare cake according to package directions for sheet cake. Punch holes in cake with a fork and spread with cherry pie filling. Dollop whipped cream topping over cherries, and spread carefully. Sprinkle chocolate chips over topping.
chill before serving. Makes about 12 servings.

RED VELVET CAKE

1½ cups sugar
1½ cups cooking oil
3 eggs
2½ cups plain flour
1 teaspoon soda
2 tablespoons cocoa
2 teaspoons vanilla
2 teaspoons vinegar
2 tablespoons red food coloring
1 cup buttermilk

Cream sugar and oil; add eggs. Mix flour, soda, and cocoa with sifter. Add vanilla, vinegar, and food coloring to sugar mixture. Add flour, alternating with milk. Bake in 3 layers at 300° for 30 minutes. Do not over cook. Ice with Cream Cheese Frosting (below).

CREAM CHEESE FROSTING

1 (16-ounce) box powdered sugar
½ cup margarine
1 (8-ounce) package cream cheese, softened
1 small can coconut
1 cup nuts, chopped

Mix all ingredients, and spread on cooled cake.

PEACHY ALMOND CAKE

1 (18-ounce) package white cake mix
1 (20-ounce) can peach pie filling
3 cups whipped cream topping
1 cup slivered almonds, toasted

Prepare cake according to package directions for sheet cake. Punch holes in cakes with a fork, and spread with cherry pie filling. Dollop whipped cream topping over peaches, and spread carefully. Sprinkle toasted almonds over topping. Chill before serving. Makes about 12 servings.

FAST AND FABULOUS FUDGE FROSTING

1½ cups granulated sugar
⅓ cup milk
⅓ cup butter
1 cup chocolate chips

Boil sugar, milk, and butter for 30 seconds. Stir in cup of chocolate chips. Cool. Makes about 3 cups.

EASY PIE SHELL

1⅛ cups flour, sifted
⅓ cup vegetable oil
2 tablespoons cold water

Mix flour and oil until grainy. Sprinkle with water. Mix to moisten. Roll out between two pieces of waxed paper. Bake according to recipe directions. Makes 1 pie crust.

BLUEBERRY BANANA TARTS

2 bananas, sliced
12 individual tart shells, baked
1 (8-ounce) package cream cheese, softened
1 cup sugar
1 (8-ounce) container whipped cream topping
1 can blueberry pie filling

Divide banana slices evenly among tart shells. Combine cream cheese, sugar, and whipped topping, beating until smooth. Dollop over bananas, spreading to seal completely. Top with blueberry pie filling. Chill until serving. Makes 12 servings.

BLUEBERRY PIE

1 cup water, divided
⅓ cup flour
Dash salt
4 cups fresh blueberries, divided
1 cup sugar
½ cup water
1 (9-inch) pie shell, baked
Whipped cream

Combine ½ cup water, flour, and salt, mixing until smooth. Combine 1 cup blueberries with sugar and remaining ½ cup water in a saucepan. Bring to a boil. Add flour mixture, cooking and stirring until thick and bubbly. Remove from heat, and stir in remaining 3 cups blueberries. Pour into pie shell, and chill. Serve with whipped cream. Makes 8 servings.

BLUEBERRY PIE №2

1 cup sugar
2 tablespoons cornstarch
1 cup water
4 tablespoons dry blackberry gelatin
4 cups fresh blueberries
1 (9-inch) pie shell, baked

Put sugar, cornstarch, and water into a saucepan and boil until clear and thick. Add blackberry gelatin. Chill slightly. Add blueberries. Stir and pour into pie shell. Chill thoroughly. Makes 8 servings.

FRESH BLUEBERRY CREAM PIE

1 cup sour cream
2 tablespoons all-purpose flour
¾ cup sugar
¼ teaspoon salt
1 egg, beaten
1 teaspoon vanilla
2½ cups fresh blueberries
1 (9-inch) pie shell, unbaked
3 tablespoons all purpose flour
3 tablespoons margarine or butter, softened
3 tablespoons pecans or walnuts, chopped

Combine first six ingredients; beat 5 minutes at medium speed of electric mixer or until smooth. Fold in blueberries; pour into shell. Bake at 400° for 25 minutes. Combine remaining ingredients, stirring well; sprinkle over top of pie. Bake 10 more minutes. Chill before serving. Makes 8 servings.

FAST AND EASY CHEESE PIE

2 (8-ounce) packages cream cheese, softened
3 eggs
1 cup sugar, divided
1 tablespoon vanilla
1 cup sour cream

Beat softened cream cheese, eggs, ¾ sugar, and vanilla until smooth. Pour into a buttered and floured pie pan. Bake at 325° for 35 minutes. Remove cheesecake from oven. Mix together sour cream and ¼ cup sugar.; pour over cake. Bake at 450° for 5 minutes. Makes 8 servings.

LEMONADE PIE

1 can frozen lemonade
1 can sweetened condensed milk
Juice of 1 lemon
Whipped cream topping
1 (9-inch) pie shell, baked

Mix lemonade, milk, and lemon juice. Fold in topping; pour into a pie shell. Chill overnight. Makes 8 servings.

SOUTHERN PECAN PIE

1 cup sugar
½ cup dark corn syrup
¼ cup margarine, melted
3 eggs, well beaten
1 cup pecans
1 (9-inch) pie shell, unbaked

Combine sugar, syrup, and melted margarine. Add eggs and pecans. Mix thoroughly. Pour into a pie shell. Bake at 375° for 40 to 45 minutes. Makes 8 servings.

PECAN PIE

6 tablespoons butter, melted and cooled
¾ cup sugar
4 eggs, beaten
1¼ cups light corn syrup
2 cups pecans, coarsely chopped
1 (9-inch) pie shell, unbaked

Combine butter, sugar, eggs, corn syrup, and pecans; pour into pie shell. Bake at 375° for about 30 minutes or until firm. Makes 8 servings.

CARAMEL PIE

1 (14-ounce) can sweetened condensed milk
1 (9-inch) graham cracker pie shell
1 (8-ounce) container whipped cream topping

Put condensed milk into a saucepan and cover with boiling water. Cook covered for 3 hours, checking level of water. Pour into pie shell. Let cool completely. Top with whipped cream topping. Makes 8 servings.

Chocolate Pecan Pie

6 tablespoons butter, melted and cooled
¾ cup sugar
4 eggs, beaten
1¼ cups light corn syrup
2 cups chocolate chips
2 cups pecans, coarsely chopped
1 (9-inch) pie shell, unbaked

Combine butter, sugar, eggs, corn syrup, chocolate chips, and pecans; pour into unbaked pie shell. Bake at 375° for about 30 minutes or until firm. Makes 8 servings.

Pecan Fudge Pie

2 (1-ounce) squares bittersweet chocolate
¼ cup butter
1 (14-ounce) can sweetened condensed milk
½ cup hot water
2 eggs, beaten
1 teaspoon vanilla extract
Dash salt
1½ cups pecans, chopped
1 (9-inch) pie shell, unbaked

Melt chocolate and butter over very low heat, stirring constantly. Add condensed milk, hot water, eggs, vanilla, salt, and pecans. Pour into pie shell. Bake at 350° for about 45 minutes. Makes 8 servings.

PEACH PIE

4 cups sliced peaches
1 (9-inch) pie shell, unbaked
1½ cups sugar
⅓ cup self-rising flour
2 eggs, beaten
4 tablespoons butter, melted and cooled
¼ teaspoon vanilla extract

Place peaches in pie shell. Combine remaining ingredients, and pour over peaches. Bake at 350° for about 30 minutes. Makes 8 servings.

PEACHES-AND-CREAM PIE

6 peaches, peeled and sliced
½ cup sugar
¼ cup flour
1 teaspoon cinnamon
¼ teaspoon nutmeg
1 (9-inch) pie shell, unbaked
1 cup sour cream
2 tablespoons brown sugar

Toss peaches with sugar, flour, cinnamon, and nutmeg. Place in pie shell. Spread sour cream over peaches and sprinkle with brown sugar. Bake at 450° for 10 minutes; reduce heat to 350°, and bake 30 minutes more. Makes 8 servings.

CREAM CHEESE PEACH PIE

1½ cups water
1¼ cups sugar
3 tablespoons cornstarch
¼ teaspoon salt
Juice and zest of 1 lemon
6 peaches, peeled and sliced
1 (9-inch) pie shell, baked
1 (3-ounce) package cream cheese, softened

Combine water, sugar, cornstarch, salt, and lemon juice and zest in saucepan; cook over low heat until thick and clear. Combine with peaches. Spread bottom of pie shell with cream cheese; pour peach mixture over. Chill until serving. Makes 8 servings.

BUTTERMILK PIE

½ cup butter, softened
1½ cups sugar
3 tablespoons flour
3 eggs
1 cup buttermilk
Juice and zest from 1 lemon
1 teaspoon vanilla extract
Dash salt
1 (9-inch) pie shell, unbaked

Cream butter and sugar until light and fluffy. Add flour, beating well. Add eggs, beating well. Stir in buttermilk, lemon juice and zest, vanilla extract, and salt. Pour into pie shell. Bake at 450° for 15 minutes. Reduce oven temperature to 350°, and bake 45 minutes more, or until set. Makes 8 servings.

STRAWBERRY CRACKER PIE

3 egg whites
½ teaspoon cream of tartar
1 cup sugar
1 teaspoon vanilla extract
2 drops almond extract
1 cup cracker crumbs
1 cup pecans, chopped
1 (9-ounce) container whipped cream topping
1 (10-ounce) package frozen sliced strawberries, thawed and
  drained

Beat egg whites and cream of tartar until stiff peaks form. Beat in
sugar, vanilla extract, and almond extract. Stir in cracker crumbs and
pecans. Spread in greased pie plate. Bake at 325° for 30 minutes.
Cool. Combine whipped cream toppingand strawberries, and spread
into cooled pie shell. Chill until served. Makes 8 servings.

CHOCOLATE CHEESE PIE

1 cup sugar
3 (8-ounce) packages cream cheese, softened
5 eggs
1 tablespoon vanilla extract
1 tablespoon lemon juice
1 (4-ounce) package German sweet chocolate, melted

Combine sugar, cream cheese, eggs, and vanilla; beat until smooth.
Divide in half. Stir lemon juice into half of cream cheese mixture, and
pour into greased pie plate. Stir melted chocolate into remaining half
of cream cheese mixture and pour over mixture in pie plate. Bake at
350° for about 45 minutes. Makes 8 servings.

CHOCOLATE COCONUT PIE

1 cup butter
1 cup chocolate chips
2 cups sugar
4 eggs, beaten
1 cup coconut, shredded
1 cup pecans, chopped
1 (9-inch) pie shell, unbaked

Melt butter and chocolate chips over very low heat, stirring
constantly, until smooth. Beat in sugar and eggs; fold in coconut and
pecans. Pour into pie shell. Bake at 350° for about 45 minutes. Makes
8 servings.

CRUSTLESS COCONUT PIE

2 tablespoons flour
1½ cups sugar
3 eggs, beaten
¾ cup butter, melted
1 (14-ounce) can evaporated milk
1 (3½-ounce) can flaked coconut
1 teaspoon vanilla extract

Whisk together flour and sugar; add remaining ingredients, mixing
until smooth. Pour into a greased 2-quart baking dish. Bake at 325°
for about 45 minutes. Makes 8 servings.

MUD PIE

1½ cups finely chopped walnuts
1 tablespoon plus ⅓ cup flour
¾ cup butter, softened and divided
1¼ cups sugar, divided
3 eggs
2 (1-ounce) squares unsweetened chocolate, melted
2 teaspoons vanilla extract
½ teaspoon baking powder
Dash salt
1 (9-inch) pie shell

Combine walnuts, 1 tablespoon flour, ¼ cup butter, and ¼ cup sugar. Press into greased pie plate and set aside. Combine remaining ⅓ cup flour, remaining ½ cup butter, remaining 1 cup sugar, eggs, chocolate, vanilla, baking powder, and salt, beating until smooth. Pour into pie shell. Bake at 325° for about 45 minutes. Makes 8 servings.

FUDGE PIE

½ cup butter
3 tablespoons cocoa
1 cup sugar
2 eggs, beaten
½ cup flour, sifted
½ cup pecans, chopped
1 teaspoon vanilla

In a saucepan, melt butter and cocoa together. Mix in sugar and then remaining ingredients. Pour into pie plate. Bake at 350° for 25 to 30 minutes. Serve warm. Makes 8 servings.

CHOCOLATE CHESS PIE

6 tablespoons butter
3 (1-ounce) squares bittersweet chocolate
4 eggs, beaten
1¾ cups sugar
2 teaspoons vanilla extract
Dash salt
1 (9-inch) pie shell, unbaked

Melt butter and chocolate over very low heat, stirring constantly. Add eggs, sugar, vanilla, and salt, blending well. Pour into pie shell. Bake at 375° for about 30 minutes or until set. Makes 8 servings.

ORANGE CHESS PIE

8 egg yolks
1½ cups sugar
3 tablespoons cornmeal
Juice and zest of 1 orange
½ cup butter, melted
1 (9-inch) pie shell, unbaked
Nutmeg to taste

Beat egg yolks until thick and lemon-colored; add sugar and cornmeal, beating well. Add orange juice and zest and melted butter. Pour into pie shell, and sprinkle with nutmeg. Bake at 375° for about 30 minutes or until set. Makes 8 servings.

LEMON CHESS PIE

8 egg yolks
1½ cups sugar
3 tablespoons cornmeal
Juice and zest of 2 lemons
½ cup butter, melted
1 (9-inch) pie shell, unbaked
Nutmeg to taste

Beat egg yolks until thick and lemon-colored; add sugar and cornmeal, beating well. Add lemon juice and zest and melted butter. Pour into pie shell, and sprinkle with nutmeg. Bake at 375° for about 30 minutes or until set. Makes 8 servings.

INDIVIDUAL CHESS TARTS

Filling for Chocolate Chess Pie (p. 403), Orange Chess Pie
(p. 403), and Lemon Chess Pie (above)
8 individual tart shells, unbaked

Pour filling into tart shells. Bake at 375° for about 20 minutes or until set. Makes 8 servings.

BLUEBERRY COBBLER

1 tablespoon cornstarch
½ cup plus 1 tablespoon sugar
4 cups fresh blueberries
1 teaspoon lemon juice
1 cup flour
1½ teaspoons baking powder
½ teaspoon salt
3 tablespoons shortening
½ cup milk

Mix together cornstarch and ½ cup sugar in a saucepan; stir in blueberries and lemon juice and cook, stirring constantly, until it thickens and boils. Cook 1 minute. Pour into casserole dish. Mix flour, 1 tablespoon sugar, baking powder, and salt; add shortening and milk. Mix until dough forms. Do not stir too much. Drop dough by spoonfuls into hot berries. Bake 25 to 30 minutes at 375°. Makes 8 servings.

PEACH CRINKLE

1 (28-ounce) can sliced peaches, drained
Juice and zest of 1 lemon
1¼ cups pie shell mix
¾ cup brown sugar
½ cup butter, melted

Combine peaches and lemon juice and zest. Combine pie shell mix and sugar, mixing well. Sprinkle over peaches, and drizzle melted butter over all. Bake at 325° for about 45 minutes. Makes 6 servings.

FAST AND EASY FRUIT CRISP

2 (21-ounce) cans apple or cherry pie filling
1 package (2-layer) yellow cake mix
½ cup butter, melted
½ cup pecans, walnuts, or raisins

Spread pie fillings in low roasting pan. Sprinkle dry cake mix over the fruit. Drizzle with melted butter. Sprinkle with nuts. Bake, uncovered, at 350° for 40 to 50 minutes or until golden brown.

PEACH COBBLER ROLL-UPS

1½ cups flour
½ cup shortening
½ teaspoon salt
1 teaspoon baking powder
½ cup milk
2 cups canned fruit, drained, juice reserved
½ cup butter, melted
2 cups sugar
Water

Mix first 5 ingredients, and roll out dough; spread fruit on it, and roll as jelly roll. Grease a cookie sheet with the melted butter. Place cut rolls onto cookie sheet. Mix 2 cups sugar with fruit juice and enough water to make 3 cups of liquid; pour over dough. Bake at 325° for 1 hour or until brown.

FAST AND EASY PEACH COBBLER

2 cans sliced peaches
1 (16-ounce) package yellow cake mix
½ cup butter
Sugar and cinnamon
Ice Cream

Drain juice from 1 can peaches. Place both cans of peaches in a 9-inch x 13-inch cake pan. Pour dry cake mix over it. Slice butter on top, and sprinkle with sugar and cinnamon. Cook at 350° for approximately 30 minutes or until golden brown. Serve with ice cream.

EASIEST FRUIT COBBLER

½ cup butter, melted
1 cup self-rising flour
1 cup milk
1 (28-ounce) can sliced fruit, drained

Combine butter, flour, and milk, stirring until smooth. Pour into greased baking dish. Arrange drained fruit over batter. Bake at 350° for about 30 minutes. Makes about 6 servings.

APPLE CRUMBLE PIE

⅓ cup flour
¾ cup firmly packed brown sugar
⅓ cup butter
6 medium tart apples, pared and sliced

Combine flour and brown sugar; cut in butter to make a crumbly mixture. Arrange sliced apples in bottom of a greased, shallow baking dish. Sprinkle sugar over the top. Bake at 375° for about 30 minutes, or until top is golden brown and the apples are tender.

APPLE TURNOVERS

¼ cup vegetable oil plus extra for brushing
2 cups multigrain biscuit mix
¾ cup apple juice
Jams, fruit butters, honey, nuts, cinnamon, nutmeg, etc.

Stir oil into dry mix with fork until mixture is uniform in color and texture. Stir in juice. Let dough set 2 minutes. Knead dough 12 to 15 times. Roll dough out to ¼-inch thickness. Cut with biscuit cutter. Roll biscuits out into larger, thin circles of dough. Spoon 1½ to 2½ teaspoons of jam into the center of each circle; fold circle in half. Press edges together. Place pies on lightly oiled cookie sheet. Brush tops lightly with oil. Bake at 375° for 12 minutes or until done. Serve with condiments.

APPLE PIE

6 apples, peeled, cored, and chopped
1 cup sugar, divided
½ cup flour plus 2 tablespoons
½ teaspoon cinnamon
¼ teaspoon nutmeg
1 (9-inch) pie shell, unbaked
½ cup butter, melted

Combine apples, ½ cup sugar, 2 tablespoons flour, cinnamon, and nutmeg. Pour into pie shell. Combine remaining ½ cup sugar, remaining ½ cup flour, and butter; sprinkle over apples. Bake at 400° for about 45 minutes. Makes 8 servings.

FAT-FREE CHERRY COBBLER

2 (16-ounce) cans water-packed sweet cherries, drained, juice
  reserved
½ cup self–rising flour
¼ cup sugar
⅔ cup skim milk

Place cherries and ⅓ cup of the reserved juice in a 9-inch-square pan.
In a medium bowl, mix together flour, sugar, and milk. Pour evenly
over cherries. Bake uncovered at 350° for 45 minutes.

PUMPKIN CREAM PIE

2 cups milk
2 (4-ounce) packages vanilla pudding mix
1 cup canned pumpkin
1 cup whipped cream topping
1 teaspoon cinnamon
Dash nutmeg
Dash ground cloves
1 (9-inch) pie shell, unbaked
1 cup pecans, chopped

Combine milk, pudding mix, pumpkin, whipped topping, cinnamon,
nutmeg, and cloves; beat until thoroughly combined. Pour into pie
shell, top with pecans, and chill until set. Makes 8 servings.

Peanut Butter Pie

1 cup peanut butter
1 cup powdered sugar
1 (8-ounce) package cream cheese, softened
½ cup milk
2 cups whipped cream topping
1 (9-inch) chocolate crumb pie shell
½ cup peanuts, chopped

Combine peanut butter, powdered sugar, cream cheese, and milk, beating until smooth. Fold in whipped cream topping, and spoon into pie shell. Top with peanuts, and chill until firm. Makes 8 servings.

Million Dollar Pie

1 (8-ounce) container whipped cream topping
1 (14-ounce) can sweetened condensed milk
½ cup lemon juice
2 (8-ounce) cans mandarin oranges, drained
1 (8-ounce) can crushed pineapple, drained
1 (14-ounce) can diced peaches, drained
2 (9-inch) pie shells, baked

Combine whipped topping, condensed milk, and lemon juice, beating until smooth. Combine oranges, pineapple, and peaches; fold gently into cream mixture. Spoon into pie shells and chill until set. Makes 16 servings.

ALMOND DIVINITY

4 egg whites
½ teaspoon cream of tartar
Dash salt
1¼ cups sugar
1 teaspoon vanilla extract
2 drops almond extract
1 cup slivered almonds

Beat together egg whites, cream of tartar, and salt until soft peaks form. Gradually beat in sugar, then extracts. Gently fold in almonds. Drop by teaspoonfuls onto well-greased cookie sheet. Bake at 250° for about 45 minutes. Cool on wire racks. Makes about 4 dozen.

CHERRY ALMOND FUDGE

1 (14-ounce) can sweetened condensed milk
2 cups semisweet chocolate chips
½ cup almonds, coarsely chopped
½ cup candied cherries, chopped
1 teaspoon almond extract

Line an 8-inch-square pan with foil. In a microwave-safe bowl, combine milk and chocolate. Microwave on high in 30-second intervals for 1½ to 2 minutes, or until chocolate is melted and mixture is smooth when stirred. Add almonds, cherries, and extract. Spread into pan. Chill. Cut into 1-inch squares. Store covered in refrigerator. Makes 64 servings.

Microwave Caramel Corn

7 large marshmallows
½ cup butter
½ cup brown sugar
¼ teaspoon baking soda
3 to 4 quarts cooked popcorn

Combine marshmallows, butter, and brown sugar in a mixing bowl.
Microwave on high for 3 minutes. Add baking soda and stir. Cook an
additional 30 seconds on high, or until marshmallows are melted. Stir
immediately and pour popcorn, stirring to coat evenly. Place on
waxed paper to cool. Makes 8 servings.

Peanut Brittle

2 cups sugar
½ cup white corn syrup
½ cup water
1 cup raw peanuts
Dash baking soda

Mix first 3 ingredients togetherk, and bring to a boil. Add nuts and
cook until they pop. Remove from heat, add baking soda, and beat.
Pour into a greased pan and cool. Makes 4 servings.

HAYSTACKS

¼ **cup butter**
½ **cup creamy peanut butter**
1 (12-ounce) package butterscotch chips
6 cups corn cereal
⅔ **cup miniature semisweet chocolate chips**

Melt butter, peanut butter, and butterscotch chips in a large saucepan over very low heat. Stir constantly until melted. Remove from heat. Pour corn cereal into a large bowl. Pour hot butterscotch mixture over cereal. Stir with large spoon until cereal is coated. Stir in chocolate chips. Spoon out mixture into mounds on waxed paper-lined baking sheets. Refrigerate until firm before serving. Makes 3 dozen 2½-inch pieces.

QUICK CHOCOLATE FUDGE

1½ **cups milk chocolate chips**
1 cup sweetened condensed milk
3 tablespoons butter
2 teaspoons vanilla extract
¾ **cup walnuts, chopped**

Melt chocolate chips in top of double boiler over very low heat. Stir until melted. Remove from heat. Stir in condensed milk, butter, and vanilla. Blend until butter is mixed with chocolate. Stir in nuts. Spread mixture immediately into a lightly oiled 8-inch square pan. Cool at room temperature. Cut into even squares. Makes 25 pieces.

No-Cook Fudge

1 (3-ounce) package cream cheese, softened
2 cups powdered sugar
2 (1-ounce) squares unsweetened chocolate, melted
½ cup pecans, chopped
1 teaspoon vanilla extract
¼ teaspoon salt
Dash salt

Beat cream cheese until very smooth. Gradually add powdered sugar and beat until well combined. Beat in melted chocolate. Stir in pecans, vanilla, and salt. Pour into greased 8-inch-square pan and chill 15 minutes or until firm. Makes 25 pieces.

Rocky Road Fudge

2 tablespoons butter
1 (12-ounce) package chocolate chips
1 (14-ounce) can sweetened condensed milk
2 cups dry-roasted peanuts, chopped
1 (10½-ounce) package miniature marshmallows

Combine butter, chocolate chips, and condensed milk in medium saucepan; cook and stir over medium-low heat until smooth. Remove from heat, and add peanuts and marshmallows. Stir thoroughly, and spread into waxed paper-lined 9 x 13-inch pan. Chill 2 hours. Cut into squares. Makes about 40 pieces.

MICROWAVE FUDGE

1 (16-ounce) box powdered sugar
⅓ cup cocoa
½ cup butter, melted
¼ cup milk
1 teaspoon vanilla extract
½ cup pecans, chopped

Combine sugar, cocoa, butter, milk, and vanilla in a microwave-safe bowl; cook on high for 1 minute. Stir and cook on high 1 minute more. Stir until smooth. Stir in pecans. Pour into small buttered dish and chill. Makes about 2 dozen pieces.

MICROWAVE PEANUT BUTTER FUDGE

1 (16-ounce) box powdered sugar
⅓ cup cocoa
½ cup butter, melted
½ cup peanut butter
¼ cup milk
1 teaspoon vanilla extract

Combine all ingredients in a microwave-safe bowl; cook on high for 1 minute. Stir and cook on high 1 minute more. Stir until smooth. Pour into a buttered 8-inch-square dish and chill. Makes about 2 dozen pieces.

SNOWBALLS

⅓ cup evaporated milk
1 cup chocolate chips
1¼ cups powdered sugar
½ cup pecans, chopped
¾ cup coconut, shredded

Combine milk and chocolate chips in a medium saucepan over very low heat; cook and stir until smooth. Stir in powdered sugar and nuts. Form into 1-inch balls and roll in coconut. Chill until set. Makes about 2 dozen.

MARSHMALLOW NUT CLUSTERS

¾ cup sugar
½ cup evaporated milk
1 tablespoon corn syrup
1 cup chocolate chips
1½ cups miniature marshmallows
1 cup pecans, chopped

Combine sugar, evaporated milk, and corn syrup. Bring to a boil and boil 2 minutes. Stir in chocolate chips and let cool for 10 minutes. Stir in marshmallows and pecans. Drop by tablespoonfuls onto waxed paper and chill. Makes about 2 dozen.

Pecan Roll

1 (7-ounce) jar marshmallow creme
1 (16-ounce) box powdered sugar
1 teaspoon vanilla
1 (14-ounce) package caramels
¼ cup water
1½ cups pecans, finely chopped

Combine marshmallow creme, powdered sugar, and vanilla, stirring until very stiff and dry. Form into 3 or 4 logs. Chill until firm. Heat caramels and water over very low heat, stirring constantly, until smooth. Dip logs in caramel and roll in pecans. Makes 3 or 4 logs.

Chocolate Pecan Clusters

1 (12-ounce) bag chocolate chips
1 (14-ounce) can sweetened condensed milk
1 pound pecan halves

Combine chocolate chips and condensed milk in medium saucepan; cook over low heat, stirring constantly, until smooth. Stir in pecans. Drop spoonfuls onto waxed paper and chill until firm. Makes 2 dozen.

Chocolate-Covered Strawberries

1 cup chocolate chips
1 tablespoon shortening
24 strawberries, washed and well dried

Melt chocolate chips and shortening in microwave-safe bowl at 50 percent power, stirring every 30 seconds, until melted and smooth. Dip berries into melted chocolate, and place on wax paper to set. Makes about 24 pieces.

PECAN DAINTIES

1 egg white
Dash salt
1 cup light brown sugar
1½ cups pecan halves

Beat the egg white with the salt. Add the sugar. Beat until stiff. Dip pecans into meringue and put on a cookie sheet. Bake at 250° for about 30 minutes.

QUICK PEANUT BUTTER CHEWS

¼ cup chunky peanut butter
2 tablespoons powdered milk
¼ cup golden raisins
4 graham crackers, broken
1 teaspoon vanilla extract
Dash cinnamon

Cream peanut butter with 2 tablespoons milk. Add raisins, graham crackers, extract, and cinnamon, and mix well. Drop on waxed paper in 1-inch balls, and place in freezer until ready to serve.

OREO BROWNIES

1 (19-ounce) package brownie mix, prepared according to
  package directions
1 cup chocolate frosting
1 cup Oreo cookies, coarsely crumbled

Spread cooled brownies with chocolate frosting and sprinkle crushed Oreos over top. Makes about 12 servings.

LEMON BARS

2 cups flour
1 cup powdered sugar
⅛ teaspoon salt
½ cup butter, softened
2 eggs
2 cups sugar
⅓ cup flour
Juice of 1 lemon

Mix the flour, powdered sugar, and salt in a bowl. Slowly cut in butter. Pour the mixture into a greased baking dish. Bake at 350° for 20 minutes. Whisk together the eggs, sugar, flour, and lemon juice in a bowl. Spoon mixture into the crust. Bake at 300° for 30 more minutes.

BROWNIES

½ cup butter
1 cup sugar
2 eggs
1 teaspoon vanilla
2 (1-ounce) squares chocolate, melted
¾ cup sifted flour
¾ teaspoon salt
½ teaspoon baking powder
⅔ cup nuts, chopped

Cream butter, add sugar gradually, continuing to cream until mixture looks light and fluffy. Beat in eggs one at a time. Add vanilla and melted chocolate; beat well. Sift dry ingredients together and blend with chocolate mixture. Fold nuts into batter. Bake in a greased 8-inch-square pan at 350° for 25 to 30 minutes.

Meltaways

1 cup butter, softened
1 cup sugar
1 egg
1 teaspoon vanilla extract
2 cups flour
1 cup pecans, chopped and divided

Beat butter and sugar until light and fluffy; beat in egg and vanilla. Gradually add flour and ½ cup pecans. Press into greased baking sheet. Sprinkle with remaining pecans. Bake at 350° for about 30 minutes. Cut into squares. Makes about 3 dozen.

Chocolate-Coconut Squares

2½ cups graham cracker crumbs
1 cup chocolate chips
½ cup coconut
1 (14-ounce) can sweetened condensed milk
½ cup pecans, chopped

Combine graham cracker crumbs, chocolate chips, coconut, and condensed milk, mixing well. Spread in a greased 8-inch square pan. Sprinkle pecans over top. Bake at 325° for about 20 minutes. Makes about 3 dozen.

ROCKY ROAD BROWNIES

1 (12-ounce) package semisweet chocolate chips
2 tablespoons butter
1⅓ cups miniature marshmallows
½ cup roasted pecans, chopped
1 (19-ounce) box brownie mix, prepared according to package
  directions

Melt chocolate chips and butter in medium saucepan over low heat, stirring constantly. Stir in marshmallows and pecans. Immediately spread over baked brownies. Cool. Makes about 3 dozen.

QUICK BROWNIES

1 (16-ounce) package semisweet chocolate chips
⅔ cup sweetened condensed milk
1 teaspoon vanilla extract
1 cup walnuts, coarsely chopped

In top of a double boiler, melt chocolate over simmering water. Stir in sweetened condensed milk. Remove from heat. Stir in remaining ingredients. Turn into greased 8-inch-square pan that has been lined wiht waxed paper or metal foil. Bake at 375°, until toothpick inserted in center comes out clean, about 25 minutes. Turn out of pan onto cake rack. Peel off paper. Cool. Cut into 2-inch squares. Makes 16 brownies.

BLONDE BROWNIES

¼ cup butter, melted
1 cup brown sugar
1 egg
1 teaspoon vanilla extract
¾ cup flour
1 teaspoon baking powder
½ teaspoon salt
¾ cup walnuts, chopped

Combine butter and brown sugar, beating well; beat in egg and vanilla extract. Combine flour, baking powder, and salt; gradually add to butter mixture. Stir in walnuts. Spread into a greased 8-inch-square pan. Bake at 350° for 25 minutes. Makes about 2 dozen.

CHEWY GOOEY BARS

1 (20-ounce) package refrigerated chocolate chip cookie dough
2 cups miniature marshmallows
1 (12-ounce) package semisweet chocolate chips
½ cup caramel fudge ice cream topping

Slice cookie dough into ½-inch slices and arrange in a 10-inch x 15-inch pan. Press evenly into pan using floured fingers so dough covers bottom of pan. Bake crust at 350° for 10 to 13 minutes until light golden brown. Sprinkle crust with marshmallows and chocolate chips. Return to oven, and bake an additional 8 to 10 minutes or until marshmallows are puffy and light golden brown. Remove from oven and drizzle caramel topping evenly over bars. Cool completely and cut into bars.

QUICK AND EASY BARS

1½ cups semi-sweet chocolate chips
1 cup peanut butter minus 2 tablespoons
½ cup butter
1 bag miniature marshmallows

Melt chips, peanut butter, and butter over low heat. Stir until melted and hot, but not boiling. Pour over small marshmallows in the bottom of a 9-inch x 13-inch pan. Refrigerate. Makes 8 servings.

HELLO DOLLIES

½ cup butter, melted
1 cup graham cracker crumbs
1 cup flaked coconut
1 cup chocolate chips
1 cup pecans, chopped
1 (14-ounce) can sweetened condensed milk

Combine butter and graham cracker crumbs; press into an 8-inch-square baking pan. Sprinkle coconut, chocolate chips, and pecans over crust. Pour condensed milk evenly over all. Bake at 350° about 30 minutes. Cool completely. Cut into 16 squares.

Chocolate Chip Cookies

1 (16-ounce) package white cake mix
½ cup oil
2 eggs
1 cup semisweet chocolate chips

Blend all ingredients together. Add a little water if dough is too thick.
Drop onto an ungreased cookie sheet. Bake at 350° for 10 to 12
minutes (top of cookies will look pale). Cool on cookie sheet for
1 minute, then remove to rack to finish cooling. Makes 12 servings.

Peanut Butter Cookies

1 cup butter
1½ cups crunchy peanut butter
1½ cups dark brown sugar
⅔ cup sugar
2 eggs
2 teaspoons vanilla
2⅔ cups plain flour
2 teaspoons baking soda

Cream butter, peanut butter, and sugars well. Add eggs and vanilla.
Sift the flour and soda together and add creamed mixture. Mix well.
Shape into small balls about 1-inch in size. Place on a cookie sheet.
Bake at 350° for 10 minutes. Makes about 12 dozen cookies.

QUICK AND EASY PEANUT BUTTER COOKIES

1 (16-ounce) package golden yellow cake mix
2 eggs
½ cup shortening
½ cup peanut butter

Blend in a large mixing bowl. Shape into balls. Place on ungreased cookie sheet and flatten with fork. Bake at 375° for 10 to 12 minutes until golden brown. Makes 12 servings.

FLOURLESS PEANUT BUTTER COOKIES

1 cup peanut butter
1 cup sugar
1 egg
1 teaspoon vanilla

Blend all ingredients well. Drop from teaspoon onto a greased cookie sheet. Criss-cross with sugar-dipped fork. Bake at 350° about 15 minutes or until brown around edges. Makes 2 dozen.

MACAROONS

1 cup coconut, shredded
⅔ cup sweetened condensed milk
1 teaspoon vanilla extract

Grease cookie sheets lightly. Combine ingredients and mix well. Drop from teaspoon about 1 inch apart. Bake at 350° for 8 to 10 minutes until delicately brown. Makes 5 to 6 dozen.

FAST AND FANCY MACAROONS

1 (14-ounce) bag coconut, shredded
1 (14-ounce) can sweetened condensed milk
2 teaspoons vanilla extract
1 teaspoon lemon or almond extract

Combine all ingredients, mixing well. Drop from teaspoon 1 inch apart on well-greased baking sheets. Sprinkle with sugar crystals, if desired. Bake at 350° for 12 to 15 minutes, or until lightly browned. Remove at once, using moistened spatula. Place cookies on wax paper.

CHOCOLATE MACAROONS

2 (1-ounce) squares unsweetened baking chocolate
¼ cup butter
1½ cups biscuit mix
¾ cup sugar
1 egg
¼ cup milk
1 teaspoon vanilla
1⅓ cups coconut, shredded

Melt chocolate and butter over very low heat, stirring constantly. Whisk biscuit mix and sugar together, and stir into melted chocolate mixture. Add egg, milk, and vanilla, mixing well. Fold in coconut. Drop by teaspoonfuls onto ungreased baking sheets. Bake at 375° for about 12 minutes. Makes about 4 dozen.

PECAN BALLS

1 cup butter, softened
½ cup sugar
2 cups flour
2 teaspoons vanilla extract
Dash salt
2 cups ground pecans
1 cup powdered sugar

Cream butter and sugar until light and fluffy; add flour, vanilla, salt, and pecans, mixing well to combine. Roll into 2-inch balls. Bake at 350° for about 20 minutes. While still hot, roll in powdered sugar to coat. Makes about 2 dozen.

NO-BAKE OATMEAL COOKIES

3 cups quick oats
⅓ cup cocoa
1 cup pecans, chopped
1 cup coconut, shredded
2 cups sugar
½ cup butter, melted
½ cup milk
1 teaspoon vanilla extract

Combine oats, cocoa, pecans, and coconut; set aside. Combine sugar, butter, milk, and vanilla in a large saucepan; bring to a boil. Pour into oat mixture, and stir well to combine. Drop by tablespoonfuls onto waxed paper, and let set. Makes about 5 dozen.

SUGAR COOKIES

1 cup butter, softened
1 cup oil
2 eggs
1 cup sugar
1 cup powdered sugar
4½ cups flour
1 teaspoon baking soda
1 teaspoon cream of tartar
1 teaspoon vanilla

Cream together butter, oil, eggs, and sugar. Add all other dry ingredients gradually. Add vanilla. Roll into walnut-size balls. Flatten with a fork. Sprinkle lightly with sugar. Bake at 350° for 10 to 12 minutes. Makes 8 to 10 dozen.

OLD-FASHIONED BUTTER COOKIES

1 cup butter, softened
1 cup sugar
1 egg
1 teaspoon vanilla
2 cups flour

Cream butter and sugar. Add egg and vanilla. Gradually add flour. Drop by teaspoon on cookie sheet. Flatten with fork. Bake about 10 minutes at 350° or until brown.

Peanut Butter Chocolate Chunk Cookies

1 cup extra-crunchy peanut butter
1 cup brown sugar
1 egg
1 teaspoon vanilla extract
1 teaspoon baking soda
1 cup semisweet chocolate chunks

Combine first 5 ingredients. Stir in chocolate chunks. Drop by tablespoonfuls on ungreased cookie sheet. Bake at 350° for 12 to 15 minutes. Makes about 16 cookies.

Coconut Oatmeal Scotchies

1 cup butter, softened
1 cup sugar
1 cup brown sugar
2 eggs
1 teaspoon vanilla extract
2 cups flour
1 teaspoon baking powder
1 teaspoon baking soda
½ teaspoon salt
2 cups quick-cooking oats
1½ cups flaked coconut
1 cup pecans, chopped
1 cup butterscotch chips

Cream butter with sugar and brown sugar until light and fluffy; add eggs and vanilla extract, beating well. Combine flour, baking powder, baking soda, and salt; gradually add to creamed mixture. Stir in reamaining ingredients. Drop by teaspoonfuls onto ungreased cookie sheets. Bake at 350° for about 10 minutes. Makes about 8 dozen.

DATE-PECAN COOKIES

1 pound dates, chopped
2 cups pecans, chopped
1 cup sugar
¾ cup self-rising flour
2 eggs
1 teaspoon cinnamon
1 teaspoon vanilla extract

Combine all ingredients; drop by tablespoonfuls onto greased cookie sheets. Bake at 300° for about 30 minutes. Makes about 3 dozen.

SNICKERDOODLES

1 cup shortening
2 cups sugar, divided
2 eggs
2 tablespoons milk
1 teaspoon vanilla
2¾ cups all-purpose flour
2 teaspoons cream of tartar
1 teaspoon baking soda
¾ teaspoon salt
2 teaspoons cinnamon

Cream shortening, 1½ cups sugar, eggs, milk, and vanilla in a large bowl until well blended. Combine flour, cream of tartar, baking soda, and salt. Mix into creamed mixture. Shape dough into 1-inch balls. Combine ½ cup sugar and cinnamon in a small bowl. Roll balls of dough in mixture. Place 2 inches apart on an ungreased baking sheet. Bake at 400° for 7 to 8 minutes. Remove to cooling rack. Makes 30 servings.

CHOCOLATE-COVERED PEANUT BUTTER SANDWICHES

100 round buttery crackers
1 cup peanut butter
1 (12-ounce) package semisweet chocolate chips
2 tablespoons shortening

Spread half of crackers with peanut butter; top with remaining crackers. Melt chocolate and shortening in microwave-safe bowl at 50 percent power, stirring every 30 seconds, until melted and smooth. Dip cracker sandwiches into melted chocolate and lay on waxed paper to set. Makes 50 servings.

ALMOND COOKIES

1¾ cups flour
½ teaspoon baking powder
¼ teaspoon salt
1 cup butter, softened
¾ cup sugar, plus additional for flattening cookies
½ teaspoon vanilla extract
½ teaspoon almond extract
⅓ cup slivered almonds

Whisk together flour, baking powder, and salt; set aside. Cream butter and sugar until light and fluffy; beat in vanilla extract and almond extract. Gradually add flour mixture to butter mixture, mixing well. Roll dough into 1-inch balls and place on an ungreased baking sheet. With a flat-bottomed glass dipped in sugar, flatten cookies. Press an almond into each cookie. Bake at 375° for 10 to 12 minutes. Makes about 5 dozen.

BUTTER PECAN COOKIES

½ **cup butter, softened**
½ **cup sugar**
1 **cup flour**
¼ **teaspoon salt**
1 **egg yolk**
1 **teaspoon vanilla extract**
2 **cups pecan halves**

Cream butter and sugar until light and fluffy. Add flour and salt, mixing well. Add egg yolk and vanilla extract, mixing well. Roll into marble-size pieces, and place on an ungreased cookie sheet. Press a pecan half into each cookie. Bake at 350° for about 5 minutes. Makes about 4 dozen.

QUICK RASPBERRY-MANGO TART

1 **sheet frozen puff pastry, thawed**
2 **cups raspberries, picked over**
1 **pound mango slices**
2 **cups vanilla low-fat yogurt, chilled**
2 **tablespoons powdered sugar**

Bake puff pastry according to package directions. Set aside and let cool. Using a sharp knife, cut puff pastry in half horizontally. Gently remove the top half. Arrange fruit over bottom half of pastry. Spread yogurt over fruit. Gently cover with top layer of puff pastry. Serve sprinkled with powdered sugar. Makes 4 servings.

QUICK PEACH DESSERT

4 peaches, sliced
½ cup sugar
4 sponge cake shells
1 cup light frozen dessert topping

Combine peaches and sugar in a bowl. Refrigerate 20 to 30 minutes for sugar to dissolve. Stir well before spooning into cake shells. Serve with a dollop of dessert topping. Makes 4 servings.

ELEGANT DESSERT

2 cups seedless grapes
¼ cup light sour cream
2 teaspoons brown sugar

Wash and remove stems from grapes and allow to dry. Cut large grapes in half; blend grapes with light sour cream and brown sugar. Chill for 1 hour or more for best flavor. Makes 4 servings.

QUICK BANANA PUDDING

2 cups vanilla wafers
4 bananas, sliced
2 (14-ounce) cans vanilla pudding
2 cups whipped cream topping

Combine vanilla wafers, bananas, and vanilla pudding, mixing well. Spread into serving dish. Spread whipped cream toppingevenly over pudding and chill before serving. Makes 4 to 6 servings.

CREAMY BANANA PUDDING WITH CHOCOLATE CHIPS

1 (14-ounce) can sweetened condensed milk
1 cup milk
1 (3½-ounce) package vanilla pudding mix
4 bananas, sliced
1 cup chocolate chips
2 cups vanilla wafers
2 cups whipped cream topping

Combine condensed milk, milk, and pudding mix; beat well. Stir in bananas, chocolate chips, and vanilla wafers, mixing well. Spread into small serving dish. Spread whipped cream toppingevenly over pudding and chill before serving. Makes 4 to 6 servings.

MEXICAN CHOCOLATE PUDDING

1 (3-ounce) package chocolate pudding mix
1 tablespoon instant coffee
¼ teaspoon cinnamon
2 cups milk

Combine all ingredients in a medium saucepan; bring to a boil, stirring constantly until smooth. Chill. Makes 4 servings.

PUDDING PARFAITS

1 (3-ounce) package vanilla pudding, prepared according to package directions
2 cups fresh sliced peaches

Layer pudding and peaches in dessert glasses; chill. Makes 4 servings.

RICE PUDDING

1 quart hot milk
⅓ cup short-grain rice
¼ cup sugar
2 tablespoons butter
¼ teaspoon salt
¼ teaspoon nutmeg

Combine all ingredients. Bake at 300° for about 1½ hours, stirring every 15 minutes. Makes 4 servings.

OZARK PUDDING

1 egg
¾ cup sugar
2 tablespoons flour
1½ teaspoons baking powder
¼ teaspoon salt
½ cup pecans, chopped
1 tart apple, peeled, cored, and chopped
1 teaspoon vanilla extract

Beat egg and sugar until smooth; add flour, baking powder, and salt, mixing well. Stir in pecans, apple, and vanilla extract. Bake in a greased pie plate at 350° for about 30 minutes. Makes 6 servings.

FRUIT TRIFLE

1 package golden egg custard
2 cups milk
2 cups fresh fruit, sweetened slightly
3 to 4 slices pound or angel food cake
Whipped cream topping

Cook custard with milk; chill until thickened. Place pound cake in bottom of a 1½-quart casserole. Spoon fruit over cake. Fold whipped cream toppinginto custard. Spoon over fruit. Garnish with fruit slices or ground walnuts. Makes 8 servings.

CREAMY FRUIT COCKTAIL

1 can fruit cocktail, drained
1 can pineapple chunks, drained
1 (3-ounce) package strawberry gelatin
1 cup sour cream
Whipped cream topping

Combine fruit cocktail, pineapple, and strawberry gelatin; let sit about 10 minutes. Stir in sour cream and whipped topping. Chill until served. Makes about 4 servings.

STRAWBERRY MERINGUE TORTE

3 egg whites
½ teaspoon baking powder
1¼ cups sugar, divided
10 saltines, crushed
½ cup pecans, chopped
4 cups strawberries, sliced
1 cup whipping cream
¼ cup powdered sugar

Beat egg whites with baking powder until frothy. Gradually beat in
1 cup sugar until stiff peaks form. Stir in cracker crumbs and pecans.
Pour in a greased 9-inch pie plate. Bake at 300° for about 30 minutes.
Toss strawberries with remaining ¼ cup sugar, and pour into meringue
shell. Beat cream and powdered sugar until soft peaks form, and
spread over strawberries. Makes 8 servings.

INDIVIDUAL MERINGUE CUPS

1 (16-ounce) box powdered sugar
6 egg whites
1 teaspoon cream of tartar
½ teaspoon vanilla extract
½ teaspoon almond extract

Beat sugar and egg whites until soft peaks form. Add cream of tartar,
vanilla extract, and almond extract, and beat until stiff peaks form.
Drop by tablespoonfuls onto greased baking sheets. Spread into
circles with the back of a spoon, leaving edges higher than centers.
Bake at 300° for about 30 minutes. Makes about 2 dozen.

FAST AND FABULOUS FRUIT

1 (4-ounce) package instant pudding, any flavor
1 (20-ounce) can crushed pineapple in juice
1 cup whipped cream topping
1 can sliced peaches or fruit cocktail, undrained
**1 cup sour cream, whipped cream cheese, cottage cheese, or plain
  yogurt**

Combine pudding mix and fruit with juice in bowl. Blend in sour
cream or your choice. Chill. Makes 8 servings.

CHEWY FRUIT TARTLETS

**1 (20-ounce) package refrigerated sugar cookie dough or
  slice-and-bake cookies**
1 (6-ounce) carton orange yogurt
1 (3-ounce) package cream cheese, softened
**Fresh fruit (strawberries, peaches, grapes, kiwi, pineapple,
  blueberries)**

Slice and bake cookies as directed on package or in recipe. Cool
cookies completely on a wire rack. In a small bowl, mix yogurt and
cream cheese, and beat until smooth. Chill for 1 to 2 hours to firm
and blend flavors. When ready to eat, spoon some of the cream
cheese mixture on cooled cookies and top with fresh fruit. Serve
immediately. Makes 24 servings.

CREAMY FRUIT PARFAITS

1 (8-ounce) package cream cheese, softened
1 (7-ounce) jar marshmallow creme
1 cup sliced strawberries
1 cup blueberries or raspberries

Beat together cream cheese and marshmallow until smooth. Layer fruit with cream cheese mixture in four dessert glasses. Makes 4 servings.

EASY BAKED CUSTARD

2 cups milk
2 eggs
⅛ teaspoon salt
2 tablespoons sugar

Beat together milk, eggs, salt, and sugar. Pour into custard cups; place cups in a pan with hot water nearly to top of custard line. Bake at 325° for about 40 to 55 minutes, until custard is set. Makes 4 to 6 servings.

NOODLE KUGEL WITH RAISINS

1 (8-ounce) package dried egg noodles, cooked and drained
¾ cup butter, melted
1 (16-ounce) carton sour cream
1 (8-ounce) package cream cheese, softened
1 (8-ounce) carton cottage cheese
1 cup warm milk
3 eggs, beaten
¾ cup sugar
½ cup raisins
2 teaspoons vanilla
Dash salt

Combine cooked noodles with butter. Combine the rest of the ingredients; add to buttered noodles. Pour into a greased 3-quart casserole. Bake covered at 350° for 1 hour. Uncover, reduce heat to 300°, and bake 30 minutes more. Makes 10 servings.

APPLE DUMPLINGS

1 cup sugar
1 cup orange juice
½ cup butter
2 tart apples, peeled, cored, and quartered
1 (8-count) can refrigerated crescent roll dough

Combine sugar, orange juice, and butter in a medium saucepan over medium-high heat; cook and stir until sugar dissolves. Roll one apple quarter up in each piece of crescent roll dough; place in greased baking dish. Pour orange juice mixture over dumplings. Cover. Bake at 350° for about 20 minutes. Uncover and bake 15 minutes more. Makes 8 servings.

CHERRY CLAFOUTI

1 (16-ounce) can dark sweet pitted cherries, undrained
1½ cups sugar, divided
½ cup milk
1 teaspoon baking powder
1 cup flour
2 tablespoons butter

Combine cherries and 1 cup sugar, stirring until sugar is dissolved. Combine remaining ½ cup sugar, milk, baking powder, and flour, stirring until smooth. Melt butter in an 8-inch-square baking dish; pour batter mixture over butter, spreading to edges. Pour in cherry mixture. Bake at 350° for about 45 minutes. Makes 6 to 8 servings.

CHOCOLATE FUDGE SAUCE

3 (1-ounce) squares unsweetened chocolate
½ cup butter
⅔ cup sugar
Dash salt
⅔ cup evaporated milk
1 teaspoon vanilla extract
2 to 3 drops almond extract

Melt chocolate and butter in a small saucepan over low heat, stirring constantly. Stir in sugar and salt, mixing well. Gradually add evaporated milk. Cook and stir just until boiling. Remove from heat and stir in vanilla extract and almond extract. Makes about 1½ cups.

APPLE CINNAMON SAUCE

½ cup brown sugar
1 tablespoon cornstarch
¾ teaspoon cinnamon
Dash allspice
Zest of 1 lemon
¾ cup water
1 (20-ounce) can sliced apples

Combine all ingredients, mixing well. Cook over medium heat, stirring frequently, until thickened. Makes 4 to 6 servings.

WARM NECTARINE-PINEAPPLE ICE CREAM SAUCE

1½ cups nectarines (about 2 large), peeled and chopped
1 (12-ounce) jar pineapple sundae topping
¼ teaspoon peppermint extract

Combine all ingredients in a small saucepan; cook and stir over low heat until warm. Makes about 2½ cups sauce.

VANILLA SAUCE

1 cup sugar
2 tablespoons cornstarch
¼ teaspoon salt
2 cups boiling water
½ cup butter
2 teaspoons vanilla extract

Combine sugar, cornstarch, and salt in a medium saucepan. Gradually add boiling water and bring mixture to a boil; reduce heat and simmer 5 minutes. Remove from heat and add butter and vanilla extract, stirring until smooth. Makes about 2 cups.

Strawberry Sauce

2 cups sliced strawberries
½ cup sugar
1 tablespoon water
1½ teaspoons cornstarch

Combine all ingredients in a small saucepan; cook over low heat, stirring constantly, until thick and bubbly. Makes about 1 cup.

Lemon Sauce

1 cup sugar
2 tablespoons cornstarch
¼ teaspoon salt
2 cups boiling water
½ cup butter
3 tablespoons lemon juice
2 teaspoons grated lemon zest

Combine sugar, cornstarch, and salt in a medium saucepan. Gradually add boiling water, and bring mixture to a boil; reduce heat and simmer 5 minutes. Remove from heat, and add butter, lemon juice, and lemon zest, stirring until smooth. Makes about 2 cups.

Walnut Praline Sauce

½ cup butter, softened
¾ cup walnuts, chopped
¾ cup light corn syrup
¼ cup brown sugar
2 tablespoons water

Combine all ingredients in a medium saucepan over medium heat; cook, stirring constantly, until boiling. Boil 3 minutes. Makes 1½ cups.

Chocolate Fondue

2 (12-ounce) packages semisweet chocolate chips
2 cups light corn syrup
1 tablespoon vanilla extract
½ cup whipping cream
Assorted dippers (fresh fruit, dried fruit, cake squares,
  marshmallows, etc.)

Combine chocolate chips and corn syrup in a medium saucepan; cook
over low heat, stirring constantly, until smooth. Add vanilla and
cream; stir until well blended. Serve with dippers. Makes about 4
cups.

Chocolate Orange Fondue

2 (12-ounce) packages semisweet chocolate chips
2 cups light corn syrup
1 tablespoon vanilla extract
½ teaspoon orange extract
½ cup whipping cream
Assorted dippers (fresh fruit, dried fruit, cake squares,
  marshmallows, etc.)

Combine chocolate chips and corn syrup in a medium saucepan; cook
over low heat, stirring constantly, until smooth. Add vanilla extract,
orange extract, and cream; stir until well blended. Serve with dippers.
Makes about 4 cups.

CHOCOLATE-MINT FONDUE

2 (12-ounce) packages chocolate chips
2 cups light corn syrup
1 tablespoon vanilla extract
¼ teaspoon peppermint extract
½ cup whipping cream
Assorted dippers (fresh fruit, dried fruit, cake squares,
  marshmallows, etc.)

Combine chocolate chips and corn syrup in a medium saucepan; cook over low heat, stirring constantly, until smooth. Add vanilla extract, peppermint extract, and cream; stir until well blended. Serve with dippers. Makes about 4 cups.

CHOCOLATE-BANANA FREEZE POPS

6 ripe bananas
12 wooden popsicle sticks
1 cup milk chocolate chips

Peel bananas and cut in half crosswise. Insert a wooden popsicle stick into each half; freeze until firm. Melt chocolate chips in a small saucepan over very low heat, stirring constantly. Quickly spread melted chocolate over each banana half, and place on waxed paper. Freeze until firm. Makes 12 servings.

Peach and Raspberry Sorbet

2 cups frozen peach slices, thawed
¾ cup frozen raspberries, thawed
1 cup milk
2 tablespoons honey
1 teaspoon vanilla

Combine all ingredients in a food processor or blender; process until smooth. Pour into freezer-safe container, and freeze until firm. Makes 4 servings.

Peach and Raspberry Granita

Follow directions for Peach and Raspberry Sorbet (above), but stir every hour during freezing to form large crystals. Makes 4 servings.

Quick Fruity Float

⅔ cup pineapple juice
⅔ cup cranberry juice
⅔ cup orange juice
¼ cup sorbet or sherbet, orange or other flavor

Mix first three ingredients. Add the sorbet and serve. Makes 2¼ cups.

Quick Sherbet Float

4 cups lime sherbet
2 cups sliced and cleaned fresh strawberries
½ cup red grape juice, or other juice

Spoon fruit and sherbet into individual cups or glasses. Pour the grape juice over it. Serve chilled. Makes 6½ cups.

Watermelon Granita

½ cup sugar
½ cup water
3 cups watermelon, seeded and cubed
2 teaspoons light corn syrup

In a heavy saucepan, combine sugar and water, and bring to a boil, stirring until the sugar dissolves. Let cool completely. Purée the watermelon in a blender and measure 2 cups of the purée. Mix with corn syrup and cooled sugar syrup. Place in freezer-safe container, and freeze for about an hour, until the mixture begins to freeze around the edges. Remove from freeze,r and beat thoroughly. Return to freezer. Repeat this process three more times every 30 minutes, until mixture is frozen to a slush consistency. Makes about 5 cups.

Ice Cream Pie

1 (9-inch) prepared graham cracker or cookie crumb crust
4 cups any flavor ice cream or sorbet, slightly softened
1 cup hot fudge, butterscotch, strawberry sauce
Whipped cream, nuts, cherries (optional)

Layer scoops of ice cream with sauce in the pie shell. Cover tightly and freeze until firm, at least 4 hours. Serve with additional toppings, if desired. Makes 8 servings.

INSTANT ÉCLAIRS

2 cups strawberries or raspberries
8 ladyfinger cookies or madeleine cookies
1 pint strawberry or raspberry ice cream or sherbet, softened

Mash or purée half of the fruit and set aside. Place one cookie on each serving plate and top with a scoop of ice cream. Place some berries on the ice cream, and top with another cookie. Spoon some of the mashed or puréed fruit over the éclairs and serve. Makes 8 servings.

FROZEN YOGURT AND STRAWBERRY PURÉE

3 cups strawberries, sliced
1 quart frozen vanilla yogurt
2 cups blueberries
1 cup raspberries

In a blender or food processor, process strawberries until smooth. Stir purée into the frozen yogurt, and top with blueberries and raspberries. Makes 8 servings.

PEANUT BUTTER ICE CREAM SQUARES

¾ cup light corn syrup
¾ cup chunky peanut butter
4 cups crisp rice cereal
½ gallon chocolate ripple ice cream, slightly softened

In a large bowl, stir together corn syrup and peanut butter. Stir in rice cereal. Press ¾ mixture on bottom of buttered 9-inch x 13-inch pan, and freeze until firm, about 30 minutes. Spread ice cream on top of crust, and sprinkle with remaining cereal mixture. Freeze until firm, about 2 to 3 hours. Cut into squares to serve.

OREO SUNDAE PIE

20 Oreo cookies, crushed
¼ cup butter, melted
½ gallon vanilla ice cream, softened
Chocolate syrup
Whipped cream
Nuts, chopped
Maraschino cherries

Combine crushed cookies and butter; press into bottom of a 9-inch pie plate. Spread ice cream over cookie crust, and top with chocolate syrup. Freeze until firm. Slice and serve with whipped cream, nuts, and maraschino cherries. Makes 8 servings.

CARAMEL ICE CREAM PIE

½ cup brown sugar
2 cups flour
1 cup butter, melted
1½ cups pecans, chopped
1 jar caramel ice cream topping
½ gallon vanilla ice cream, softened

Combine brown sugar, flour, butter, and pecans; spread on baking sheet. Bake at 350° for 15 minutes. Cool and crumble, reserving ½ cup. Press remaining pecan mixture in bottom of a 9-inch pie plate. Pour caramel topping over crumbs, and spread ice cream over. Sprinkle with reserved ½ cup pecan mixture and refreeze. Makes 8 servings.

MILK SHAKE

Ice cream, any flavor
2 tablespoons chocolate syrup
4 ounces milk

Put 2 scoops of ice cream into a glass. Pour the chocolate syrup over the ice cream. Add the milk, and mix well with a spoon. Makes 1 serving.

MOCHA MILKSHAKE

2 scoops vanilla or chocolate ice cream
1 cup cold coffee
1 cup milk

Combine all ingredients in a blender; blend until smooth. Makes 1 or 2 servings.

STRAWBERRY-PECAN FREEZE

1 (8-ounce) package cream cheese, softened
1 quart strawberry ice cream, softened
2 cups strawberries, sliced
1 cup pecans, chopped

Combine all ingredients, mixing well. Pour into a freezer-safe dish, and freeze until firm. Makes 6 to 8 servings.

BREAKFAST

EGG AND SAUSAGE CASSEROLE

6 eggs, beaten
⅛ teaspoon dry mustard
Dash salt
Pepper to taste
2 cups milk
1 pound sausage, browned and drained
1 pound Cheddar cheese, grated
6 slices white bread, crusts removed and cubed

Beat eggs; add spices, milk, sausage, cheese, and bread. Pour into a buttered 3-quart casserole. Bake for 40 minutes. Makes 8 servings.

SPICY SAUSAGE CHEESE SQUARES

1 cup all-purpose baking mix
⅓ cup milk
2 tablespoons sour cream
1 pound spicy sausage
1 onion, chopped
1 egg, beaten
2 cups shredded Monterey Jack cheese
2 (4½-ounce) cans chopped green chiles, drained

Combine baking mix, milk, and sour cream; press into a greased 3-quart baking dish. Brown sausage and onion until cooked; drain and sprinkle over biscuit mixture. Combine egg, cheese, and chiles; spread over sausage. Bake at 350° for about 30 minutes. Makes 8 servings.

CHEESY SCRAMBLED EGGS WITH CHIVES

4 eggs, beaten
2 tablespoons water
1 tablespoon chopped chives
Salt and pepper to taste
2 tablespoons butter
½ cup shredded Cheddar cheese

Combine eggs, water, chives, and salt and pepper to taste. Melt butter in a large skillet over medium heat; add eggs and cook, stirring occasionally, until cooked to desired degree of doneness. Stir in cheese. Makes 2 servings.

HAM AND SPINACH SOUFFLÉ

1 (10-ounce) package frozen spinach, thawed and drained
½ pound ham, cubed
1 (8-ounce) container cottage cheese
2 cups Swiss cheese, shredded
6 eggs, beaten
½ cup butter
⅓ cup flour

Combine all ingredients; pour into a greased 3-quart casserole. Bake at 350° for about 1 hour. Makes about 8 servings.

BAKED GARLIC CHEESE GRITS WITH BACON

2 cups chicken broth
1 cup milk
1 cup grits
1 pound bacon, cooked and crumbled
½ cup butter, melted
1 (3-ounce) roll garlic cheese
1 cup shredded sharp Cheddar cheese
Dash hot sauce
Salt and pepper to taste

Combine chicken broth and milk; bring to a boil. Whisk in grits, and cook according to package directions. Stir in remaining ingredients. Pour into greased 3-quart baking dish. Bake at 350° for about 30 minutes. Makes about 8 servings.

FRIED GRITS CAKES

⅓ cup grits
2 tablespoons self-rising flour
1 egg, beaten
Salt and pepper to taste
2 tablespoons vegetable oil

Cook grits according to package directions. Add flour, egg, and salt and pepper to taste. Drop by tablespoonfuls into hot vegetable oil. Cook patties until brown on both sides. Makes about 8 servings.

COUNTRY PANCAKES

2 cups buttermilk
2 eggs, separated
2 teaspoons butter, melted
1 teaspoon salt
2 tablespoons sugar
2 cups flour, sifted
2 tablespoons baking soda

In bowl, blend buttermilk, egg yolks, and melted butter. Beat egg whites until stiff but not dry. Fold gently into batter. Combine salt, sugar, flour, and baking soda. Add to batter. Fry 4-inch cakes on hot griddle, turning once. Serve with Strawberry Devonshire Cream (below). Makes 4 servings.

STRAWBERRY DEVONSHIRE CREAM

½ cup sour cream
½ cup whipping cream
2 tablespoons sugar
1 cup fresh strawberries, sliced
Squeeze of lemon or lime juice

Pour sour cream and whipping cream into bowl. Beat until soft peaks form. Beat in sugar. Fold in berries and lemon juice. Serve on pancakes or waffles. Makes about 2 cups.

POTATO BACON TART

6 slices bacon, cooked and crumbled
6 eggs, beaten
1 (12-ounce) bag frozen hash browns, thawed
1 cup shredded Cheddar cheese
2 chopped green onions
½ cup sour cream
Salt and pepper to taste

Combine all ingredients; pour into a greased pie plate. Bake at 350°
for about 25 minutes. Makes about 6 servings.

CARAMEL ROLLS

1 teaspoon cinnamon
½ cup sugar
3 (10-ounce) cans refrigerator biscuits
½ cup brown sugar

Combine ¾ teaspoon cinnamon and ½ cup sugar. Cut biscuits into
quarters. Roll each piece in cinnamon and sugar mix. Layer in a
well-greased Bundt pan. Combine brown sugar, the remaining
cinnamon, and butter in a sauce pan. Bring to a boil. Allow to boil for
3 minutes, and pour over biscuits. Bake for 30 minutes at 350°. Cool
for 10 minutes before removing from pan and serving. Makes 24
servings.

CHERRY BREAKFAST SCONES

3 cups all-purpose baking mix
¼ cup sugar
1 cup dried cherries, chopped
1⅓ cups cream plus more for brushing

Combine biscuit mix, sugar, and cherries. Stir in 1⅓ cups cream, stirring just until combined. Drop by tablespoonfuls onto greased cookie sheet. Bake at 425° for about 10 minutes. Brush hot scones with remaining cream. Makes 2 dozen.

CREAMY SAUSAGE SQUARES

2 (9-ounce) cans refrigerated crescent roll dough
1 pound sausage, cooked and drained, still warm
1 (8-ounce) package cream cheese, softened
1 egg, beaten
1 tablespoon poppy seeds

Unroll 1 can of crescent roll dough, pinching seams together to seal into one large dough sheet. Place on greased cookie sheet. Combine sausage and cream cheese, stirring well to combine. Spread sausage mixture over dough sheet. Unroll second can of crescent roll dough, pinching seams to seal; lay over sausage mixture, and pinch edges to seal filling in. Brush beaten egg over top layer of dough, and sprinkle with poppy seeds. Bake at 350° for about 15 minutes, or until golden brown and heated through. Cut into squares. Makes about 3 dozen.

CANDIED BACON

½ cup brown sugar
¼ cup honey mustard
1 egg, beaten
1 pound thick-cut bacon
1 cup breadcrumbs

Combine brown sugar, honey mustard, and egg. Dip each bacon slice in sugar mixture and roll in breadcrumbs. Bake at 350° for about 30 minutes. Makes about 6 servings.

BACON-CHEDDAR TART

1 (9-ounce) can refrigerated crescent roll dough
1 pound bacon, cooked and crumbled
2 cups shredded Cheddar cheese
2 chopped green onions
2 eggs, beaten

Unroll crescent roll dough, and press into greased pie plate. Combine remaining ingredients, and pour over crescent roll dough. Bake at 325° for about 1 hour. Makes 4 to 6 servings.

HAM AND SWISS CRESCENTS

1 cup ham, finely chopped
½ cup Swiss cheese, shredded
2 tablespoons honey mustard
1 green onion, finely chopped
1 (9-ounce) can refrigerated crescent roll dough

Combine ham, cheese, honey mustard, and green onion. Place about 2 tablespoons ham mixture in center of each crescent and roll up. Place seam-side down on greased baking sheet. Bake at 350° for about 15 minutes. Makes 8 servings.

BROCCOLI-CHEESE CRESCENTS

1 cup broccoli, cooked and finely chopped
½ cup grated Parmesan cheese
2 tablespoons mayonnaise
1 teaspoon Italian seasoning
1 (9-ounce) can refrigerated crescent roll dough

Combine broccoli, cheese, mayonnaise, and Italian seasoning. Place about 2 tablespoons broccoli mixture in center of each crescent and roll up. Place seam-side down on greased baking sheet. Bake at 350° for about 15 minutes. Makes 8 servings.

BREAKFAST BURRITOS

6 eggs, beaten
2 tablespoons milk
¼ teaspoon cumin
Salt and pepper to taste
2 tablespoons butter
½ cup shredded Cheddar cheese
6 slices bacon, cooked and crumbled
4 (10-inch) flour tortillas, warmed

Combine eggs, milk, cumin, and salt and pepper to taste; scramble in butter. Stir in cheese and bacon. Divide egg and bacon mixture among tortillas; wrap up, burrito-style. Makes 4 servings.

QUICK STRAWBERRY JAM

2 to 3 cups strawberries
3 cups sugar
1 (3-ounce) package strawberry gelatin

Wash and pick strawberries, and mix with sugar. Let stand overnight. Bring to a hard boil. Reduce heat to medium, and cook 10 minutes. Add the gelatin, mix until well dissolved, and bring to a boil again. Remove from heat, and let stand a few minutes. Stir again. Put into jars, and keep in refrigerator or store in freezer-safe containers in freezer. Makes 5 to 6 cups.

BATTERED FRENCH TOAST

1 cup flour
1 tablespoon sugar
1½ teaspoons baking powder
½ teaspoon salt
½ teaspoon cinnamon
1 cup milk
1 egg, beaten
1 teaspoon vanilla extract
8 slices stale French bread
1 cup vegetable oil
Powdered sugar

Combine flour, sugar, baking powder, salt, and cinnamon, whisking to blend. Add milk, egg, and vanilla to flour mixture, whisking until smooth. Dip bread slices into batter. Cook in hot oil, turning once, until golden brown. Drain on paper towels, and sprinkle with powdered sugar. Makes 4 servings.

BROILED GRAPEFRUIT WITH MARMALADE GLAZE

1 grapefruit, halved and seeded
¼ cup orange marmalade

Spread each grapefruit half with 2 tablespoons marmalade; broil in preheated broiler about 5 minutes. Makes 2 servings.

Overnight French Toast with Glazed Apples

4 tart apples, peeled, cored, and sliced
2 tablespoons butter
1 cup brown sugar
1 teaspoon cinnamon
8 thick slices French bread
3 eggs
1 cup milk
1 teaspoon vanilla extract

Cook apples in butter until tender; stir in brown sugar and cinnamon, cooking until thoroughly coated. Pour into a greased 3-quart baking dish. Lay bread slices over apples. Combine eggs, milk, and vanilla extract and pour over bread. Chill overnight. Bake at 375° for about 30 minutes. Makes 8 servings.

Potato and Onion Frittata

2 tablespoons olive oil
2 tablespoons butter
2 medium onions, thinly sliced
1½ pounds potatoes, thinly sliced
1 large tomato, sliced
8 eggs, beaten
4 chopped green onions
Salt and pepper to taste

Heat olive oil and butter in a very large ovenproof skillet over medium-high heat; add onions and potatoes, and cook about 15 minutes, stirring occasionally. Arrange tomato slices over potato mixture; cover and cook 1 minute. Combine eggs, green onions, and salt and pepper to taste. Pour over tomatoes, cooking and stirring gently until eggs are almost set. Cook under preheated broiler about 3 or 4 minutes, or until eggs are set. Makes about 6 servings.

ASPARAGUS FRITTATA

2 tablespoons olive oil
2 tablespoons butter
1 bunch asparagus, trimmed and chopped
1 red bell pepper, seeded and chopped
8 eggs, beaten
Salt and pepper to taste

Heat olive oil and butter in a very large ovenproof skillet over medium-high heat; add asparagus and red bell pepper, cooking and stirring until tender. Pour eggs over asparagus, and season with salt and pepper. Let cook several minutes, stirring gently, until eggs are almost set. Cook under preheated broiler about 3 or 4 minutes, or until eggs are set. Makes about 6 servings.

HOT APPLE-CRANBERRY CRISP

3 cups apple, peeled, cored, and chopped
2 cups fresh cranberries
½ cup sugar
⅔ cup brown sugar, divided
1 cup rolled oats
½ cup pecans or walnuts, chopped
¼ cup butter, melted

Combine apples, cranberries, sugar, and ⅓ cup brown sugar. Pour into a 3-quart casserole that has been coated with cooking spray. Combine remaining ⅓ cup brown sugar with oats, pecans, and melted butter. Sprinkle over apple mixture. Bake at 350° for 30 to 45 minutes or until hot and bubbly. Makes 10 to 12 servings.

GLAZED CIDER APPLES

⅔ cup apple cider
¼ cup brown sugar
¼ cup raisins
¼ teaspoon cinnamon
4 tart apples, peeled, cored, and sliced

Combine cider, brown sugar, raisins, and cinnamon in a medium saucepan over medium heat, stirring until sugar is dissolved. Add apples; reduce heat, cover, and simmer for about 15 minutes, stirring occasionally. Makes 4 to 6 servings.

STRAWBERRY-ALMOND BUTTER

½ cup butter or margarine, softened
⅓ cup strawberry preserves
¼ teaspoon almond extract

Cream butter with preserves and extract until smooth. Chill. Serve with biscuits, toast, or muffins. Makes about 1 cup.

HONEY BUTTER

½ cup butter, softened
¼ cup honey

Combine butter with honey, mixing until smooth. Makes ¾ cup.

CINNAMON BUTTER

½ **cup butter, softened**
2 **tablespoons brown sugar**
1 **tablespoon honey**
½ **teaspoon cinnamon**
Dash nutmeg

Combine all ingredients, mixing until smooth. Makes about ¾ cup.

COFFEE CAKE

¼ **cup oil**
1 **(16-ounce) package white cake mix**
2 **eggs**
½ **cup water**
1 **(15-ounce) can pie filling**
Powdered sugar

Pour oil into a 9-inch x 13-inch; tilt pan, covering bottom and sides. Put cake mix, eggs, and water in pan; stir until blended (about 2 minutes). Spread batter evenly in pan. Spoon favorite pie filling onto batter. Using a fork, fold filling, making a marbled effect. Bake at 350° for 35 to 45 minutes, until toothpick inserted in middle comes out clean. Cool. Sift small amount of powdered sugar over the top. Use a knife to loosen cake from sides of pan. Serve with ice cream or whipped cream if desired. Makes 12 servings.

APPLESAUCE COFFEE CAKE

2 cups self-rising flour
2 cups sugar
1 cup vegetable oil
1 cup applesauce
3 eggs
1 teaspoon cinnamon
1 teaspoon ground cloves

Combine all ingredients, mixing well. Pour into a greased Bundt pan.
Bake at 350° for 1 hour. Makes about 16 servings.

DUTCH PANCAKES

3 eggs
¼ teaspoon salt
½ cup flour
½ cup milk
2 tablespoons butter

In a medium bowl, beat eggs until light colored and thick. Add salt,
flour, and milk, and beat well to combine. Spread butter in a 10-inch
pie plate, coating sides, and pour in batter. Bake at 425° for 20
minutes. The pancake should be brown at this time, but if it isn't,
reduce heat to 350° and bake 5 to 10 minutes longer until brown.
Makes 4 servings.

CORNMEAL WAFFLES

2 cups self-rising cornmeal
2 cups self-rising flour
½ cup sugar
4 eggs, beaten
2 cups milk
6 tablespoons butter, melted

Combine all ingredients to make waffle batter. Pour into preheated waffle iron and bake until done. Makes about 8 waffles. Serve with Blueberry Topping (below).

BLUEBERRY TOPPING

1 (20-ounce) can blueberry pie filling
1 teaspoon vanilla
1 teaspoon lemon zest
Dash cinnamon

Combine all ingredients, cooking over low heat until just warmed through. Makes about 1½ cups.

CRÈME FRAÎCHE

1 cup whipping cream
1 tablespoon buttermilk

Combine cream and buttermilk in a glass jar; cover tightly and shake to combine. Leave out for 18 to 36 hours. Cream will thicken slowly; when desired consistency is reached, refrigerate for about 2 weeks. Spread over sweet biscuits or scones, or dollop on fruit desserts. Makes 1 cup.

SAUSAGE WAFFLES

4 eggs, beaten
2 cups milk
2 tablespoons butter, melted
3½ cups flour
½ cup sugar
2 tablespoons baking powder
½ teaspoon salt
1 pound sausage, cooked and drained

Combine eggs, milk, and butter. Whisk together flour, sugar, baking powder, and salt; add to egg mixture, mixing well. Stir in sausage. Cook in preheated waffle iron. Makes about 8 waffles.

FRUITY YOGURT PARFAIT

4 (8-ounce) containers lemon yogurt
2 cups strawberries, sliced
½ cup blueberries
3 tablespoons granola

Layer half of yogurt in each of 4 dessert glasses. Mix strawberries and blueberries; divide evenly over yogurt, and top with remaining yogurt. Sprinkle granola over tops. Makes 4 servings.

MICROWAVE OMELET

2 tablespoons butter
5 eggs
2 slices American cheese
½ cup bacon bits
½ cup picante sauce

Melt butter in a small glass dish. Break eggs in dish. Tear sliced cheese in pieces, and add to eggs. Add remaining ingredients, blending together. Cook in microwave approximately 6 minutes, stirring every 2 minutes. Cooking time will vary depending on microwave oven. Let set 5 minutes before eating. Makes 2 servings.

PEACH CRÈME BRÛLÉE

2 cups canned peach halves, drained
1 cup sour cream
½ cup brown sugar

Place drained peach halves in a shallow glass baking dish. Spoon sour cream over peaches, and sprinkle evenly with brown sugar. Broil 4 to 6 inches from heat until sugar melts and caramelizes. Makes about 3 cups.

PEAR CRÈME BRÛLÉE

2 cups canned pear halves, drained
1 cup sour cream
½ cup brown sugar

Place drained pear halves in a shallow glass baking dish. Spoon sour cream over pears, and sprinkle evenly with brown sugar. Broil 4 to 6 inches from heat, until sugar melts and caramelizes. Makes about 3 cups.

BAKED PEACHES

4 large ripe peaches
5 tablespoons butter, softened
⅔ cup sweet granola

Cut peaches in half and remove the pit. Leave the skin on so that the peaches hold their shape while baking. Place peaches, cut side up, on a baking sheet with sides. Pour 2 tablespoons water into bottom of pan. Place 1 teaspoon butter into each peach half. Bake at 350° for 20 to 30 minutes, or until peaches are soft and slightly brown.

Meanwhile, melt remaining butter in a small saucepan, and stir in granola. Cook for 2 to 3 minutes, or until granola is well coated with butter. Remove peaches from oven, place on serving dish, and sprinkle with warm granola. Makes 8 servings.

SPARKLING FRUIT COMPOTE

3 cups melon balls
2 cups strawberries, sliced
3 bananas, peeled and sliced
1½ cups peaches, sliced
1 cup blueberries
1 bottle sparkling white grape juice, chilled

Layer fruits in individual serving glasses. Pour sparkling grape juice evenly over fruit in each glass. Makes 8 to 10 servings.

INDEX

INDEX

INDEX

INDEX

INDEX

INDEX

INDEX

INDEX

INDEX